INTRODUCTION TO THE

WORLD OF BUSINESS

SECOND EDITION

Dr. John Mago

Anoka–Ramsey Community College

Dr. Jill Friestad-Tate

Des Moines Area Community College

Kendall Hunt

publishing company

Cover image © Shutterstock, Inc.

Kendall Hunt
publishing company

www.kendallhunt.com
Send all inquiries to:
4050 Westmark Drive
Dubuque, IA 52004-1840

CONTENTS

CHAPTER 1

UNDERSTANDING THE BUSINESS ENVIRONMENT

> *"Successful people take big risks knowing that they might fall hard. But, they might succeed more than they ever dreamed, too."*
>
> ~Robert Kiyosaki, Financial literacy activist and author of the best-selling book "Rich Dad, Poor Dad"

OUTCOMES:

➢ Explain the difference between a for-profit and non-profit organization.

➢ Define the risk/reward trade-off and how it affects revenues and/or profits in an organization.

➢ Outline eras that have framed business development in the United States throughout history.

➢ Discuss the changing dynamics of business and the workforce.

➢ Understand and identify stakeholders in organizations.

➢ Analyze the effect government has on business operations.

Rawpixel/Shutterstock.com

WHAT IS BUSINESS?

pedrosek/Shutterstock.com

Business: An organized effort of producing and selling goods and services.

Profit: The money remaining after business expenses are deducted from sales revenue.

Risk/Reward Tradeoff: The potential gain one might receive when taking a risk.

Have you ever wondered what the word *business means*? The term business is utilized in many ways. For instance, one may reference a business by its name such as McDonalds, Wal-Mart, or Ford Motor Company. Others reference a business by the type of industry such as fast-food, medical, or insurance. Understanding the term business is important as it is connected to whatever job or career you may perform in your life as everything relates to business in some form or another.

In general terms, a **business** is an organized effort of producing and selling goods and services. There are many types of businesses, which we will explore as we move through the textbook. However, in most businesses, it is fundamental to earn a profit. A **profit** is the money remaining after you deduct all business expenses (costs) from revenue (sales). Profits are important to a business because they drive future growth potential as well as provide incentives for investors and business owners.

Sometimes, taking risks in business increases the level of profit that can be earned; however, there can be drawbacks to taking risks as a business may lose money. The decision to accept risk in order to make a profit is known as the **risk/reward** or **risk/return tradeoff**, which refers to the potential gain one might receive when taking a risk to do something. In relation to business, it refers to the

FIGURE 1.1

Is the reward worth
the risk?

phloxii/Shutterstock.com

potential profits that can be made when an individual decides to open a business or put savings into a particular type of investment such as stocks, bonds, or mutual funds. It is the type of relationship that reacts to a change in one variable, as there will likely be a corresponding change in the other variable—the more risk, the greater the reward (higher profits). Based on this tradeoff, individuals determine what types of businesses they will operate and where to invest their money. This is where the phrase, "No risk, no reward," comes from. For example, the gentleman in **Figure 1.1** could jump from one side to the other and enjoy the reward of the thrill of jumping as well as saying he made it across. However, if he doesn't make it, he stands the risk of falling to the bottom. It is important to ask yourself what risk you are willing to accept in order to gain a particular reward.

Along with determining an acceptable risk level, an organization must determine what type of business they will operate, which leads to the two classifications of organizations: for-profit and non-profit.

FOR-PROFIT ORGANIZATIONS

The majority of businesses you encounter are for-profit organizations. These are companies whose primary goal is to earn a profit after all business expenses have been paid. Although this is not the only focus of such businesses, it does show the value in creating a profit. It should be noted that many companies today also see value in bettering society and creating a better environment, which be covered in more detail in Chapter 2 when we discuss social responsibility.

For-profit Organization:
A company engaged in selling
a product or service primarily
for a profit.

NON-PROFIT ORGANIZATIONS

Non-profit Organization: An organization whose primary purpose is to serve society versus making a profit.

Rob Wilson/Shutterstock.com

Although making profit is the goal for most businesses, non-profit businesses' primary objectives are focused on serving society. Without donations of time and money from individuals or companies around the world, these organizations could not exist. Some well-known organizations include: The Red Cross, the U.S. Post Office, the Ronald McDonald House, and The Salvation Army. Non-profit organizations can include private sector entities (libraries, trade associations, religious and charitable organizations, and museums) and public sector entities (government agencies, labor unions, and political parties). Most non-profit organizations rely on charitable contributions to perform their services. You might be surprised to find out that there were over 1.5 million non-profit organizations registered with the Internal Revenue Service (IRS) in the United States at the end of 2015.[1] So, the next time you donate your time or money to a charitable organization, remember that you are helping others in need but also contributing to the success of business functions around the world.

concept check

Explain the difference between a for-profit and non-profit organization.

HISTORY OF BUSINESS

The beginning of business in the United States started over 400 years ago when the first European settlements arrived. As shown in **Table 1.1**, there are six eras associated with the development of business in the United States.

TABLE 1.1

Six Eras in U.S. Business History

ERA	CHARACTERISTICS	TIME FRAME
Colonial	Mostly agricultural	Prior to 1776
Industrial Revolution	Mass production and use of machines	1760–1850
Industrial entrepreneurs	Technological advancements and increased demand for manufactured products, lead to entrepreneurial opportunities	Late 1800s
Production	Focus on faster production of goods, introduction of assembly lines	Through the 1920s
Marketing	Consumer focused, research consumer needs	Since 1950s
Relationship	Promote benefits of relationships with individuals, customers, employees, suppliers, and other stakeholders	Beginning 1990s

COLONIAL PERIOD (PRIOR TO 1776)

This time period's main economic focus was centered on rural and agricultural production. Towns were small and functioned as marketplace centers for farmers. A key reference point is that many colonists still relied on England for manufactured goods and financial backing for their early businesses.

INDUSTRIAL REVOLUTION (1760–1850)

This period included major developments in production history as business operations started to focus on a factory system of mass-produced or large-scale production of goods. This allowed for growth in profits as machines increased production capabilities, specialized labor created production efficiencies, and purchasing large quantities of raw materials reduced production costs.

Stacey Newman/Shutterstock.com

In this era, the United States began a time of rapid industrialization. Factories developed in cities and agricultural production increased due to new technologies, which reduced the number of workers needed in the agricultural industry. Fortunately, more workers were needed in the factories and a shift of population to cities began. Newly built railroad systems provided efficient and economical transportation for goods and raw materials. A good example of this was the California Gold Rush (1848–1855), which began on January 24, 1848, when gold was discovered

Michael Rega/Shutterstock.com

at Sutter's Mill. As news of the discovery spread, approximately 300,000 people migrated to California from around the United States and abroad to capitalize on the wealth. These early gold-seekers, called "forty-niners," along with the railroad construction, created huge demand for new businesses including construction, industry, and merchants of all trades. The business boom was on!

INDUSTRIAL ENTREPRENEURS (LATE 1800s)

The industrial revolution brought many opportunities for entrepreneurs (business owners) in the United States. The new market transformation raised the overall standard of living for individuals and increased the demand for manufactured goods. Many new giants in industry used this time to solidify their presence in

Everett Historical/Shutterstock.com

the U.S. business landscape. Some of the most notable names associated with this era include John D. Rockefeller (oil), Andrew Carnegie (steel), Cornelius Vanderbilt (railroad), and J.P. Morgan (banking).

Keep in mind, that during this era, inventors created many commercial products and new production methods that are still used today. Eli Whitney, inventor of the cotton gin, introduced the concept of interchangeable parts that aided in the facilitation of mass production. The large-scale production capacity of manufactured goods opened up many new opportunities for both businesses and consumers.

PRODUCTION ERA (THROUGH THE 1920s)

During the production era, businesses were not concerned with what customers wanted to buy but rather what businesses could produce most efficiently. The goal was to sell as much of what businesses wanted to make without regard to whether or not it was what was needed. Through the 1920s, demand for manufactured goods continued to increase. This marked the creation of the assembly line where efficiency in mass production meant higher profits for producers and increased product availability for consumers.

The creator of the assembly line was Henry Ford. He used the assembly line to produce his Ford Model T automobile, offered only in black. The assembly line became commonplace in major industries. Business owners used trained managers to run their operations and focused attention on internal processes rather than external influences. Marketing was almost obsolete as little attention was paid to consumer wants and needs but instead to businesses who decided what to produce. We will discuss in Chapters 7 and 9 how this era affected management practices and organizational structures—many of which still exist in organizations today.

Olga Popova/Shutterstock.com

MARKETING ERA (SINCE 1950s)

The shape of U.S. business was changed again in the early 1930s due to the Great Depression. As businesses began to analyze consumers' wants and needs, consumer orientation became the focus before production actually occurred. Consumers wanted choices and businesses began to distinguish themselves from the competition through their marketing and advertising focus. As businesses focused on consumer needs, brand names such as Coca-Cola, IBM, GE, McDonald's, Apple, and Microsoft were created. The effect of the marketing era on business today has been tremendous as business owners realize the importance of understanding what consumers want and why they buy specific products.

Bloomua/Shutterstock.com

RELATIONSHIP ERA (BEGAN IN 1990s)

Once businesses started analyzing why customers purchased specific products, they realized how important relationships are to their long-term success. Thus, the Relationship Era was born and continues today. This new focus on developing and maintaining connections between businesses and existing customers is important as it is much cheaper to maintain current customers than find new ones. Retaining customers allows companies to develop relationships, increase revenue, and avoid costs associated with attracting new customers, which is said to be at least five times more than keeping an existing customer.[2] Managing customer relationships helps

create company and brand loyalty. This era is all about connections and how relationships can provide essential benefits for businesses and consumers alike.

A potentially new era has been termed the Social Era, where social media technology such as Facebook and Twitter is the focus. It is now possible to market and sell products or services using social media, which historically has not been possible. This potential is changing the way businesses operate and will be a major indicator of and change in businesses' success in the future.

concept check

Discuss the importance of each era of U.S. business history.

WORKFORCE DYNAMICS

Each era brought about new workplace challenges. Today, the dynamics of the workforce are changing as well. Employers seek highly skilled, educated, and motivated employees in order to compete in the global economy. Technological advancements have contributed to "shrinking" the world so that organizations can conduct business via methods such as the internet, video conferencing, and remote access portals. In other words, the sky is the limit for any business. By creating a world-class workforce, businesses can develop a competitive advantage and differentiate themselves from their competition.

WORKFORCE CHALLENGES

There are multiple trends that challenge employers in today's changing workforce. Managers and human resource departments face challenges related to workplace diversity, a shrinking labor pool, an aging population, outsourcing, the work-life balance, and workplace innovation. As you learn more about business operations, maybe you will come up with innovative solutions to help deal with these workplace challenges.

Rawpixel/Shutterstock.com

WORKFORCE DIVERSITY

Effectively managing and embracing differences in a business are challenges employers face. Workplace diversity includes similarities and perceived differences among employees in relation to race, age, gender, religion, physical and mental disabilities, sexual orientation, and cultural background (ethnicity). Of course, merging these differences can be cumbersome at times as each person is unique and brings individual characteristics to the workplace. However, diversity allows companies to "see" viewpoints and experiences from a variety of perspectives, which is important in a global economy.

Workplace Diversity: Similarities and differences among employees related to race, age, gender, religion, physical and mental disabilities, sexual orientation, and cultural background.

In a 2014 survey of 1,215 companies, DiversityInc.com released a list of businesses that value diversity. **Table 1.2** provides a few of the top companies as well as the industries in which they operate.

COMPANY	INDUSTRY
Novartis Pharmaceuticals Corporation	Pharmaceuticals
Kaiser Permanente	Pharmaceuticals
Proctor & Gamble	Consumer goods
Marriott International	Hospitality
AT&T	Communications
PricewaterhouseCoopers	Financial consulting service
Mastercard	Credit card
Prudential Financial	Insurance

Source: Diversityinc.com (2015). Top 50 Companies for Diversity. Retrieved on February 1, 2016, from: http://www.diversityinc.com/the-diversityinc-top-50-companies-for-diversity-2015/. Note: Not all companies on the listed are represented.

marcogarrincha/Shutterstock.com

The U.S. workforce has been growing more diverse in many areas and particular focus has been placed on the aging population and increase in the number of minorities in the workplace. As the population ages, more diversity of generational ideas and beliefs exist in the workplace. As the age of retirement rises, so does the number of older workers who remain in the workforce, each with different life experiences than younger generations joining them. Although the benefits of multiple generations working together outweigh the challenges, it is nonetheless an area that management must approach wisely in order to help individuals effectively work together.

Another focus for management is the growth in the Hispanic and Asian populations over the past few decades, which will continue into the future. It is reported that by 2060, the Hispanic population will increase from 17 percent to 31 percent of the U.S. population whereas the Asian population will increase from 5.1 percent to 8.2 percent of the U.S. population.[3] Although this growth should be viewed as positive for U.S. businesses, it presents challenges to the status quo and business operations that have existed in the United States for centuries.

POPULATION AND LABOR POOL

Despite the focus on ethnic and racial changes in the United States, it is likely that businesses today are more concerned about the aging population. Combined with a shrinking labor pool, businesses are struggling to find skilled, experienced employees to fill available positions. The Baby Boomer generation (1946–1964) is starting to retire whereas younger generations are delaying entry into the workforce for various reasons. There simply are not as many workers entering the workforce as those leaving it. In the near future, Millenials will make up 50% of the workforce , which will force businesses to pay attention to their views on the workplace, lifestyles, and family.

Businesses conduct research and monitor labor projections to evaluate considerations such as future expansions, employee needs, and workplace diversity. Recent data, as well as projected growth or decline in each area by 2022, are included in **Table 1.3**. A continued analysis will need to take place to ensure employees are available for jobs that need to be filled. This is an exciting time for individuals in the workforce with the necessary skills and education businesses desire!

Rawpixel/Shutterstock.com

TABLE 1.3

Civilian Labor Force by Age, Sex, Race, and Ethnicity Projected 2022

GROUP	LEVEL (000'S)	ANNUAL GROWTH RATE (PERCENT)
	2022	2012–2022
Age		
16 to 24	18,462	−1.4
25 to 54	103,195	0.2
55 and up	41,793	2.6
Race		
White	126,923	0.3
Black	20,247	1.0
Asian	10,135	2.2
All other (*)	6,145	2.7
Ethnicity		
Hispanic origin	31,179	2.5
Other than Hispanic Origin	132,271	0.1
White non-Hispanic	99,431	−0.2

*The all other group includes: (1) those classified as being of multiple racial origin, (2) the race category of American Indian and Alaska Native, and (3) Native Hawaiian and Other Pacific Islanders.

Source: Bureau of Labor Statistics (2014). Retrieved on December 9, 2014.

OTHER CHALLENGES

Another factor companies need to consider is job flexibility. With the adaptation of technology, workers of all ages have developed skills that allow them to perform job functions from remote locations. Employers need to consider options such as *telecommuting* and *job sharing* with other employees to afford these workers the flexibility they are seeking. Meeting the demands of skilled employees and managing this process will be challenging for management. Managers need to trust employees and ensure that all employees act ethically and are contributing their fair share with reduced supervision.

Another aspect to retaining employees relates to the work-life balance, which means providing an environment that allows an employee to balance his professional life with his personal life. This is important to management as a productive workplace exists where employees are satisfied with both their work and home life. Many businesses try to accomplish this balance by providing flexible sched-

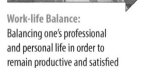

Work-life Balance:
Balancing one's professional and personal life in order to remain productive and satisfied in both worlds.

ules, on-site daycares, and paid-time off that can be used at an employee's discretion. For example, Google provides many benefits for employees that help provide work-life balance, some of which include free food, the ability to bring pets to work, and a death benefit of half of a spouse's salary for 10 years if an employee who works for the company passes away.[4]

Finally, with technological advancements and global access, workplace innovation allows for access to lower-wage earning labor forces in other countries that create new opportunities for less expensive goods and services. In order to reduce costs and remain competitive, businesses use **outsourcing**, the utilization of vendors outside of the organization, to produce goods and services instead of performing certain functions in-house (within the business). This can happen within U.S. borders as well as outside the United States as a means to reduce costs. Outsourcing is utilized for a variety of reasons beyond cost reductions as is shown in **Table 1.4**.

Outsourcing: Using outside vendors to produce goods and services.

TOP REASONS TO OUTSOURCE
1. Lower operational and labor costs;
2. Allows companies to focus on core business functions and focus on areas of strength;
3. Allows access to global knowledge and talent;
4. Frees up internal resources to be utilized more efficiently;
5. Allows access to resources not available internally;
6. Reduces risks involved in working or expanding in areas that are not strengths for the organization;
7. Allows closer proximity to end users, which can expand the market.

Table 1.4

Reasons for Outsourcing

Source: Flatworld Solutions (2016). The Top 10 Reasons To Outsource. Retrieved on February 1, 2016, from: https://www.flatworldsolutions.com/articles/top-ten-reasons-to-outsource.php.

This, of course, can result in loss of jobs, quality issues, and a reduction in tax base for the U.S. economy. However, many would argue that by outsourcing lower-paying jobs and responsibilities to other countries, opportunities for increasing higher-skilled jobs are created in the United States. The challenge is ensuring that workers displaced by outsourced jobs increase their skills and educational level in order to fill the new, higher-skilled jobs. The top 10 countries to outsource business to are listed in **Table 1.5**.

TABLE 1.5

Top 10 Countries to Out-
source Business To

TOP COUNTRIES TO OUTSOURCE BUSINESS TO	
1. India	6. Indonesia
2. China	7. Bulgaria
3. Malaysia	8. Philippines
4. Thailand	9. Chile
5. Brazil	10. Japan

Source: http://www.ranker.com/list/the-top-ten-countries-for-outsourcing-business/
mcorn310?page=2

concept check

What workplace challenges face businesses today?

BUSINESS STAKEHOLDERS

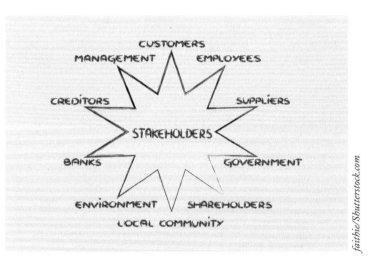

faithie/Shutterstock.com

Stakeholder: A person, group, or organization affected by the operations of a business.

Internal Stakeholders: Individuals within a firm who are affected by its actions.

External Stakeholders: Individuals outside a firm who are affected by its actions.

A **stakeholder** is a person, group, or organization that has an interest or concern in a business. There are two types of stakeholders: **internal stakeholders** (employees, managers, and owners) who are within an organization, and **external stakeholders** (customers, suppliers, society, government, creditors, and shareholders) who are outside of the organization. Stakeholders can directly affect or be affected by the organization's actions, decisions, and practices. However, not all stakeholders are equal. A company's customers are entitled to fair practices but they are not entitled to the same consideration as the company's employees.

An example of a negative impact on stakeholders is when a company needs to reduce costs and plans a reduction in the workforce. This negatively affects the community of workers in the area and in essence the local economy. Someone owning shares in a business (stockholder or shareholder) such as Microsoft is positively affected, for example, when the company releases a new device and sees stock prices increase.

Stockholder/shareholder: An investor who owns shares of an organization.

concept check

Who are considered internal stakeholders of an organization? External stakeholders?

GOVERNMENT'S ROLE IN BUSINESS

The U.S. government's role in business is as old as the country itself. The Constitution gives the government the power to regulate commerce when necessary. Though the government's role has increased over the decades, business industry still enjoys considerable freedom. The government exercises its authority in several ways including requiring registration for business operations, passing legislation to enforce consumer and business rights, and enforcing contracts in order to protect businesses.

PERMISSION

Most businesses need to register with a state government in order to operate. This registration defines the type of business structure an organization will operate such as a sole proprietorship, partnership, or corporation. Registration also allows the government to monitor companies as they execute business functions such as accounting, marketing, and human resources.

CONTRACT ENFORCEMENT

Businesses contract with other businesses. These contracts may be complex, such as mergers, or they may be as simple as a warranty on supplies purchased. The government enforces these contracts. If one party fails or refuses to meet its obligation under a contract, a company will turn to the legal system for enforcement.

Francisco Javier Gil/Shutterstock.com

HOW DO BUSINESSES & GOVERNMENT RELATE?

We will further this discussion in upcoming chapters, but for now, it is important to know that the government plays a role in protecting consumers, employees, investors, and the environment.

LOVEgraphic/Shutterstock.com

CONSUMER PROTECTION

Consumers are protected by the government. This is a key role that the government plays in business. For example, if a business fails to honor a product or service guarantee, the customer has rights written in the law. Also, if a product or service causes harm to consumers, the courts may hold the business or manufacturer responsible. The Truth in Lending Act was established to help consumers understand credit terms and limit liability to $50 if someone uses a credit card without your authorization. Although consumer rights in the United States have been expanded over the past few decades, there is an ongoing need to protect consumers.

EMPLOYEE PROTECTION

Employee rights are protected by both state and federal agencies. The Department of Labor administers and enforces 180 federal laws related to employee rights. These laws cover over 10 million employers and 125 million workers. One example is the Occupational Health and Safety Administration (OSHA), which is an agency that monitors safe and healthy work environments. Another agency, the Equal Employment Opportunity Commission (EEOC), works to protect employees from workplace discrimination.[5]

ENVIRONMENTAL PROTECTION

The Environmental Protection Agency (EPA) is an agency within the U.S. federal government created for the purpose of protecting human health and the environment. Its mission is to conduct environmental assessments, research, and provide education. It has the responsibility of maintaining and enforcing national standards under a variety of environmental laws, in consultation with state, tribal, and local governments.

TAXATION

Governments at all levels (local, state, and federal) tax businesses in order to gain revenue (income). Taxes are used to pave roads, repair bridges, pay for public education, and provide benefits to individuals in need. Tax revenues create the basis for developing budgets and allow policy makers to determine which government programs or initiatives to fund.

INVESTOR PROTECTION

The government mandates that publicly traded companies make financial information available to others, thereby protecting the rights of investors. This is generally done through filings with the Securities and Exchange Commission (SEC), a government agency established to protect investors and the public from fraudulent business practices.[6]

All of these areas will be discussed more in-depth throughout the book, but for now, this brief introduction helps illustrate the relationship between the government and businesses in the United States.

WRAPPING UP...

Chapter 1 provided an introduction to what business is, why it functions, its development over time, challenges faced by businesses, and the role government plays in business operations. We will discuss these and many other business-related topics more in-depth as we move forward. Remember the risk/reward tradeoff and take the risk to study this information as the reward for knowing and understanding it will be increased knowledge and skill in navigating whatever business situations you encounter in the future!

In Chapter 2, we will examine actions individuals take when operating a business which are determined by society to be "right" or "wrong." This is the study of business ethics and social responsibility.

BUSINESS TERMINOLOGY

Business	Work-life balance
Profit	Outsourcing
Risk/reward or risk/return tradeoff	Stakeholder
For-profit organizations	Internal stakeholder
Non-profit organizations	External stakeholder
Workplace diversity	Stockholder or shareholder

DISCUSSION QUESTIONS

1. Identify changes businesses have made due to recent economic crises, and discuss how these problems have affected employees.

2. Peter Drucker, business guru, stated that there is no functional difference between a for-profit and a non-profit business. What did he mean by this statement?

3. How is diversity playing a role in today's businesses? How has it affected the workforce?

4. Describe how outsourcing has affected U.S. business practices. Discuss the pros and cons of outsourcing.

5. Pick a company in any industry and identify the various stakeholders who are affected by the company.

6. Identify roles the government plays in the business sector.

LEARNING ACTIVITIES

1. Nearly all companies, regardless of whether they are for-profit or non-profit, have web sites. Find web sites for two non-profit businesses and two for-profit businesses. Compare and contrast the sites to determine how the sites are similar and/or different, the type of information being shared with consumers, and the purpose of each web site. Be prepared to present your findings using a chart or presentation.

2. Research a recent article (within the past year) that displays how the government protected a consumer, business, or society through a law or its actions. Use a search engine or library database source to locate an article. Summarize the details of the article, how the government protected the individual, business or society, and consider what might have been the result had the government not been involved in the situation.

3. In Chapter 1, a chart about the changing workforce through 2022 was included. Visit the U.S. Department of Labor web site (www.bls.gov) and examine demographic changes that are projected to take place over the next decade or two. Write a one-page summary discussing what changes are projected, how these changes will affect you personally, and how you believe businesses should adapt to the projected changes in the workforce.

4. Understanding the culture of an organization is important as you search for a business in which to work. Choose two organizations that you are interested in working for and research the benefits offered to employees by those firms. This information can typically be found on company web sites; however, other articles can be easily located that discuss benefits and perks provided to employees. Analyze the benefits offered compared to your values in creating a work-life balance and determine if those companies would, in fact, be a good fit for you personally.

Note: *Because web sites often change, use a search engine to find alternative web sites to access required information when necessary.*

CASE STUDY: TO DIVERSIFY OR NOT?

Manny's Movers is a regional moving company that specializes in residential and commercial moving. Laury Anderson is the current CEO and has noticed a trend to have a more diverse workforce in the employment market over the past several years. Manny's Movers currently employs over 1000 movers and its employee demographic breakdown by race and ethnicity over the last several years is as follows:

RACE/ETHNICITY:	2010	2013	2016
Caucasian	75%	60%	55%
Hispanic	24%	38%	43%
Other	1%	2%	2%

A recent market analysis of Laury's region shows that many of the new businesses and certain sections of the community are comprised of individuals from the Hmong culture. Laury's future plans include serving this community at higher levels than she is currently; however, she is concerned that this population is underrepresented in her current workforce as the majority of employees are Caucasian and Hispanic. Laury has heard that some cultures clash with each other and wants to provide movers for various demographics in order to improve customer satisfaction levels of the business.

There are two ways Laury feels that Manny's could profit from this "new" market: (1) diversify its workforce to include Hmong and/or Asian employees; and (2) try and purchase a competitor that serves this community. The first option is viable; however, she does not know how to recruit employees in this community successfully as previous efforts did not result in many new hires. The second option is potentially too costly to undertake at this time and may cause hardships on her current business.

CASE STUDY ANALYSIS

Based on the information provided, answer the following questions:

(1) What advice would you offer Laury in regard to expanding her business?

(2) What type of diversity program should Laury develop in order to include other ethnic cultures in her business and employee base?

(3) What type of recruiting efforts would you suggest to diversify Manny's workforce?

CHAPTER 2

CORPORATE SOCIAL RESPONSIBILITY AND ETHICS

"We make a living by what we get, but we make a life by what we give."

~Winston Churchill, Former British Prime Minister

OUTCOMES:

➤ Distinguish between law and ethics.
➤ Summarize the ethical responsibilities organizations have to various stakeholders.
➤ Explain management's role in setting ethical standards and encouraging employees to act ethically.
➤ Compare compliance-based and integrity-based ethics codes.
➤ Discuss corporate social responsibility and its importance to an organization and the business environment.
➤ Review ethical behaviors as Americans conduct business internationally.

Ken Wolter/Shutterstock, Inc.

LAW VERSUS ETHICS

Nearly every day, stories about businesses engaged in some sort of unethical actions—stealing, lying, harassing, endangering others, or some other behavior—in the name of increasing profits for an organization or oneself can be seen. In 2013, for example, Trader Joe's, a specialty grocery store chain known for selling natural products, had a class action lawsuit filed against it accusing the store of

Stuart Miles/Shutterstock, Inc.

selling food products that were improperly labeled, marketed, supplied, and sold as "all natural" and/or "100% natural," even though they contained one or more synthetic ingredients. Trader Joe's denies it did anything wrong or unlawful and declared that the products' labels were truthful, consistent with the law, and not misleading. However, to avoid further expenses and to avoid additional negative press, Trader Joe's agreed to a settlement.[1] By agreeing to settle out of court, many people question the innocence of the company. Similar cases have been filed against other companies whose products claim to be all natural.

Acting in an ethical way involves distinguishing between "right" and "wrong" and then making the "right" choice. In order to "be ethical," individuals must understand what is meant by the term ethics and how to apply ethics personally and professionally. Ethics is the study of right and wrong and is considered a moral philosophy that guides individual or group behavior within society. Moral standards create ethics, which come from laws, situational ethics, or religious beliefs.

Ethics: The study of right and wrong within a society.

In theory, the same principles that determine an individual's actions also apply to business; however, there is often a conflict between what shareholders want (a profit) and what employees want (a safe working environment and secure jobs). **Business ethics** is the practical application of moral standards within business situations.

Asking whether it is okay to label products a certain way, knowing that it is really not what it claims to be, is an ethical dilemma. An ethical question might be, "What acceptable actions can be taken in order to make a profit?" These are challenging questions to answer as each person has individual behaviors he or she feels are acceptable. Some of the most common unethical behaviors in the workplace, based on a report from an Ethics Resource Center study (2016), are listed in **Table 2.1**.

Business ethics: The practical application of moral standards within business situations.

MOST COMMON UNETHICAL BEHAVIORS IN THE WORKPLACE
Abusive behavior or behavior that creates a hostile work environment
Lying to employees
A conflict of interest—behavior that places an employee's interests over the company's interests
Violating company policies related to Internet use
Discriminating against employees
Violations of health or safety regulations
Lying to customers, vendors, or the public
Retaliation against someone who has reported misconduct
Falsifying time reports or hours worked
Stealing or theft
Violating employee wage, overtime, or benefit rules

TABLE 2.1

Most Common Unethical Behaviors in the Work-place

Source: Ethics Resource Center, 2016 National Business Ethics Survey.

concept check

Explain the difference between ethics and business ethics.

BUSINESS LAW

Challenges often arise as individuals and organizations determine what is ethical and what is legal. An individual's actions can be legal but not ethical or actions can be ethical and not legal. For example, in business, an individual might feel it is appropriate to market a product in any way that attracts customers; however, the advertising may not be fully honest. If the advertising is untrue, then it would be false advertising, which is illegal. However, if the advertising states something that is exaggerated but hard to verify, such as, "We have the best deals around," then it would be unethical as determining what is meant by "best" or "around" would be difficult.

Therefore, a contradiction between business law, which includes all laws that dictate how to establish and operate a business, and ethics often occurs. If the sole purpose of a business is to make a profit, then unethical behaviors could take place such as hiding information from customers or suppliers, taking unfair advantage of others, or using one's buying influence to gain an advantage over other businesses. Practices such as *price-gouging*, which occurs when merchants raise the prices of consumer goods during an emergency or natural disaster, could be perceived as being unethical.

Alexander Remy Levine/Shutterstock, Inc.

For example, after Hurricane Katrina in 2005, people were forced to pay $7.00 for a bottle of water when the normal price was typically $1.00 per bottle. Some businesses justified raising prices by citing shortages in certain products, which necessitated an increase in price. Fortunately, there are legal protections against price-gouging in many states which allows the attorney general to investigate and prosecute instances of price-gouging once a state of emergency is declared.[2] As you can see, the line between ethical behaviors and legal actions can be blurred.

concept check

How can business law conflict with ethics?

DETERMINING ETHICAL BEHAVIORS

It is important to use various methods to determine if actions might be considered unethical within an organization or by the public. *Blanchard and Peale* use a three-question analysis of a situation to determine if, in fact, actions are ethical. The three questions include: (1) Is it legal? (2) Is it balanced? (3) How does it make me feel? If the answers to all questions are positive, then the dilemma is typically not an ethical concern. But, if there is a negative answer, an organization should further examine the situation to be sure nothing unethical or illegal is taking place. *Laura Nash* suggested viewing the problem from another person's perspective. If you can discuss the decision with your family and friends, then it might be on track to being an ethical decision.

The *Wall Street Journal Model* examines three C's—compliance, contribution, and consequences. When analyzing an ethical situation, this model examines if laws are being violated (compliance), what it does to help stakeholders (contribution), and how the action will affect others (consequences). Another method for determining whether or not a situation is an ethical issue is to ask how you might feel if the story was published by an objective, informed reporter. This *"Front-Page-of-the-Newspaper Test"* might make some think twice before behaving unethically as often this type of behavior ends up on the front page of the newspaper, in social media, or on television![3]

ATTEMPTING TO JUSTIFY UNETHICAL BEHAVIOR? YOU MIGHT BE IF YOU SAY SOMETHING LIKE THIS:
"Everybody else does it."
"That's the way it has always been done."
"It really doesn't hurt anyone."
"No one will know."
"I was just following orders."
"We'll wait until the lawyers tell us it's wrong."

Source: Jennings (2015). Business, its legal, ethical, and global environment, 10th edition. Cengage Learning.

concept check

Discuss methods businesses can use to determine if their actions are ethical.

CONCERNS OF STAKEHOLDERS

Because a variety of stakeholders are affected by a business, ethical issues often arise. Each stakeholder has specific concerns and can exert pressure on management to act in an ethical (or unethical) manner. It is important to identify each stakeholder's concerns; **Table 2.2** lists ethical concerns of a few organizational stakeholders.

TABLE 2.2

Stakeholder Ethical Concerns

STAKEHOLDER	ETHICAL CONCERN
Customer	Expectation that products are safe, dependable, and realistic in price
Employee	Demand fair treatment, safe work conditions, and equitable compensation
Investor	Require that management make sound financial decisions that increase return on their investment
Competitor	Anticipate business practices and dealings will be reasonable and truthful
Creditor	Require timely payment on accounts and accurate accounting information provided by the business

concept check

List five types of stakeholders and provide an example of an ethical concern each might express.

RESPONSIBILITIES TO STAKEHOLDERS

CUSTOMERS

Although a major goal of businesses is to make a profit, they cannot do so at the expense of consumers. Without customers, a business will not operate. A business must consider consumerism, which includes all actions taken to protect consumer rights. The concept of consumer rights includes consumer protection and provides legal protection of consumer interests.[4] When the product a business offers to customers results in harm, this can be devastating for individuals and businesses. Organizations must guarantee that rigorous checks and balances are in place to create products that meet safety standards. Businesses must also make sure consumer and employee safety are a priority.

Consumerism: Actions taken to protect consumer rights.

Due to the government's responsibility to protect consumers, in 1962, President John F. Kennedy introduced the **Consumer Bill of Rights**. The following are the six basic consumer rights:

1. *The Right to Be Safe*—ensures consumer safety against injuries caused by a purchased product.

2. *The Right to Choose Freely*—states that consumers will have a variety of products and services provided by different companies.

3. *The Right to Be Heard*—ensures the opportunity for consumers to voice complaints and concerns about a product and have the issue handled efficiently and responsively.

4. *The Right to Be Informed*—states that businesses should always provide consumers with complete and truthful information to help make informed product choices.

5. *The Right to Education*—ensures that consumers are educated to make better marketplace decisions.

6. *The Right to Service*—ensures that quality services are provided to consumers.

Consumer Bill of Rights: Six basic rights introduced by President John F. Kennedy in 1962 to protect consumers.

concept check

Explain the six rights protected in the Consumer Bill of Rights.

EMPLOYEES

Many believe employees are the most important stakeholders in an organization as the success of the business rests upon their execution of company goals and objectives. Because this is true, it is important for management to set the culture of the organization through its actions and policies. This is often done through the creation of a code of ethics.

A **code of ethics** is a written statement of how an organization expects employees to behave within the organization. As various cultures merge in a work environment, ethical dilemmas may occur as ethics and morals vary between cultures. Companies, therefore, must develop and implement a code of ethics that creates a standard policy to be followed by its employees.

Code of ethics: A written statement of how an organization expects employees to behave within the organization.

Compliance-based: Rules and regulations to ensure ethics compliance in an organization.

Integrity-based: Views ethics as an opportunity to implement core values of the organization.

There are two types of ethics codes a company can create: compliance-based and integrity-based. A compliance-based approach includes rules and regulations to ensure compliance in an organization. This approach deters illegal behavior and promotes a culture of avoidance. An integrity-based approach views ethics as an opportunity to implement core values of the organization. Leaders take responsibility for the firm's ethical culture and hold employees accountable for practicing ethical behaviors and core practices. This type usually includes individuals who directly oversee the enforcement of the code such as chief officers, human resource managers, and board member committees.[5]

concept check

Differentiate between a compliance-based and an integrity-based code of ethics.

MANAGEMENT'S ROLE IN ETHICAL STANDARDS

It is not enough to simply create a code of ethics in an organization. Management must educate employees, act responsibly, and allow for action to be taken when ethics codes are violated. Educating employees provides employees with the necessary policies and expectations established by the employer. Training should educate employees on relevant laws and regulations, empower employees to ask tough questions and make ethical decisions, and make employees aware of available resources, support systems, and appointed personnel who can help with advice in regards to ethical and legal advice. If properly designed, ethics training can make employees aware of ethical issues, increase their understanding of the importance of ethical training, and increase confidence that they can make correct ethical decisions. In order to create an effective ethics program, an organization should do the following (see **Table 2.3**).

TABLE 2.3

Keys to Creating an Effective Ethics Program

KEYS TO CREATING AN EFFECTIVE ETHICS PROGRAM
1. Assess organizational values and vulnerabilities to misconduct.
2. Create opportunities for management to discuss organizational values and risks.
3. Develop and communicate clear standards of conduct.
4. Refine management systems and practices to support the ethics program.

Source: Perry, D. (n.d.). Keys to Creating an Effective Ethics Program. Retrieved from http://home.earthlink.net/~davidlperry/healthex.htm.

"We're getting back to first principles ...
which means we're going to have some."

Cartoonresource/Shutterstock.com

(1) *Assess organizational values and vulnerabilities to misconduct.* Many organizations make the mistake of assigning a small group of staff (usually from the legal department) to write a code of ethics, without first making any attempt to find out what types of ethical issues employees face in their day-to-day jobs. When this happens, it is possible to overlook problems that cannot be addressed in a code alone.

(2) *Create opportunities for management to discuss organizational values and risks.* Management must reach agreement on high-priority concerns as well as action plans that must be formulated to address those issues. Management must schedule periodic reviews of such plans to ensure their continued relevance as well as demonstrate their commitment to ethical actions within the organization. If management does not develop a sense of ownership of the ethics program, employees will perceive it to be merely an unenforced policy and not a long-term commitment.

(3) *Develop and communicate clear standards of conduct.* Once management understands the issues, a written code of ethics can be created or revised. This code should encourage a basic set of organizational values, principles or commitments, establish ground rules, provide guidelines for challenging areas, and explain how employees can obtain further advice and counsel without fear of retaliation.

(4) *Refine management systems and practices to support the ethics program.* This is the most difficult and important step, because it relates to basic tools that managers use to manage: goal-setting (strategic, departmental, individual), incentive and reward systems, performance appraisals, and disciplinary practices. All of these practices need to be evaluated according to whether they serve to reinforce the ethics program or could unintentionally or intentionally encourage unethical behaviors. This process is not a one-time review, but rather an ongoing process of refinement and improvement.[6]

WORKPLACE SAFETY

Employees are important stakeholders in any business. They provide the labor yet are in a subordinate position within the business. State and federal laws have been created to guarantee that employees are treated properly and are fairly compensated. The U.S. Department of Labor (DOL) is the federal organization that implements and governs the workplace activities of approximately 10 million employers and 125 million employees. The DOL enforces more than 180 federal employment laws to protect the employment rights of job seekers and wage earners.[7]

Laws are established to protect both employees and management within the business. Examples of employee rights found under the National Labor Relations Act (1935) include: (1) the ability to form unions; (2) the right to earn minimum pay; (3) the right to earn equal compensation regardless of sex; (4) the right to have safe work environments; (5) the right to earn unemployment benefits; (6) the right to nondiscriminatory hiring practices; (7) the right to take family and medical leave (FMLA); and (8) the ability to voice concerns without employer retaliation.

concept check

Explain how employment law relates to ethics.

INVESTORS

The Sarbanes Oxley Act of 2002 (SOX) is federal legislation that established new rules and regulations for accounting practices and securities trading. This was created to deter and punish corporate and accounting fraud while protecting the interests of employees and shareholders. This act required greater and more transparent financial disclosures, mandated criminal penalties for Chief Executive Officers (CEO's) and Chief Financial Officers (CFOs) who defraud investors, provided protection for whistle-blowers, and established a new regulatory body for public accounting firms. In addition, the U.S. Sentencing Commission has minimum requirements for compliance as companies who have codes of ethics are required to publish them as well as notify the public when any changes are made.[8]

July 30, 2002
[H.R. 3763]

Sarbanes-Oxley Act of 2002. Corporate responsibility. 15 USC 7201 note.

Ethical behavior is the responsibility of everyone within an organization; however, many employees are afraid to notify anyone of wrong-doing for fear of retaliation by management. For this reason, laws have been put in place to protect individuals who "blow the whistle" on wrongful events or actions within organizations. Whistleblowers are employees who disclose to company administration, government agencies, or the media any illegal, unethical, or immoral business practices committed by a company. Usually whistleblowers have exhausted all avenues to resolve a dilemma before going outside the company about an issue.

Sarbanes Oxley Act of 2002 (SOX): Federal legislation that established new rules and regulations for accounting practices and securities trading.

Whistleblowers: Employees who disclose illegal, unethical, or immoral business practices committed by a company.

External reporting can often be prevented by promoting an ethical culture. The Ethics Resource Center conducted a whistleblower study, which surveyed 4,700 working people in mid-September 2011, and found that only 18% of whistleblowers reported externally and 84% of those did so after first trying to report internally. The results of the study found that, in companies where employees trust senior management, 86% reported internally.[9]

GOOD FAITH AND FAIR DEALING

Much of what a business does is defined by the agreements or contracts it has with vendors, employees, and customers. Beyond the explicit rights and responsibilities defined by a contract, the business also has an implicit agreement of good faith and fair dealing. Good faith means honesty in the conduct of a business or within the transaction (not to steal, cheat, or lie). An example of dealing in good faith is focusing on the terms parties have agreed upon in a con-

Good faith: Honesty in business transactions and conduct.

Peter Bernik/Shutterstock, Inc.

tract and fulfilling reasonable expectations of the other party. For example, if a company contracted with a cleaning service to utilize that service exclusively but willfully contracted with another cleaning service to provide those same services, it would violate the notion of acting in "good faith."

An agreement made in good faith is an ethical obligation that courts attempt to enforce. This standard forces all contracting parties to avoid doing anything that would make satisfying the terms of the contract impossible. Examples of acting in good faith include granting the other party access to physical resources under the business's control or providing appropriate information to complete a contracted job. To consider what constitutes good faith, a court relies on the doctrine of equity, which requires that a court resolve a case based on the principles of fairness and justness as defined by the circumstances of the situation.

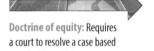

Doctrine of equity: Requires a court to resolve a case based on principles of fairness and justness.

concept check

Why is "good faith" important?

SOCIAL RESPONSIBILITY

wk1003mike/Shutterstock.com

In business, one of the main goals is to make a profit by playing within the rules of the game. However, many businesses and individuals see their role as far more than making a profit. Some view the advancement of society or the environment as an additional role of the business, which has led to the idea of being socially responsible. Social responsibility is the ethical basis that advocates that a business or individual has a responsibility to act for the benefit of society at large. Social responsibility can include a variety of strategies such as giving a portion of profits to non-profit organizations, providing products or services to individuals or groups in need, or giving away a product or service to a cause for every purchase.

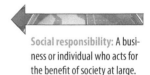

Social responsibility: A business or individual who acts for the benefit of society at large.

The level of social responsibility a business subscribes to begins with the attitude of management. Management's attitude toward social responsibility can be classified into two perspectives: the economic model or the socioeconomic model. The economic model perspective promotes the idea that management's main responsibility is to increase shareholders' wealth and maximize profits. According to the traditional concept of business, a company exists to produce quality goods and services, earn a reasonable profit, and provide jobs. The economic model of social responsibility holds that society will benefit more when business is left alone to produce and market profitable products that society needs.

Economic model: Focused on maximizing profits and returns to shareholders.

The opposing perspective is the socioeconomic model, which supports the idea that a business has responsibilities to society beyond simply maximizing profits. A recent trend shows an increasing number of managers and companies have adopted the socioeconomic model for at least three reasons: (1) a business is dominated by the corporate form of ownership and the corporation is a creation of society;

Socioeconomic model: Business has responsibilities to society at large beyond maximizing profits.

Competitive advantage: A distinct advantage a business has over its competition.

(2) companies are starting to take pride in their social responsibility records; and (3) business people consider it a competitive advantage or a distinct advantage over any of its competition.[10]

PROS OF SOCIAL RESPONSIBILITY

Social responsibility increases a business's accountability and provides transparency with media, stakeholders, local communities, and investors. According to a study conducted by the branding company Landor Associates and cited by the University of Pennsylvania's Wharton School, 77 percent of consumers think that companies should be socially responsible. Consumers are attracted to companies that are known for being socially responsible.[11] A social responsibility program enhances profitability, value, and the image of a company. In fact, research from the Ethics Resource Center showed that, over a 30-year period, socially responsible companies outperformed companies that were not socially responsible in the stock market.[12]

CONS OF SOCIAL RESPONSIBILITY

The amount of time, money, and resources utilized to maximize profits and shareholder return can influence whether an organization invests in socially responsible behaviors. A major disadvantage of social responsibility is the cost: investing in the right equipment, hiring service providers, adding new space, and investing in employee education and training. Another disadvantage for businesses is the potential for negative reactions by shareholders. Some shareholders may be happy to invest in businesses that are socially responsible whereas others may not support the expense of implementing socially responsible strategies.[13]

concept check

How can social responsibility be a benefit to a company?

Corporate social responsibility (CSR): A business's duty to maximize its positive impact on all stakeholders, the community, and the environment.

A socially responsible business believes it has an obligation to the people it works with directly as well as anyone who may be affected by their activities. Corporate social responsibility (CSR) is a business's duty to positively impact all stakeholders while minimizing its negative impact on society and the environment. A business can meet this goal by promoting employees' charitable acts, reducing waste, or minimizing pollution output. By being socially responsible, a business can meet its ethical obligations, promote its public image, or possibly avoid violating laws.

Although many companies now practice some form of social responsibility, a few have made it a core value within their operations.[14] For companies that decide to invest in being socially responsible, the options for contributing to society are endless. **Table 2.4** displays a few examples of socially responsible efforts practiced by businesses today.

COMPANY	SOCIALLY RESPONSIBLE EFFORTS
Google (Technology)	Google Green is a corporate effort to use resources efficiently and support renewable power. Google has seen an overall drop in power requirements for their data centers by an average of 50 percent.
Xerox (Printing)	The printing giant has multiple programs for donating and supporting others. Their *Community Involvement Program* encourages employees to get directly involved with socially responsible efforts in their areas.
Target (Retail)	Since 2010, the company's efforts—from growing sustainable practices to educational grants—have amounted to 5 percent of its profit going to local communities. In the area of education alone, Target has donated more than $875 million.

TABLE 2.4

Examples of Corporate Social Responsibility Initiatives

Moreno, C. (2015). Doing Their Part: 3 Excellent Examples of Corporate Social Responsibility. Retrieved from: http://lineshapespace.com/doing-their-part-3-excellent-examples-of -corporate-social-responsibility/.

Although the Environmental Protection Agency (EPA) does regulate some areas related to the environment, many businesses go above and beyond what they are required to do in order to help decrease their impact on the environment. Environmentalism is the effort made by an organization to protect the environment from destruction or pollution. Businesses, in general, have a large carbon footprint, which is the amount of carbon dioxide or other carbon compounds released into the atmosphere by an individual, company, or country. Any steps taken to reduce those footprints are considered positive for the company as well as society and include everything from curbing pollution to developing clean energy solutions.

Environmental Protection Agency (EPA): Governmental agency that regulates business effects on the environment.

Environmentalism: The effort made by an organization to protect the environment.

Carbon footprint: Carbon compounds released into the atmosphere by an individual, company, or country.

mangostock/Shutterstock.com

Corporate philanthropy is an organization's ability to give back to the community around them and the world at large. Businesses can be philanthropic by donating money, resources, or time to international, national, or local charities. Businesses have many resources that have the potential to reach further than individuals are capable of doing on their own. Forbes provided a list of the top ten most generous companies, which included names such as Wells Fargo, Walmart, Chevron Corporation, Bank of America, Target Corporation, and Google.[15] Corporations are not obligated to contribute to society; however, the trade-off in giving back to society can bring rewards in the form of customer loyalty and positive public relations. Non-profit volunteering at places like Ronald McDonald houses, Habitat for Humanity, or donation matching are common forms of corporate philanthropy. If you donate time, money, or resources to an organization, check with your employer to see if they are willing to match your contributions as many organizations have matching programs, which doubles your good deeds!

INTERNATIONAL BUSINESS AND ETHICAL BEHAVIORS

Social responsibility is a core value in many organizations in the United States and around the globe; however, there are challenges to being socially responsible as not all global organizations value social responsibility nor support the costs necessary to be socially responsible.

SUPPLY CHAIN

Businesses that work with global suppliers can find it challenging to address socially irresponsible or unethical business practices. Apple came under fire from the media and its customers when sub-par working conditions were reported at one of its supplier's plants. Apple insisted it was not aware of the labor conditions and sent a team to the Foxconn plant in China to investigate the allegations. Similarly, Walmart came under intense pressure from its shareholders to disclose and monitor how its international suppliers treat workers. Walmart admitted that addressing this issue was a challenge for the company as it conducts business with numerous suppliers.[16]

arka38/Shutterstock.com

ETHICAL LABOR PRACTICES

Treating employees fairly and ethically is another form of corporate social responsibility. This is especially true of businesses that operate in international locations with different labor laws than those in the United States.[17] **Sweatshops**, or sweat factories, is a term for a workplace that has socially unacceptable working conditions. The work may be difficult or dangerous and employees may not be paid a wage that is adequate for a livable wage. Workers in sweatshops may work long hours for low pay, regardless of laws mandating overtime pay or a minimum wage; child labor laws may also be violated or ignored in countries around the world that rely on such labor to make products.

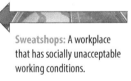

Sweatshops: A workplace that has socially unacceptable working conditions.

These types of workplace violations are the norm in the global apparel industry. Brand name companies such as Nike, The Gap, Walmart, Victoria's Secret, and even Disney have been caught selling products that utilize sweatshops.[18] The challenge in dealing with suppliers in other countries is that they do not have to follow U.S. laws within their borders. Organizations do have some leverage as foreign businesses will comply to some degree in order to maintain business relationships with U.S. companies.

EMPLOYEE PAY

In a perfect world, every employee would earn wages high enough to live well, but unfortunately, every business has specific goals and objectives that require economic decisions to be made about employee compensation. Socially responsible companies understand that paying employees a fair or above average wage may cost more but has significant advantages in the long run. However, the challenge lies in keeping stockholders happy as employees' salaries are always the highest expense in an organization and being socially responsible can add considerable costs to the company.

Sustainability: Methods used to promote proper use and extension of ecological resources.

Sustainability refers to methods used to promote proper use and extension of ecological resources. Recycling bottles and cans or reducing paper and energy consumption are ways that businesses can incorporate sustainable practices in their operations. Old habits are hard to change, and companies have to remain committed to training employees on how to incorporate these practices in their daily activities. Sustainability practices should be employed company-wide and tracked or measured to determine success. Businesses can document their efforts to be environmentally responsible in their annual reports.[19]

Green marketing: The practice of selling products and/or services based on their environmental benefits.

Green marketing refers to the practice of selling products and/or services based on their environmental benefits. To monitor this effort, the Federal Trade Commission (FTC) mandates that marketers show evidence that products they sell as "green" qualify as "recyclable," "recycled content," "compostable." Other terms including "carbon offsets," "nontoxic," or "renewable energy" are often used and must be verified in order to qualify as green products."[20]

Vlad Karavaev/Shutterstock.com

WRAPPING UP...

Chapter 2 focused on the challenging and ever-changing areas of ethical behavior and social responsibility. Due to many viewpoints regarding both topics, there are myriad ways organizations are implementing and enforcing policies in the United States and around the globe. It is important to understand acceptable ethical practices and behaviors in an organization and to develop your own moral code in order to avoid personal and professional dilemmas.

In Chapter 3, we will discuss economic systems and basics components of economics. This will lay the groundwork for you to understand how businesses operate within the United States and in a competitive environment.

BUSINESS TERMINOLOGY

Ethics	Socioeconomic model
Business ethics	Economic model
Business law	Competitive advantage
Consumerism	Corporate social responsibility
Consumer Bill of Rights	(CSR)
Code of ethics	Environmental Protection Agency
Compliance-based	(EPA)
Integrity-based	Environmentalism
Sarbanes Oxley Act of 2002 (SOX)	Carbon footprint
Whistleblowers	Corporate philanthropy
Good faith	Sweatshops
Doctrine of equity	Sustainability
Social responsibility	Green marketing

DISCUSSION QUESTIONS

1. Do you feel that there is a general decline in business ethics in today's world?

2. Select a company you believe is socially responsible and provide evidence that proves they are socially responsible.

3. What are the pros and cons of requiring all companies to be socially responsible?

4. Why was the Sarbanes Oxley Act established, and do you think that it has worked?

5. Do you feel that the use of sweatshops affects consumers' decisions to purchase products from companies who use them?

6. Do you believe green marketing is a response to consumer demand, or is it another marketing ploy?

LEARNING ACTIVITIES

1. Think about the use of a code of ethics from a current or past employer. Evaluate the organization's use of the code of ethics based on how individuals were made aware of the code; the initial, as well as the on-going, training within the organization to enforce the code; and the ethical behaviors of management. (*If you have not been employed, ask someone about an organization he/she is familiar with or look up information about a company on their web site.*) Share this information in a small group and discuss the use of a code of ethics within different organizations.

2. Conduct an Internet search for an "online business ethics quiz." Several choices will show in your results; however, select one and take the quiz. Write a short summary of the business quiz you selected (include URL, title of quiz, and who sponsors it) as well as your individual results and what they mean in relation to your ethical behavior. Do you feel the results are an accurate reflection of who you are and how you operate in your personal and professional life?

3. The top 100 "Best Companies to Work For" list is published each year by Fortune magazine. In addition, local newspapers publish the top companies to work for in their respective areas. Use the Fortune web site or a local newspaper to locate two companies listed on a "Best Companies" list and discuss what makes each company a great place to work and what socially responsible efforts the organization is involved in.

4. Select an organization and research their efforts to "Go Green" in recent years. What areas of controversy have surrounded the organization in moving toward green efforts? And, what improvements have been made by the organization and what are its plans moving forward?

Note: *Because web sites often change, use a search engine to find alternative web sites to access required information when necessary.*

CASE STUDY: PERCEPTIONS MATTER

Riley and Associates recently acquired a public relations firm to complement their management consulting company. Riley Glidden is the managing partner of the firm and was approached by a local fast food chain, Sir Friendly's, to help develop their public image. Upon researching the business, Riley found that over the past three years, Sir Friendly's has been cited for various food violations and has not established a good name within the communities they serve due to unclean facilities and rumors of being unethical in their business practices.

The company president's goal is to become the "restaurant of choice", and he vowed to do anything to make this happen. A quick survey of the marketplace found that the food was good and service adequate. Upon further investigation, Riley found that the current owner purchased the chain three years ago. She contacted area businesses regarding their perception of this particular business and found that, prior to new ownership, the company was a contributing business to the local community and provided support to local charities and school clubs. These activities ceased when the new president took over.

CASE STUDY ANALYSIS

Based on the information provided, answer the following questions:

(1) What suggestions can Riley offer to the company president in regard to his goal of becoming the "restaurant of choice"?

(2) How do you believe expectations by the community for Sir Friendly's to be socially responsible have affected the business? Is this fair?

(3) Knowing that social responsibility is a volunteer process, what suggestions should Riley offer the company president to help him establish positive public relations without adding exorbitant costs?

CHAPTER 3

UNDERSTANDING
ECONOMIC SYSTEMS

OUTCOMES:

- ➤ Define macroeconomics and microeconomics.
- ➤ Describe the business cycle.
- ➤ Discuss key economic indicators and what they demonstrate to businesses, the government, and society.
- ➤ Compare and contrast capitalism, socialism, communism, and mixed economies.
- ➤ Explain the difference between fiscal and monetary policy.
- ➤ Analyze financial institutions in the United States and internationally and the Federal Reserve Board's importance to business.

ECONOMICS

Economics is a social science concerned with the description and analysis of how societies use scarce resources to produce, distribute, and monitor consumption of goods and services around the world. Three main questions that come from economics are: (1) What goods and services will be produced? (2) How they will be produced? (3) How they will be distributed among the members of society?

Adam Smith is widely considered the father of modern economics. Smith's book, *The Wealth of Nations*, describes the "invisible hand" theory, which shows how an individual's personal gain benefits others and a nation's economy.[1] For example, when an individual stops to get the morning paper and a cup of coffee from a local business, that individual makes life better for himself as well as the business owner as the business owner profits and the individual is satisfied with the coffee and newspaper.

This in turn benefits both parties, which is the idea of the invisible hand. Smith believed that if individuals were left to make their own decisions about what was bought and sold in the marketplace, it would lead to the right products at the right prices being offered without government involvement.

Economics is customarily divided into two areas of study: microeconomics and macroeconomics. Microeconomics is a division of economics that studies the behavior of individual consumers and suppliers as they make decisions in the market. The key factors that impact market prices are supply and demand. Supply is the amount of goods or services producers are willing and able to produce in the market at different prices. Demand is the readiness and capability of buyers to purchase goods or services at different prices. Because consumers and suppliers want different prices to maximize their resources, an agreeable price for goods and services must be determined in the marketplace. The point at which buyers and sellers agree upon price and quantity is known as the equilibrium price. Stated differently, the equilibrium price is the point at which supply matches demand for a particular good or service (see **Figure 3.1**).

As you examine **Figure 3.1**, you can see that at $30, the demand for a new DVD is fairly low (less than 5); however, as the price drops, consumers are willing and able to purchase more DVDs (at $5, quantity demanded is roughly 45). The supply side is just the opposite as producers are willing to supply more at higher prices (40 at $25) than at lower prices (five at $5) because they will make more money from each DVD sold. At $15, supply and demand meet, which indicates that, at the equilibrium point, 25 DVDs should be produced and sold in the marketplace.

Economics: An analysis of how societies use scarce resources to produce, distribute, and monitor consumption of goods and services around the world.

Adam Smith: The father of modern economics.

Invisible Hand: Smith's philosophy that describes how an individual's personal gain benefits others and the economy.

Microeconomics: A division of economics that studies the behavior of individual consumers and suppliers as they make decisions.

Supply: The amount of goods or services producers are willing and able to produce in the market at different prices.

Demand: The readiness and capability of buyers to purchase goods or services at different price levels.

Equilibrium price: The point at which supply matches demand for a particular good or service.

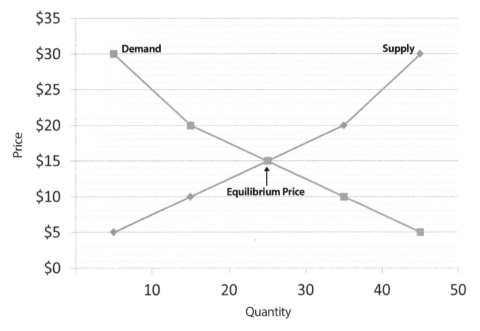

FIGURE 3.1

Equilibrium Price

Macroeconomics: The study of economic indicators such as unemployment, inflation, and gross domestic product, and their influence on the economy as a whole.

Gross Domestic Product (GDP): The total value of goods and services produced within a country's borders over some unit of time.

Productivity: A measure of how much is produced with available resources.

Per capita GDP: A measure of a country's economic strength and standard of living as compared to other countries.

Macroeconomics involves the study of economic indicators such as unemployment, inflation, and gross domestic product, and their influence on the economy as a whole. Business owners, individuals, and the government are all concerned with these factors as they provide an indication of whether a nation's economy is growing, remaining stable, or declining.[2] The following discussion explains indicators that help determine the overall growth of a country in a given period.

concept check

Explain the difference between macroeconomics and microeconomics.

Gross domestic product (GDP) represents the total value of goods and services produced within a country's borders over some unit of time, typically one year. This calculation measures a country's **productivity**, which is a measure of how much is produced with available resources.[3]

Analysts divide total GDP by the population of a country in order to determine **per capita GDP**. This allows for a comparison of economic strength and standard of living across the globe. The United States enjoys a high per capita GDP, which is an indication that citizens live fairly well as compared to those countries with lower per capita GDP. **Figure 3.2** shows the countries of the world with the highest GDP. The United States had roughly $18 trillion of GDP in 2016, whereas the lowest GDP of less than $40 million was from Tuvalu, which is north of New Zealand and east of Australia in the Pacific Ocean.

FIGURE 3.2

Countries with
Highest GDP

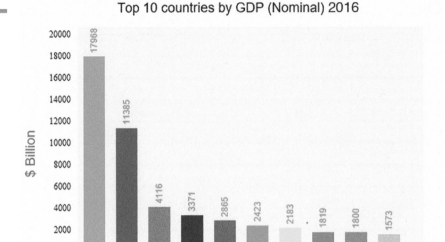

Top 10 countries by GDP (Nominal) 2016

Source: Projected Global GDP Rankings (2016). Retrieved from: http://statisticstimes.com/economy/projected-world-gdp-ranking.php.

concept check

Why is GDP used as a measure of economic strength?

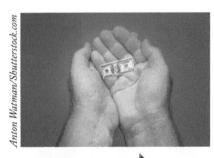

Inflation: A sustained increase in the general price level of goods and services.

Another economic indicator used to evaluate the strength of a country's economy is the **inflation** rate. Inflation is defined as a sustained increase in the general price level of goods and services. It is measured as an annual percentage increase or decrease and affects an individual's purchasing power or how much can be purchased with a given amount of money. When inflation rates go up, there is a decline in the purchasing power of money. For example, if the inflation rate is 2% annually, then it would cost 2% more every year to buy the same goods and services purchased previously. If your wages do not increase with inflation rates, you will be able to purchase less next year than this year. This can be good if your income rises more than the inflation rate but negatively impacts individuals whose incomes do not increase, or do not increase as much as the inflation rate, from year to year.

Lisa S./Shutterstock.com

The **Consumer Price Index (CPI)** measures the average prices of a basket of consumer goods and services used by urban families, such as transportation, food, and medical care. In order to determine if prices have increased, the Bureau of Labor Statistics (BLS) compares basket items monthly. If prices increase, it is an indication of rising inflation rates. Changes in the CPI are used to assess price changes associated with the cost of living.[4]

Another indicator of an economy's strength involves the workforce and its ability to provide jobs for those seeking employment. In the United States, individuals counted in the **total labor force** include those over 16 years of age who are actively seeking employment.[5] Those individuals included in the total labor force who cannot find employment are included in the unemployment rate. The **unemployment rate** is calculated by dividing the number of unemployed individuals by the total labor force. The unemployment rate is sometimes criticized as not being fully accurate as it does not include individuals who have simply stopped looking for work (called **discouraged workers**) or those who are not utilizing their education or full skill set in their current position (called **underemployed workers**).

Consumer Price Index (CPI): Measures the average prices of a basket of consumer goods and services in order to determine inflation rates

Total labor force: All individuals who are 16 years or older and actively seeking employment.

Unemployment rate: Total unemployed workers in the total labor force.

Discouraged workers: Individuals who have given up looking for employment.

Underemployed workers: Individuals working but not utilizing their skills or education.

concept check

Explain the types of economic indicators used to measure the strength of the U.S. economy.

All of these economic indicators ebb and flow over time, which lead to changes in the economy. The **business cycle** describes the various stages of growth and decline in an economy and includes four phases: expansion, boom, recession, and depression. Each phase influences consumer, producer, and governmental actions. The National Bureau of Economic Research (NBER) determines what phase of the business cycle the United States is in by examining GDP, employment numbers, personal income, and retail sales.

Business cycle: The phases of growth and decline in an economy.

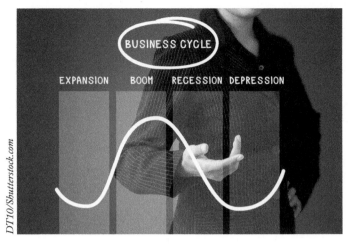

A trough is the low-point in a business cycle from which the economy starts improving. In the *expansion stage*, sometimes referred to as recovery, there is steady growth in the economy and GDP increases. The *boom stage* is the high-point of economic growth, sometimes referred to as the peak, where individuals and businesses experience high rates of inflation and GDP maximizes. What goes up must come down and when it does, there is a "downturn" in the economy, which can lead to a *recession*. This stage is characterized by a steady decline in GDP, which lasts for six months or longer. A sustained decline in economic growth and GDP over an extended period of time is called a *depression*. After the Great Depression of the 1930s, economists are hesitant to use this term as it causes a loss in consumer confidence and potentially panic, which would drive the economy into a worse state.[6]

concept check

Explain each phase of the business cycle.

TYPES OF ECONOMIC SYSTEMS

Capitalism: An economic system characterized by a free market and private control of production and consumption exists.

Capitalism is an economic and political system characterized by a free market and private control of production and consumption. The United States is considered the leader in capitalism. Characteristics of capitalism include: privately owned businesses, large numbers of businesses, limited government interference, and the ability to retain profits. These characteristics provide incentives for individuals to create and expand businesses in a capitalistic country, which increases the level of innovation and motivation of entrepreneurs.

Socialism: An economic system in which major industries are controlled by the government, while private owners operate noncritical industry businesses.

Socialism is an economic system in which major industries are controlled by the government, whereas private owners operate noncritical industry businesses. It is characterized by production for use rather than profit, by equality of individual wealth, by the absence of competitive economic activity, and, usually, by government determination of investments, prices, and production levels. Socialism is an economic system in which the production and distribution of goods are controlled substantially by the government rather than by private enterprise, and in which cooperation, rather than competition, guides economic activity. In such a system, motivation and innovation are limited in state-run businesses but do exist in private enterprise. A list of several socialist countries is found in **Table 3.1**.

SOCIALIST COUNTRIES IN THE WORLD	
Denmark	Sweden
Finland	Norway
Netherlands	Ireland
Canada	Belgium

Source: http://blog.peerform.com/top-ten-most-socialist-countries-in-the-world/.

TABLE 3.1

Socialist Countries in the World

Communism is an economic system in which all activity is controlled by a centralized government and profits are not allowed for individual business owners. In the mid-1800s, Karl Marx formed the basis of communist theory with **Marxism**, which holds that private enterprise has an unfair advantage in the market as they control the majority of resources; therefore, it is best to allow a centralized government to control production and share resources equally among citizens. Today, there are only five countries considered communist: China, North Korea, Vietnam, Laos, and Cuba. It is important to note that China has made movement toward more of a mixed economy as it blends capitalistic and socialistic elements into its current economy. This will likely continue to happen as China grows economically, adapts to Western culture, and increases its use of Western products.

Communism: An economic system in which all activity is controlled by a centralized government.

Marxism: Theory that states it is best to allow a centralized government to control production and to share resources equally among citizens.

Mixed economies: Economies that combine elements of capitalism and socialism.

Mixed economies are economies that combine elements of capitalism and socialism as some industries are privately owned while others are publicly owned or nationalized. France, for example, employs what is often referred to as state capitalism. In this type of mixed economy, the state owns the majority share in private enterprises. In Great Britain's history, it was common for the state to own some industries while allowing others to be privately held.[7] In mixed economies, the private sector owns most businesses and is expected to make a profit, but state-run business entities are also expected to make a profit on their endeavors.

concept check

Compare and contrast the various types of economic systems.

TYPES OF COMPETITION

Most industrialized countries operate under the private enterprise system (capitalism). In most cases, this system rewards businesses for meeting consumer demands in the form of profit. In general, government tends to adopt a hands-off approach toward business owners in order to allow competition to determine who is successful in the marketplace. The competitive market regulates economic life, creating both opportunities and challenges for business owners. Because competition drives business activities and decisions, it is important to understand the various types of competition that exist in the business world including: pure competition, monopolistic competition, monopolies, and oligopolies (see **Figure 3.3**).

FIGURE 3.3

Market Structure Continuum

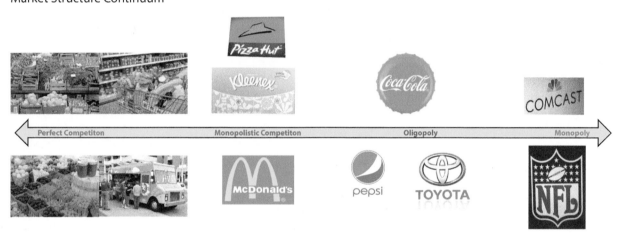

Products and services on the various types of competition. Source: Shutterstock.com.

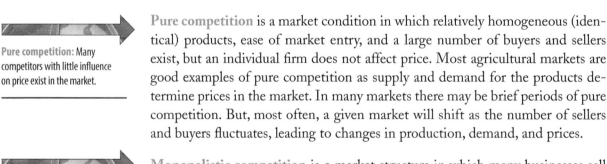

Pure competition: Many competitors with little influence on price exist in the market.

Pure competition is a market condition in which relatively homogeneous (identical) products, ease of market entry, and a large number of buyers and sellers exist, but an individual firm does not affect price. Most agricultural markets are good examples of pure competition as supply and demand for the products determine prices in the market. In many markets there may be brief periods of pure competition. But, most often, a given market will shift as the number of sellers and buyers fluctuates, leading to changes in production, demand, and prices.

Monopolistic competition: Many heterogeneous products are sold by firms and are differentiated in the marketplace.

Monopolistic competition is a market structure in which many businesses sell products that are similar but not identical. The characteristics of a monopolistic competition are as follows: there are many sellers and many buyers in a given market; no business has total control over the market price; consumers perceive that there are nonprice differences among the competitors' products (*product* *differentiation*); and there are few barriers to entry and exit. Some examples include cereal, shoes, computer software, books, or furniture as products are available from private label producers to brand names. These varied products in the market allow customers to select which level of product they want to purchase, even though the products have similarities. For example, a parent can purchase Target's Up & Up Diapers less expensively than a name brand such as Huggies or Pampers. It is up to companies to influence consumer purchasing by persuading them that the company's products offer features, benefits, or cost advantages the other products do not.

A **monopoly** is a market environment where there is only one provider of a certain economic good or service. Entry into these markets is restricted due to high costs or economic, social, or political barriers. A government can create a monopoly over an industry that it wants to control. The most common monopoly in most areas is the utilities industry. Typically, only one company exists in a geographical area and customers do not have a choice of provider. When this happens, the government regulates pricing so consumers are not taken advantage of or treated unfairly.

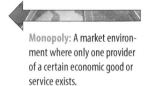

Monopoly: A market environment where only one provider of a certain economic good or service exists.

Another barrier to entry in a monopolistic industry occurs when one organization has exclusive rights to a natural resource. For example, in Saudi Arabia, the government has sole control over the oil industry. A monopoly also exists when a company has a copyright or patent that prevents others from entering the market. Pfizer, for instance, holds a patent on Viagra that lasts for 20 years. Microsoft, which was considered a monopoly for combining their operating system and other software on personal computers, settled on charges of following monopolistic practices in the early 2000s.

cberezoff/Shutterstock.com

An **oligopoly** is a market situation in which a small group of firms control the market. An oligopoly is much like a monopoly; however, in an oligopoly, at least two firms control the market. Whether by noncompetitive practices, government mandate, or technological savvy, these companies take advantage of their position to increase profitability. Companies in technology, pharmaceuticals, and health insurance have become successful in establishing oligopolies in the United States.[8] Industries that are examples of oligopolies include: the steel industry, aluminum, film, television, cell phones, and gas (see **Figure 3.4**). **Table 3.2** displays a summary of the differences in the types of business competition.

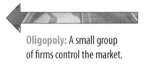

Oligopoly: A small group of firms control the market.

FIGURE 3.4

Oligopolies in Industry

Gas
Royal Dutch Shell,
Chevroon, and British
Petroleum (BP)

Cell Phone Makers
Samsung, Nokia,
and Apple

Television
NBC, CBS, and ABC

Film Studios
20th Century Fox,
Warner Bros., and
Paramount

TABLE 3.2

Differences in the Types of Business Competition

CHARACTERISTICS OF MARKET MODEL	PURE COMPETITION	MONOPOLISTIC COMPETITION	MONOPOLY	OLIGOPOLY
NUMBER OF FIRMS IN MARKET	Many	Many	One	Few (more than one)
TYPE OF PRODUCTS SOLD	Homogeneous (similar)	Heterogeneous (differentiated)	Unique, no substitutes	Similar or differentiated
BUSINESS CONTROL OVER PRICE	No control	Limited control	High level of control (though regulations may limit)	High level if other businesses agree
EASE OF ENTRY INTO MARKET	Very easy	Fairly easy	Blocked	Difficult
EXAMPLES	Agriculture	Fast food, retail stores	Utility companies, oil industry in Saudi Arabia	Car companies, soft drink companies

concept check

Evaluate the various types of competition in the marketplace.

HISTORY OF ECONOMIC THEORY

Everett Historical/Shutterstock.com

The **Great Depression** was a severe worldwide economic depression that started in 1929 following the stock market crash and lasted until 1939. During this time, personal income decreased, tax revenue dropped, and unemployment rose to nearly 25%, which greatly influenced the development of macroeconomics theory. Citizens of the United States wanted to improve economic conditions; therefore, different ideas about how to fix the economy developed and continue to frame present day discussions. Two opposing views about how to fix the economy emerged, including Keynesian and Monetarism schools of thought.

In 1936, John Maynard Keynes published The *General Theory of Employment, Interest and Money*, which theorized that government spending and tax policies could be used to stabilize economies. The **Keynesian** school of economic thought argues that an increase in government spending or a reduction in taxes could be used to stimulate the economy; likewise, a reduction in government spending or an increase in taxes could be utilized to slow down the economy and reduce inflation. Individuals who support government intervention to alter the economic conditions of a country subscribe to the Keynesian school of economic thought.

Great Depression: A severe worldwide economic depression during the late 1930s through the middle 1940s.

Keynesian: School of economic thought that supports government intervention to stabilize the economy.

Monetarism: School of thought that the Federal Reserve System should control the supply of money as the chief method of stabilizing the economy.

Milton Friedman developed another well-known macroeconomic school of thought called Monetarism. This theory supports having the Federal Reserve System control the supply of money as the chief method of stabilizing the economy. This would be done through regulating banking systems, interest rates, and the money supply. This philosophy rejects Keynes's idea that government involvement will correct a faltering economy.[9] Proponents of each theory continue to argue about how to correct or stimulate the economy when it is perceived as stagnating or declining.

concept check

Discuss the difference between the Keynesian and Monetarism schools of economic thought.

MANAGING ECONOMIC PERFORMANCE

A solid economy must have individuals who control the money supply and create policies to provide for and protect the public's well-being. This is done through the use of two types of policies: fiscal and monetary. Depending on one's view of how a free market should operate, either Keynesian or Monetarism, individuals support the use of different policy actions.

Monetary policy: The actions of the Federal Reserve System to achieve macroeconomic policy objectives such as price stability, full employment, and economic growth.

Expansionary monetary policy: Stimulating the economy by increasing the money supply and lowering interest rates.

Restrictive monetary policy: Slowing down the economy by decreasing the money supply and raising interest rates.

Monetary policy refers to the actions of the Federal Reserve System to achieve macroeconomic policy objectives such as price stability, full employment, and economic growth. The U.S. Congress established full employment and price stability as macroeconomic objectives for the Federal Reserve. Congress determined that operational conduct of monetary policy should be free from political influence, so the Federal Reserve, an independent agency of the federal government, was established in 1913. The Federal Reserve System is tasked with monitoring interest rates, the money supply, and bank reserve requirements.

Increasing or decreasing the money supply, changing banking requirements, and adjusting interest rates to influence spending alters bankers' willingness to make loans. Expansionary monetary policy increases the money supply by reducing interest rates, which encourages businesses to invest or expand, and in turn stimulates employment and economic growth. Restrictive monetary policy reduces the money supply by raising interest rates to control rising prices, overexpansion, and concerns about overly rapid economic growth. Taking these actions typically slows the economy.

Fiscal policy refers to the "tax and spend" policies of the federal government. Fiscal policy decisions are determined by Congress and the current administration; the Federal Reserve plays no role in determining fiscal policy.[10] Many programs are offered by the federal government to help individuals in the United States; however, taxes may be increased or other budget items cut in order to pay for such programs. Individuals have strong opinions about fiscal policy decisions and vote for candidates that support their beliefs about what policies should be in place to help drive economic growth. Some individuals prefer more government intervention whereas others prefer little government intervention. If individuals in Congress do not agree on actions to be taken to improve the economy, little is accomplished.

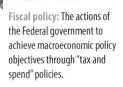

Fiscal policy: The actions of the Federal government to achieve macroeconomic policy objectives through "tax and spend" policies.

concept check

What is the difference between monetary policy and fiscal policy?

FEDERAL RESERVE BANK CREATION

maigi/Shutterstock.com

On December 23, 1913, the Federal Reserve Bank, which serves as the nation's central bank, was created by an act of Congress. The Federal Reserve System (The Fed) consists of a seven member Board of Governors with headquarters in Washington, D.C., and 12 Reserve Banks located in major cities throughout the United States. The Federal Reserve Districts are shown in **Figure 3.5**.

Federal Reserve Bank: The central bank of the United States, which regulates banking institutions.

FIGURE 3.5

The 12 Federal Reserve Bank Districts

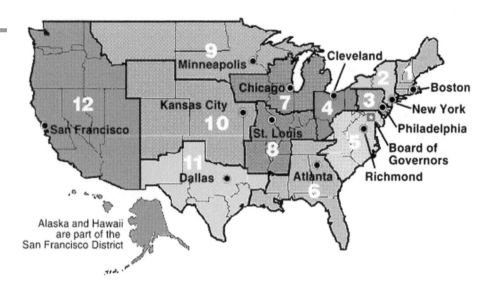

Source: http://www.federalreserve.gov/otherfrb.htm.

The Fed has supervisory and regulatory authority over many banking institutions. In this role, the Fed promotes the safety and soundness of the banking system, fosters stability in financial markets, and ensures compliance with laws and regulations under its jurisdiction. The Fed encourages banking institutions to meet the financial needs of their communities by making sensible loans and evaluating banks' compliance with laws and regulations.[11] Without this oversight, banking institutions would not be as secure as they are today; however, even with such oversight, failures occur in the banking system as was evidenced in the 1930s, 1980s, and as recently as 2008.

concept check

What is the purpose of the Federal Reserve System?

THE GREAT RECESSION OF 2008

In 2008, the United States experienced a major financial crisis that led to the most serious recession since World War II. The recession was caused by the failure of several major industries in the United States, including banks, financial institutions, automakers, and other companies. The effects created a global crisis and caused the housing market to collapse. In 2008 and 2009, the U.S. labor market lost 8.4 million jobs, or 6.1% of all payroll employment. This was the most dramatic employment contraction of any recession since the

Great Depression in the 1930s. By comparison, a recession in the 1980s had job losses of 3.1%, about half as severe. The Great Recession brought the worst of both worlds: extraordinarily severe job loss combined with an extremely sluggish recovery.

On September 15, 2008, Lehman Brothers, one of the largest investment banks in the world, failed. Following their failure, the U.S. stock market dropped by half, cash was not available, and reputable companies laid off thousands of employees. When these events took place, there was no doubt a recession was upon the American economy. In the fall of 2008, the economy began to decline at more than a 6% annual rate and the stock market had fallen by over 54%, down to roughly 6500 points from its high of nearly 14,200 points in 2007.[12]

In 2008, Congress responded by passing the Troubled Asset Relief Program (TARP). This plan was designed to decrease the severity of the recession by treating its cause: the financial crisis. TARP was established as a response to the economic crash, which put the U.S. economy into a recessionary state. The program was created by the United States Department of Treasury and $700 billion was made available with the intent to spur economic growth.[13] By December 2013, the government stated it was wrapping up TARP funds and gave credit to the program for saving the auto industry, foreclosures, banks, and jobs in the United States. Many disagreed with the government's involvement to fix the recession and called it a bailout.

Troubled Asset Relief Program (TARP): Plan created in 2008 by the U.S. Congress to assist failing financial institutions and save the U.S. economy from collapse.

Dodd-Frank Act: Law passed in 2010 to help lower risks in the financial system and protect consumers.

Because of the severe financial crisis of 2008, Congress passed the Wall Street Reform and Consumer Protection Act of 2010 in an effort to lower risks in the financial system. The law, known as the Dodd-Frank Act, affected the Fed in many ways. It changed the Fed's governance, increased its transparency, expanded its regulatory responsibilities, and transferred most Fed-consumer protection responsibilities to a new Consumer Financial Protection Bureau. This act caused changes to consumer credit card statements so information is more easily understood and to loan offerings to avoid predatory lending. The Dodd-Frank Act serves as a supervisory approach to safeguard the financial system and avoid future occurrences of the financial crisis experienced in 2008.

concept check

Explain what caused the Great Recession of 2008 and new legislation that resulted from it.

JMiks/Shutterstock.com

Both the financial crisis and the downturn in the U.S. economy spread to many foreign nations, resulting in a global economic crisis. The interconnectivity of nations will continue to be an issue moving forward in the 21st century, but other challenges also exist such as the widening gap between the rich and the poor, the rapid growth in population, and the persistence of environmental destruction. **Table 3.3** shows a few examples that global economies will contend with in the future and that must be collectively addressed by all nations.

U.S. firms and the government must determine how to interact with the global community to solve these challenges. Global capitalism and economic globalization have rested, and must continue to rest, on a secure political and economic foundation. To safeguard existence of the global economy, the United States and other major powers must recommit themselves to working together to rebuild its weakened political and economic foundations as well as prepare for the challenges that lie ahead.

TABLE 3.3

Global Economic
Challenges

TYPE OF RISK	CHALLENGES
Technological	Massive incidences of data fraud/theft, cyber attacks, infrastructure breakdowns
Societal	Pandemic outbreak, water crisis
Geopolitical	Small- or large-scale terrorist attacks interstate conflicts, weapons of mass destruction
Environmental	Extreme weather conditions, failure of climate change adaptations
Economic	Fiscal crises in key economies, unemployment or underemployment, energy price shock

Source: World Economic Forum (2015). Global Risks 2015, 10th Edition. Retrieved from: http://www3.weforum.org/docs/WEF_Global_Risks_2015_Report15.pdf

WRAPPING UP...

Chapter 3 examined the economic system of the United States as well as how competition, economic systems, and business cycles affect the outcomes of current economic policy. This foundation should help you understand the basics of what is taking place in the business world as well as politically.

As we move on to Chapter 4, we will discuss small business ownership and the entrepreneurial spirit it takes to succeed in starting your own business. Ready, set, open your business!

BUSINESS TERMINOLOGY

Economics	Socialism
Adam Smith	Communism
Invisible hand	Marxism
Microeconomics	Mixed economies
Supply	Pure competition
Demand	Monopolistic competition
Equilibrium price	Monopoly
Macroeconomics	Oligopoly
Gross Domestic Product (GDP)	Great Depression
Productivity	Keynesian
Per capita GDP	Monetarism
Inflation	Monetary policy
Consumer Price Index (CPI)	Expansionary monetary policy
Total labor force	Restrictive monetary policy
Unemployment rate	Fiscal policy
Discouraged workers	Federal Reserve Bank
Underemployed workers	Troubled Asset Relief Program
Business cycle	(TARP)
Capitalism	Dodd-Frank Act

DISCUSSION QUESTIONS

1. Which economic indicator do you feel measures economic strength best?

2. How does inflation affect the economy—businesses, consumers, and the government?

3. What affect does the CPI have on businesses? Consumers?

4. What are the four stages of the business cycle? What stage is the U.S. economy in currently?

5. Which type of policy do you feel most affects economic performance—fiscal or monetary? Why?

6. Which global economic challenge do you feel businesses face most often? How can a business prepare to meet global challenges?

LEARNING ACTIVITIES

1. Visit *The People History* web site (www.thepeoplehistory.com) and locate the Years and Decades section to determine the economic conditions present in the year you were born. Gather data regarding the inflation rate, interest rate, average income, the Dow Jones Index, and gas prices. Determine, based on what you know about economic indicators, what type of business cycle the United States may have been in during that time and what areas of the economy are better or worse today than in the year you were born.

2. The U.S. Debt Clock web site (located at: www.usdebtclock.org) provides up-to-date data related to various types of debt held in the United States. Review the information and then use the "Debt Clock Time Machine" button, located in the top right corner, to prepare a spreadsheet to compare current debt to a previous year's debt in the following areas:

    a. U.S. National Debt
    b. Debt per citizen
    c. U.S. population
    d. U.S. Work Force
    e. Student Loan Debt
    f. Personal Debt per Citizen
    g. Median Income
    h. Living in Poverty
    i. Without Insurance

3. Research supply and demand in today's oil market. Based on your research, be prepared to discuss why oil prices currently are priced where they are and what changes in the market would have to exist to change prices. Think about the effects additional demand for oil or alternative fuels being created might have on current prices.

4. You are a retail business owner who wants to expand your company, "Fit for All," into states across the country; however, you need to open stores where you will have employees willing and able to work as well as a stable economy. In order to determine which states are best suited for expansion, visit the Bureau of Labor Statistics (http://www.bls.gov) and review employment information. Which states do you feel are best suited for expansion based on employment numbers and economic strength? Be able to support your decision with data from the BLS or other credible sources.

Note: *Because web sites often change, use a search engine to find alternative web sites to access required information when necessary.*

CASE STUDY: MARKETPLACE DECISIONS

Eva's Designs is a regional textile manufacturer with two locations, one in New York and one in California. Business has been good in spite of a recent economic downturn. An expansion opportunity into Norway, a socialist market, has presented itself, and Eva, the CEO, knows that her business has prospered in the free market capitalism system of the United States. If she expands to Norway, Eva knows that the government will have most of the control, which is a concern. She has a personal contact in Norway who is providing further information for her prior to making a decision.

After researching the opportunity further, Eva discovers that her contact is well connected in the political environment and has assured her that she can be successful with his help. In addition, a new government election will be taking place in the next two years with potential leadership changes that could affect her contact's position. With this opportunity, her business could double in size in a matter of two years.

CASE STUDY ANALYSIS

Based on the information provided, answer the following questions:

(1) Discuss the differences between capitalism and socialism.

(2) What advice would you offer Eva regarding the pros and cons of her potential expansion opportunity?

(3) If you were Eva, would you expand based on the information provided? Is there additional information you would need in order to make a decision?

CHAPTER 4

ENTREPRENEURSHIP

"Many of life's failures are people who did not realize how close they were to success when they gave up."

~Thomas Edison

OUTCOMES:

- ➤ Evaluate the advantages and disadvantages of being an entrepreneur.
- ➤ Identify the role the Small Business Administration plays in helping small businesses succeed.
- ➤ Analyze the advantages and disadvantages of small business ownership.
- ➤ Compare and contrast the various types of business ownership.
- ➤ Discuss the importance of developing a business plan and the various forms of capital available for a start-up company.
- ➤ Evaluate franchising as an option for business ownership.

ENTREPRENEURSHIP

Entrepreneur: A person who starts a business and is willing to risk loss in order to make money.

An **entrepreneur** is a person who starts a business and is willing to risk loss in order to make money. The terms business owner, small business, and entrepreneur can be synonymous; however, the term entrepreneurship is unique in its definition. **Figure 4.1** illustrates the differences between entrepreneurship and small business ownership in relation to the creation of wealth, the speed of wealth creation, risk, and innovation. The size and scope of innovation is what separates entrepreneurship from small business ownership as new ideas being brought to the marketplace in a timely fashion create wealth beyond simply opening a small business to earn a living.

FIGURE 4.1

Entrepreneurship versus Small Business

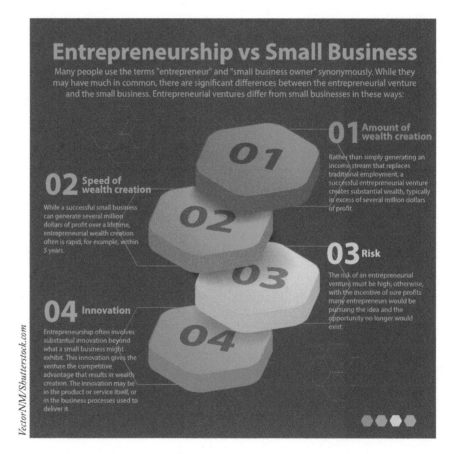

concept check

What makes entrepreneurship different than small business ownership?

CHARACTERISTICS OF ENTREPRENEURS

The key to being a successful entrepreneur lies in the ability to take an idea, and, through the process of innovation, develop it in such a way that it becomes a unique product or service in the market. Research indicates that there are a number of characteristics that are likely to be present in high-achieving entrepreneurs. Gallup studied more than 1,000 entrepreneurs to create a list of 10 qualities that highly successful entrepreneurs possess (see **Table 4.1**).[1]

1. Focus on profit	They make decisions based on the ability to make a profit.
2. Self-confidence	They know themselves well and can deal well with others.
3. Ability to think creatively	They can take existing products or ideas and make them into something better.
4. Ability to delegate to others	They do not try to do everything and give tasks to others who are competent.
5. Driven	They persist when faced with challenges.
6. Self-sufficient	They work tirelessly to build their business.
7. Life-long learner	They continually seek information that will help the business grow.
8. Passionate promoter	They act as a spokesperson for the business and have passion for their product/service.
9. Personable	They understand networking and how to develop relationships that support growth.
10. Ability to assess risk well	They make good decisions as they manage high-risk situations.

TABLE 4.1

Ten Key Characteristics of Successful Entrepreneurs

Adapted from: Pofeldt, E. (n.d.). Gallup: The 10 Qualities of Highly Successful Entrepreneurs. Retrieved on January 10, 2015, from: http://www.forbes.com/sites/elainepofeldt/.

TYPES OF ENTREPRENEURS

Today, the vast number of entrepreneurs and startups in the United States are small businesses. These **small business entrepreneurs (classical)** are people who start a small business, usually with their own savings or money acquired from rel-

Small business entrepreneurs: People who start a small business with their own savings or money acquired from relatives or friends.

atives or friends. They are willing to take all of the risk associated with owning a small business and are accountable to themselves. The goal of starting a business is to provide a good life for their family, but not necessarily to develop a chain of stores or large organization. However, this is not the only type of entrepreneurial organization that exists. **Table 4.2** provides a brief description of the various types of entrepreneurs, the level of personal risk involved, and their financial goal.[2]

TABLE 4.2

Types of Entrepreneurs

TYPE	PERSONAL RISK	FINANCIAL GOAL
Small (classical)	High	Feed the family
Scalable	High	Get rich quickly
Large (corporate)	Low	Expand current corporate profits
Social	Moderate	Improve societal problems
Serial	Moderate	Continuous innovation and profit

Source: Blank, S. (2010). You're Not a Real Entrepreneur. Retrieved on January 9, 2015, from: http://innovationfactory.ca/the-four-types-of-entrepreneurship/.

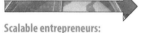

Scalable entrepreneurs: Those seeking to create large businesses by starting on a smaller scale.

Corporate entrepreneurship: The development of new ideas and opportunities within large or established businesses.

Scalable entrepreneurs are those working to start large businesses by starting on a smaller scale. These entrepreneurs need an education that helps them pull together resources and lead a company toward fast, organized growth. They have visions of expanding once they develop a successful business model and often seek outside investors to help the business grow. They largely coordinate and work through others. It is common to find this type of entrepreneur in technology startups or fast-paced environments.

Corporate entrepreneurs refer to individuals who develop new ideas and opportunities within large or established businesses, directly leading to the improvement of organizational profitability and an enhancement of competitive position. IBM used this type of entrepreneurship in 1980 when it sent a team of employees to Florida to develop the IBM PC. The company's business practices were not flexible enough to allow for such innovation, so it sent a team 1000 miles away to develop the PC. It was a success for the company and generated over $1 billion in sales.[2]

The individuals who developed the IBM PC were employed by the company to create a new product and, therefore, were considered intrapreneurs. **Intrapreneurs** are employees within a company who are assigned a special idea or project and have the resources and capabilities of the firm at their disposal. The intrapreneur's main job is to turn a special idea or project into a profitable venture for the company by using entrepreneurial skills. The benefit of being an intrapreneur is that an individual can take risks without incurring the potential losses associated with entrepreneurial activities.

padu_foto/Shutterstock.com

A **skunkworks** is a special or secret project worked on by a group of employees in an organization in order to achieve unusual results. A skunkworks is often led by a small team that assumes or is given responsibility for developing something in a short time with minimal management constraints. Skunkworks projects have been used by Lockheed Martin, Apple, and Google to develop special products.

A **serial entrepreneur** is someone who continuously comes up with new ideas and/or starts new businesses. A serial entrepreneur comes up with the idea, gets things started, and then gives responsibility to someone else in order to move onto a new idea or venture. This is different than a classical entrepreneur, who comes up with an idea, starts a company, and continues to play an important role in the day-to-day functions of the company.

Mark Cuban, known for his involvement in cable companies, the NBA, and Shark Tank, is considered a serial entrepreneur as he continually seeks new and innovative businesses to develop. While it takes business savvy to become successful, Cuban also believes in good, old-fashion, hard work: "*Sweat equity is the most valuable equity there is. Know your business and industry better than anyone else in the world. Love what you do or don't do it.*"[3]

Intrapreneurs: Employees within a company who are assigned a special idea or project and have the resources and capabilities of the firm at their disposal.

Skunkworks: A special or secret project worked on by a group of employees in an organization.

Serial entrepreneur: An individual who continuously comes up with new ideas and/or starts new businesses.

Helga Esteb/Shutterstock.com

Social entrepreneur: An individual with innovative solutions to social problems.

Social entrepreneurs are individuals with innovative solutions to social problems. Social entrepreneurs act as change agents for society, seizing opportunities others miss to improve systems, invent new approaches, and create solutions to change society for the better. Social entrepreneurs present user-friendly, understandable, and ethical ideas that engage widespread support in order to maximize the number of citizens that will stand up for their idea and implement it. A social entrepreneur develops innovative solutions to social problems and then implements them on a large scale.[4] **Table 4.3** offers examples of social entrepreneurs.

TABLE 4.3

Examples of Social Entrepreneurs

Susan B. Anthony (U.S.): Fought for Women's Rights in the United States, including the right to control property and vote.		**Vinoba Bhave (India):** Founder and leader of the Land Gift Movement that redistributed more than 7,000,000 acres of land to aid India's untouchables and landless.	
Dr. Maria Montessori (Italy): Developed the Montessori approach to early childhood education.		**Florence Nightingale (U.K.):** Founder of modern nursing, she established the first school for nurses and fought to improve hospital conditions.	
John Muir (U.S.): Established the National Park System and helped found The Sierra Club.		**Jean Monnet (France):** Helped with the reconstruction of the French economy following World War II and the establishment of the European Coal and Steel Community (ECSC), which were direct precursors of the European Union.	

Travis Klein/Shutterstock.com
rook76/Shutterstock.com
Harmony Gerber/Shutterstock.com
rook76/Shutterstock.com
Everett Historical/Shutterstock.com
Boris15/Shutterstock.com

Source: What is a Social Entrepreneur? Retrieved on January 9, 2015, from: https://www.ashoka.org/social_entrepreneur.

concept check

Compare and contrast different types of entrepreneurs.

SMALL BUSINESSES

Rob Wilson/Shutterstock.com

Although there are many different types of entrepreneurship, some individuals simply want to open a small business using the skills, knowledge, and resources they possess and those that are currently available in the marketplace. Small business enterprise is different than entrepreneurship; however, both are vital pieces of the U.S. economy.

Small businesses may not generate as much money as large businesses, but they are a critical component of, and major contributor to, the strength of national and local economies. A small business is defined as a business with 500 or less employees. According to the U.S. Small Business Administration (SBA), small businesses represent 99.7 percent of all employer firms. Since 1995, small businesses have generated 64 percent of new jobs and paid 44 percent of the total United States private payroll, according to the SBA.

Small business: A business with 500 or less employees.

Small Business Administration (SBA): Governmental agency designed to aid in small business development.

Small businesses contribute to local economies by bringing growth and innovation to the community in which the business is established. They help stimulate economic growth by providing employment opportunities to citizens. They tend to attract talent who invent new products or implement new solutions for existing problems. In fact, of those businesses who are considered "high-patenting," creating 15 or more patents in a four-year period, small businesses produced 16 times more patents per employee than larger businesses.[5]

There are additional ways that small businesses serve the local economy. Small businesses often serve larger companies by outsourcing goods or services. Outsourced services can be provided in multiple ways such as cleaning, accounting, marketing, print media, or consulting services. Finally, when customers visit local small businesses, they support the community by increasing the revenue of a small business, which typically means that the business will pay higher taxes. This money is in turn used for local police and fire departments as well as schools.[6]

Although there are benefits to local economies, there are risks involved in opening a small business, which are listed below:

- *Strategic risks*—industry specific risks associated with conducting business in a given industry;

- *Compliance risks*—risks associated with regulatory and legal laws;

- *Financial risks*—risks associated with all business transactions and the financial systems currently being used;

- *Operational risks*—risks associated with a business' operational and administrative procedures;

- *Market/Environmental risks*—external risks such as natural disasters, economic chaos, global events, or government regulation that a company has little control over.

Dusit/Shutterstock.com

Risks are unavoidable in business; however, it is important to mitigate risks and eliminate them when possible. Businesses must determine how to handle risk, which can be done through avoidance, accepting risk, transferring it to another department or time, or reducing risk through specific actions taken by the organization.

You can put risks into categories; however, some can be classified in multiple categories. An example of this relates to the securing of confidential information. Laws may mandate securing information, which makes it a compliance risk, but it can be also be an operational risk if daily business activities do not secure customer or company information. **Table 4.4** lists common risks associated with small businesses including:[7]

TABLE 4.4

TYPE OF RISKS FOR SMALL BUSINESSES	
Bad debts created by customers	Theft
Negative cash flow	Increased competition
Internet fraud and scams	Insufficient insurance coverage
Breakdown of machinery and equipment	Failure to comply with legislation, regulation and/or standards
Natural disasters such as fires and storms	Technological issues
Securing breaches and intellectual property (patents/trademarks)	High staff turnover or loss of key staff members with unique skills

INTRODUCTION TO THE WORLD OF BUSINESS

concept check

What types of risk are associated with small business ownership?

Successful companies typically have characteristics that allow them to prosper in spite of risks. Characteristics successful businesses incorporate include:

1. A *company culture* that attracts and hires the most successful people and provides an environment to retain those individuals;

2. Excellent *customer service*. Many companies incorporate customer service into their business culture through training and the design of important business processes;

3. A *positive attitude* by the owner who accepts 100 percent of the responsibility for the results of the business. Successful business owners recognize that people are the most important asset in the business;

4. A *business strategy* that includes a financial plan, marketing differentiators, product strategy and a plan for employee retention;

5. The *discipline* to execute strategies and remain on track with plans, and;

6. A team of advisors who help *plan and execute strategy* in the organization as one individual cannot possibly find success on his/her own![8]

karen roach/Shutterstock.com

Even though many individuals have wonderful ideas and passion for a product or service, the lack of knowledge related to starting and operating a business cause many new businesses to fail. **Figure 4.2** shows the percentage of businesses that fail within the first three years of operation as well as percentages of businesses in operation after four years in several industries.[9]

FIGURE 4.2

Business Failure Rates
by Year and Industry

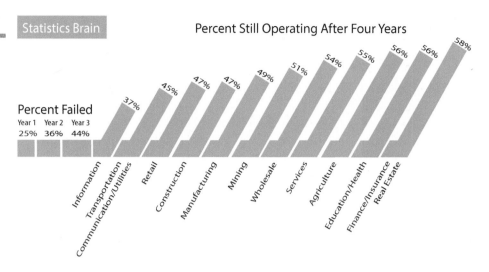

Source: Statistic Brain (2015). Startup Business Failure Rate By Industry. Retrieved on March 11, 2015, from: http://www.statisticbrain.com/startup-failure-by-industry/.

There are many reasons why small businesses fail. The ability to adapt and overcome obstacles increases the odds that a business will be successful in the long run. Below are common reasons that cause small businesses to fail:[10]

- Lack of experience
- Poor location
- Over-investment in fixed assets
- Personal use of business funds
- Competition
- Economic conditions

- Insufficient capital (money)
- Poor inventory management
- Poor credit management
- Unexpected growth
- Low sales
- Little expertise

Even though many small businesses fail, organizations exist to provide assistance to small business owners who need to develop their knowledge, skills, or abilities in given areas. One such organization, which has helped thousands of small businesses succeed, is the SBA.

SMALL BUSINESS ADMINISTRATION (SBA)

Since its founding in 1953, the U.S. SBA has delivered millions of loans, loan guarantees, contracts, counseling sessions, and other forms of assistance to small businesses. The SBA provides assistance and guides small business development, primarily through its four programmatic functions (included in **Table 4.5**).[11] To further explore their extensive offerings, visit the SBA's comprehensive web site at www.SBA.gov.

SBA FOUR PROGRAMMATIC FUNCTIONS	TABLE 4.5
1. Access to Capital (Business Financing)	SBA Four Programmatic Functions
SBA provides an array of financing from the smallest needs in microlending to substantial debt and equity investment capital (venture capital).	
2. Entrepreneurial Development (Education, Information, Technical Assistance, and Training)	
SBA provides free individual face-to-face and internet counseling for small businesses and low-cost training to emerging entrepreneurs and established small businesses in over 1,800 locations throughout the United States and U.S. territories.	
3. Government Contracting (Federal Procurement)	
In keeping with the mandate of Section 15(g) of the Small Business Act, SBA's Office of Government Contracting sets goals with other federal departments and agencies to reach the statutory goal of 23 percent in prime contract dollars to small businesses. This office also provides small businesses with subcontracting procurement opportunities, outreach programs, and training.	
4. Advocacy (Voice for Small Business)	
Created in 1978, this office reviews Congressional legislation and testifies on behalf of small businesses. It also assesses the impact of government regulations on small businesses. Additionally, it conducts research on American small businesses and the small business environment. The Chief Counsel of this office is appointed by the President of the United States.	

Sources: US Small Business Administration (n.d.). Retrieved on January 12, 2015, from: https://www.sba.gov/about-sba/what_we_do 2.

concept check

What support does the SBA provide for small businesses?

CREATING A BUSINESS PLAN

When the SBA assists small businesses in the development of a business, an important first step is creating a business plan to increase the chances for success. A **business plan** is a roadmap that provides a detailed plan of how a company will reach its goals. This document generally projects 3–5 years ahead and outlines the route a company intends to take to grow.

Business plan: A detailed plan of how a company plans to achieve its goals.

A business plan supplies answers to a comprehensive list of questions. The first and most essential question answered in the plan is: *where do you want your business to go?* **Table 4.6** provides questions to be addressed prior to developing a business plan.[12]

BUSINESS PLAN DEVELOPMENT
1. **Company Analysis:** What products and/or services do you offer now and/or what will you develop and offer in the future?
2. **Industry Analysis:** How big is/are your market(s) and how are they changing? What trends are affecting them and do these trends bode well for your future success?
3. **Competitive Analysis:** Who are your competitors and what are each of their key strengths and weaknesses? In what areas will you have or gain competitive advantage? How?
4. **Customer Analysis:** Who are your target customers? What are their demographic and/or psychographic profiles? What are their needs?
5. **Marketing Plan:** How will your reach your target customers? What promotional tactics and marketing channels will you use? How will you price your products and/or services? What brand positioning do you desire?
6. **Management Team:** Who comprises your current team and what key people must you hire in order to execute your plan? Will you build a Board of Advisors or Directors, and if so, who?
7. **Operations Plan:** What is your action plan? What are the milestones you must achieve by year's end? By the end of five years?
8. **Financial Plan:** How much external funding (if applicable) do you need to build your company? In what areas will these funds be invested? What are your projected revenues and profits over the next one to five years? What assets must you acquire?

Source: Lavinsky, D. (2014). How to write a business plan. Retrieved on January 11, 2015, from: http://www.forbes.com/sites/davelavinsky/2014/01/30/how-to-write-a-business-plan/.

Once these questions are answered, a business plan can be developed. There are key components of a business plan that must be included such as a(n):

- *Executive Summary:* A brief overview of the business plan;

- *Company Description:* A description of the company;

- *Organization and Management:* The organizational structure and profiles of the management team;

- *Services or Product Line:* A description of services offered or products sold;

- *Marketing and Sales:* Details the marketing strategy, sales projections, etc.;

- *Funding Request:* An overview of the funding needed and how will it be used;

- *Financial Projections:* Various financial data with 5-year operating projections;

- *Appendix:* Other documents as needed.[13]

Comprehensive guidelines for setting up and writing a business plan are included in **Appendix B**. Once ideas have been thoroughly developed and solidified, it is important for a business owner to determine what type of business ownership is best for the organization as well as how the development of the business will be funded.

BUSINESS OWNERSHIP OPTIONS

There are many types of small business ownership options including a sole proprietorship, a partnership, a corporation, or a franchise. Each type of business ownership has advantages and disadvantages, as will be discussed in the following paragraphs.

A sole proprietorship is owned and operated by one person and is the simplest form of business ownership to set up. A sole proprietorship is easy to form, does not require special tax filings, and allows an individual total control over the business. However, the biggest drawback of this type of ownership is that there is no separation between the business and the individual who owns it. This means the owner has **unlimited liability**, or that all debts of the business are the responsibility of the owner. In addition, because only one person owns the business, it is difficult to raise capital to start or grow the business beyond what one personally has saved or has access to. Another disadvantage is the amount of time an individual must dedicate to the business in order to find success, often without the help of others.[14] Finally, it is important to note that when the owner passes way, the business ends and cannot be transferred to another person or family member.

Sole proprietorship: The simplest form of business ownership operated by one individual.

Unlimited liability: All debts of the business are the responsibility of the owner.

ADVANTAGES OF A SOLE PROPRIETORSHIP	DISADVANTAGES OF A SOLE PROPRIETORSHIP
• Easy and inexpensive to form • Complete control • Low tax rates and income included on personal taxes	• Unlimited liability • Limited funds • Personal responsibility for success

Partnership: A business where two or more people share ownership.

Another form of business ownership is a partnership. A **partnership** is a business entity where two or more people share ownership. Although partnership agreements are not legally required, they are strongly recommended as it is considered extremely risky to operate without one. A partnership can be formed in a variety of ways to protect individuals involved with the business. Some of the types of partnerships, and the advantages and disadvantages of each, are listed below:

- *General Partnerships* assume that profits, liability, and management duties are divided equally among partners. If you opt for an unequal distribution, the percentages assigned to each partner must be documented in the partnership agreement.

- *Limited Partnerships* (also known as a partnership with limited liability) are more complex than general partnerships. Limited partnerships allow partners to have limited liability as well as limited input with management decisions. These limits depend on the extent of each partner's investment percentage. Limited partnerships are attractive to investors and businesses involved with short-term projects.[15]

ADVANTAGES OF A PARTNERSHIP	DISADVANTAGES OF A PARTNERSHIP
• Easy and inexpensive to set up • Shared financial commitment • Shared skills and expertise • Motivates employees with partnership incentives	• Joint and/or individual liability • Conflict among partners • Shared profits

CORPORATIONS

C-corporation: A business entity owned by shareholders but separates assets and liabilities from them.

A **C-corporation** is an independent legal entity owned by shareholders, which separates assets and liabilities from them. This means that the corporation is legally liable for the actions and debts the business incurs.[16] Only the amount of money invested in stocks can be lost by shareholders, regardless of the actions of the corporation, which is an advantage of a corporation. Another advantage is the ability to raise large amounts of capital through the sale of stocks (ownership in the corporation) to investors. Disadvantages of operating a corporation include the expense in legal fees to set it up and the time it takes to maintain records properly. One of the largest drawbacks includes the concept of double-taxation, which means the corporation pays taxes on profits (one tax) and then investors pay personal taxes on dividends paid out to shareholders (second tax). A corporation can continue indefinitely as stocks are transferred between shareholders, which allows it to operate into the future even upon one's death.

ADVANTAGES OF A CORPORATION	DISADVANTAGES OF A CORPORATION
• Limited financial risk • Ability to raise capital through the sale of stocks • Filing taxes separately from owners • Ability to offer competitive benefits to employees	• Expensive • Time consuming to start and operate • Double taxation • Increased paperwork and recordkeeping

There are other types of corporations, other than c-corporations, which provide similar advantages to business owners. An S-corporation (sometimes referred to as an S-Corp) is a special type of corporation where an organization has less than 100 stockholders and avoids double taxation by distributing profits as dividends to shareholders, who then pay individual taxes on the dividends. This provides protection for the owners of the business as there is limited liability and allows for any loss or gain to be reported on individual tax returns instead of filing business tax returns. Having this protection means that owners must maintain specific records and hold meetings, which can add to the cost and time of operation. The IRS continually monitors activities of S-corps to be sure businesses meet the legal requirements to form such businesses.

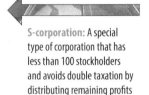

S-corporation: A special type of corporation that has less than 100 stockholders and avoids double taxation by distributing remaining profits as dividends.

ADVANTAGES OF AN S-CORPORATION	DISADVANTAGES OF AN S-CORPORATION
• Eliminates double taxation • Ability to declare profits on individual tax returns • Ability to transfer or continue corporation over time	• Higher levels of structure and operation • Close monitoring by the IRS

Limited-liability corporations (LLC) are a hybrid-type legal structure that provides limited liability like a corporation with the tax benefits and flexibility of a partnership.[17] The advantages of this type of business include limited liability, less record-keeping for owners, lower initial start-up costs, and the ability to determine which members in the organization get specified percentages of the profits and/or losses. Disadvantages of LLCs include the dissolution of the business when a member leaves the business (for any reason) after obligations of the business have been fulfilled as well as payment of self-employment taxes toward Medicare and Social Security.

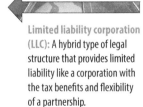

Limited liability corporation (LLC): A hybrid type of legal structure that provides limited liability like a corporation with the tax benefits and flexibility of a partnership.

ADVANTAGES OF AN LLC	DISADVANTAGES OF AN LLC
• Limited personal liability • Less recordkeeping and lower start-up costs • Members decide the percentage of the profits or losses each receives	• Limited life • Members must pay the self-employment tax contributions toward Medicare and Social Security

FRANCHISING

The most obvious example of a business owner is someone who starts a new business; however, you can be considered a business owner by buying an existing business or owning a franchise, too. In fact, many of the businesses you see today are franchises including McDonald's, Starbucks, Subway, and Dunkin' Donuts.

Charlesimage/Shutterstock.com

Franchising: Paying for the use of a firm's successful business model and brand for a prescribed period of time.

Franchisor: The supplier who allows a franchisee to use the supplier's trademark and distribute the supplier's products or services.

Franchisee: An individual or business that purchases a franchise.

Franchising involves paying for the use of a firm's successful business model and brand for a prescribed period of time. A franchisor is a supplier who allows an operator, or a franchisee (one who purchases a franchise), to use the supplier's trademark and distribute the supplier's products or services. In return, the operator pays the supplier a fee. The franchisor's success depends on the success of the franchisees. The franchisee is said to have a greater incentive than a direct employee because he or she has a direct stake in the business. **Table 4.7** lists the top ten franchises in the United States in 2016.

RANK	FRANCHISE NAME	INDUSTRY
1	Jimmy John's	Sandwiches
2	Hampton by Hilton	Midprice Hotels
3	Supercuts	Hair salons
4	Servpro	Insurance/disaster restoration and cleaning
5	Subway	Subs, salads
6	McDonald's	Fast food
7	7-Eleven Inc.	Convenience stores
8	Dunkin' Donuts	Coffee/baked goods
9	Denny's Inc.	Family restaurants
10	Anytime Fitness	Fitness centers

TABLE 4.7

The Top 10 Franchises in the United States

Source: Entrepreneur, Inc. (2016). 2016 Top franchises from Entrepreneur's Franchise 500 list. Retrieved on May 18, 2016, from: https://www.entrepreneur.com/franchise500.

Franchises offer important initial support for an owner, such as selecting the best site, designing and building the business, financing, training, and assisting with the grand-opening program. In addition, franchises provide on-going support in the form of training, national and regional advertising, guidelines for operating the business, management support, and access to organizational resources and volume discounts.[18]

ADVANTAGES OF A FRANCHISE	DISADVANTAGES OF A FRANCHISE
• Provides brand name and recognition from the start • Allows owner freedoms in operating his/her own business • Increased chance of success • Consumer-base already established with quality and consistency of the franchisor • Support from franchisor to help make business a success	• Not fully independent as an owner due to contractual agreements • Payment of initial fees and ongoing royalties to franchisor • Restrictions on product offerings and price • Potential for some franchises to damage reputation of other stores

An individual may start a business and grow to the point where franchising is a viable option for future growth and expansion. A franchisor must follow steps in order to develop a successful franchise beyond an individual storefront. Knowledge of the business and industry is vital to the growth of a franchise. Learning legal issues that surround expansion and determining how much growth is desired are the next steps. Once an owner determines these components of expansion, it is important to screen potential franchisees carefully in order to find franchisees who are passionate and knowledgeable when operating other locations. Setting restrictions related to operating procedures and providing support will also help ensure the success of all involved. **Figure 4.3** displays the steps to consider when moving from a small business to a franchise.

FIGURE 4.3

Steps to Franchising a Business

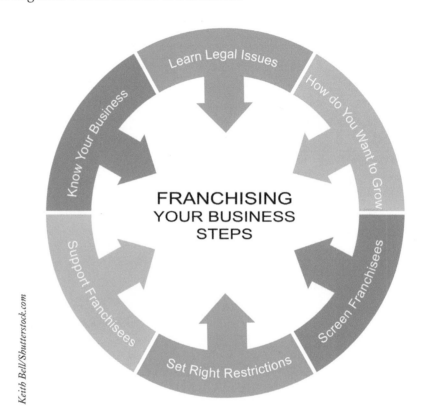

Keith Bell/Shutterstock.com

concept check

Compare and contrast the various types of business ownership options.

There are other ways for a business to be successful using established businesses beyond franchising. Three methods companies use to position themselves for future growth are acquisitions, mergers, or joint ventures.

Acquisitions involve one firm purchasing most or all of another company's assets in order to assume control of it. Acquisitions are often made as part of a company's growth strategy when it is beneficial to take over an existing firm's operations and niche versus expanding its own. Two of the most successful acquisitions include Apple purchasing Steve Jobs' NeXT software company for $429 million and Google purchasing Android for $50 million. Both have paid off handsomely for the acquiring companies. However, there are failures when it comes to acquisitions including the acquisition of Time Warner by AOL. The two giants thought they would own the media/internet business but failed to recognize other options in the market that attracted consumers, which led to the split of the merger.[19]

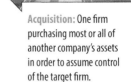

Acquisition: One firm purchasing most or all of another company's assets in order to assume control of the target firm.

Merger: Combining of two or more companies into one company.

Joint Venture: A partnership in which two or more companies agree to develop a new, combined organization.

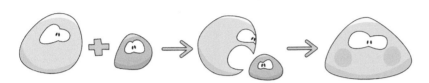

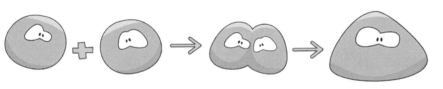

Duettographics/Shutterstock.com

A merger is combining two or more companies into one company. Mergers can be classified as vertical, horizontal, or conglomerate and are differentiated by what type of firms are joining together. A *vertical merger* exists when firms at different levels of the distribution channel combine, such as a manufacturer and a retailer. A *horizontal merger* occurs when two companies in the same industry merge. And a *conglomerate merger* combines firms that are not related to each other. Companies may elect to use this type of merger in order to diversify their holdings. Disney–Pixar, Exxon–Mobil, and Sirius–XM radio are examples of successful mergers.[20]

A joint venture is a partnership in which two or more companies agree to develop a new, combined organization. They share risks, costs, and management, as well as profits. Many companies enter joint ventures when they enter foreign markets as each organization contributes specific skills and knowledge in the joint venture.

FUNDING OPTIONS

Once an organization develops a business plan and determines what type of business ownership it will operate under, financing the business is the next step. Regardless of the length of time a business has been operating, acquiring funds is often necessary. However, it is important to evaluate what type of financing is best for each business decision. There are many factors to consider and choosing a path to follow can be overwhelming.

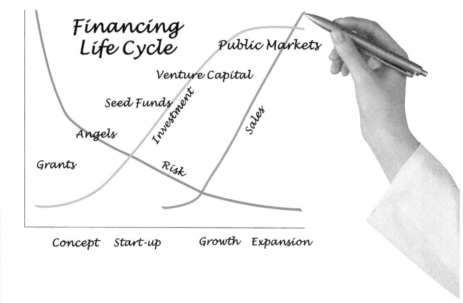

arka38/Shutterstock.com

At various stages of the financing life cycle, businesses require different types of funding. Initially, individuals rely on personal savings or loans from family and friends. Once an idea takes hold and the business starts to grow, grants and angel investors are targeted for funding. When growth is beyond these resources, an individual or organization looks to venture capitalists or the public to expand their resources. The following types of funding are available for businesses at various stages of the financing life cycle:

Seed capital: The initial capital used to start a business.

Seed capital is the initial capital used to start a business. Seed capital often comes from the company founders' personal assets or from friends and family. The amount of money is usually reasonably small because the business is still in the idea or conceptual stage and resources are limited. Such companies are generally in pre-profit stages, so seed capital is needed for research and development, to cover initial operating expenses, and to attract the attention of additional investors.

Microloans are part of the SBA loan program, which provides loans up to $50,000 to help small businesses and certain not-for-profit childcare centers start up and expand. The average microloan is about $13,000. The U.S. SBA provides funds to non-profit, community-based organizations with experience in lending. These organizations administer the microloan program for eligible borrowers. Businesses can use microloans for working capital, inventory or supplies, furniture or fixtures, or machinery or equipment. However, proceeds from an SBA microloan cannot be used to pay existing debts or to purchase real estate.[21]

Microloans: SBA loans up to $50,000 to help small businesses start up or expand.

Business incubator: Shared facilities to nurture startup firms.

patpitchaya/Shutterstock.com

Business incubators are facilities established to nurture young (startup) firms during their early stages. They provide shared offices, affordable space and services, management training, marketing support and, in many instances, access to some form of financing.

VENTURE CAPITAL

The venture capital business is just that—a business. The people we call venture capitalists are business people who look for innovative products and/or services to invest in, often in exchange for a percentage of ownership. Simply having a successful business will not attract a venture capitalist as the goal in investing is to own a share of a company with growth potential. Technology is a popular focus for venture capitalists as well as pharmaceuticals and scientific inventions. Creative, useful products and services are most likely to be funded by venture capitalists.

Venture capital: Investors who provide funds in exchange for ownership in a company.

A venture capitalist typically requires a reasonable chance of producing a tenfold increase in business value within three years in order to invest in a company. The names and addresses of venture capitalists are available in annual directories such as *The Western Association of Venture Capitalists* and *Pratt's Guide to Venture Capital Sources.*

ANGEL INVESTORS

Angel investors: Wealthy individuals who provide capital in exchange for ownership equity.

An angel investor or angel (also known as a business angel or informal investor or angel funder) is a wealthy individual who provides capital for a business start-up, usually in exchange for ownership equity. They are similar to venture capitalists; however, most angel investors work to help start-up businesses find success, so the focus is on new business versus established businesses. Angel investor networks have been formed to match investors with startup companies, which can be found using the SBA's Active Capital listings. Individuals can also post their business plans on sites that bring angel investors together such as gust. com and angel.co.

ADDITIONAL FORMS OF FUNDING

Commercial Lenders

Banks are even less likely than venture capitalists to invest in, or loan money to, startup businesses due to the lack of resources and collateral individuals possess to secure the loan. However, they are the most likely source of financing for most small businesses. Banks commonly make loans to small businesses and secure the debt with the companies' inventory or accounts receivable. A great deal of small business financing is accomplished through bank loans based on the business owner's personal collateral, such as home ownership.

The Small Business Administration

As mentioned earlier, the SBA makes loans to existing small businesses and startup businesses. SBA loans are typically applied for through and administered by local banks. The SBA will normally require that at least one third of the required capital be supplied by the new business owner whereas the rest of the amount must be guaranteed by reasonable business or personal assets. The SBA works with "certified lenders," which are banks. It sometimes takes a certified lender as little as one week to get approval from the SBA.

Other Lenders

An established small business can sell its accounts receivables in order to gain equity, which is called factoring. For example, if a customer owes you $100,000, you can sell the account to a third party for a smaller amount (say $80,000) in order to gain access to cash. The factor (purchaser of the account) takes on the risk of payment, so discounts are quite steep. Factoring is used to obtain cash when working capital is not available. Costs may be relatively high, but it is a viable source for small business financing.

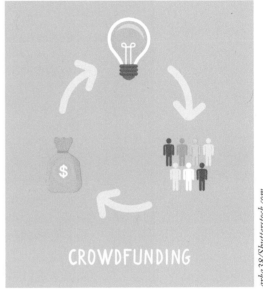

arka38/Shutterstock.com

Factoring: Selling accounts receivables in order to gain funding for a business.

Crowdfunding: Raising money from multiple individuals for a project.

A relatively new way to raise funds is using social media and the Internet in the form of crowdfunding. Crowdfunding is a method used to raise funds for a project from multiple investors, usually the Internet. It has become popular due to its relative ease to set up and ability to reach millions of potential investors quickly. Individuals and businesses have found success using crowdfunding from small projects by high school students to LeVar Burton's efforts to raise over $1 million to bring Reading Rainbow to schools and various platforms. Gofundme, Kickstarter, and Indiegogo are three of the most popular and profitable sites according to Crowdfunding.com.

Credit cards can be used for funds, but it is important to limit the use of such funding unless outstanding balances can be paid off in full or without high interest costs. Credit is often used for emergency purposes or short-term needs.

Of course, you can utilize family members or friends to obtain funds; however, this should be limited. If your parents, siblings, good friends, cousins, and in-laws will invest in your business, they have paid you an enormous compliment. Be sure you understand how easily this money can be lost and have all parties sign a contract regarding how and when the money will be repaid.[22]

concept check

What funding options are available for small business owners to start or expand their businesses?

WRAPPING UP...

Chapter 4 included information related to entrepreneurship, small business ownership and set up, as well as funding options. In Chapter 5, we will review how accounting factors into successful business operations and decision-making as well as how accounting information is utilized internally and externally. Accounting has become an important part of all companies in the past decade.

BUSINESS TERMINOLOGY

Entrepreneur
Small business entrepreneur
Scalable entrepreneur
Corporate entrepreneurship
Intrapreneurs
Skunkworks
Serial entrepreneur
Social entrepreneur
Small business
Small Business Administration
   (SBA)
Business plan
Sole proprietorship
Unlimited liability
Partnership
C-corporation

S-corporation
Limited liability corporation (LLC)
Franchising
Franchisor
Franchisee
Acquisition
Merger
Joint Venture
Seed capital
Microloan
Business incubator
Venture capital
Angel investors
Factoring
Crowdfunding

DISCUSSION QUESTIONS

1. What type of ownership structure do you feel is best? Why?

2. What challenges are faced by franchise owners (franchisees)?

3. What potential problems might arise when purchasing an existing business?

4. Why might an individual purchase an existing business versus start a new one?

5. Describe three core values you would incorporate in your own business.

LEARNING ACTIVITIES

1. Interview a small business owner in your area. Create a summary report of the interview that includes, but is not limited to, the following information: how the business started, what type of business ownership the owner decided upon (and why), what challenges the owner faces in operating the business, what future opportunities are anticipated for the business, and what the owner would have done differently if starting the business over were an option. The goal is to learn as much about business ownership as possible, so be prepared with additional questions.

2. Research an article about a recent small business, either successful or not successful. After reviewing the article, analyze elements of the business that contributed to its success or demise.

3. Imagine you are planning to start your own business. What type of business would you start, and what type of business ownership would you prefer? Also, what type of funding would you utilize and why?

4. The Small Business Administration web site (www.sba.gov) provides a wealth of information for individuals researching, starting, or managing a small business. Visit the site and locate two articles related to small business ownership. Summarize the articles and discuss why you believe the articles are of value to you as a business person.

Note: *Because web sites often change, use a search engine to find alternative web sites to access required information when necessary.*

CASE STUDY: STARTING A BUSINESS TOGETHER

Jonah, Dalton and Luke have each been involved in the performing arts for over eight years. They have planned to start a talent search company and are ready to begin after developing their business plan. The business will offer services to up-and-coming music and performing artists. Each partner contributes a unique and valuable skill set to help the business be successful.

It will cost approximately $85,000 to start the business. Luke is currently a performing artist and cannot contribute any money for the start-up but has key contacts in the music industry. Dalton can contribute $50,000 and will provide the necessary management skills needed to operate the business. Jonah can contribute $35,000 and is an excellent salesperson and spokesperson. Although the initial capital contributed by Dalton and Jonah will get the business stated, additional funds will be required. Dalton and Jonah both have excellent credit and Luke has had credit problems. Some of Luke's and Jonah's friends have expressed interest in investing money in the business if needed.

CASE STUDY ANALYSIS

Based on the information provided, answer the following questions:

(1) What organizational structure would you recommend for Jonah, Dalton, and Luke? Why?

(2) What should be considered by Jonah, Dalton and Luke as they start a new business together?

(3) Discuss potential pitfalls this group might face as they start and grow their business as well as how those pitfalls might be addressed.

CHAPTER 5

UNDERSTANDING ACCOUNTING AND FINANCE

"For every dollar spent in failure, learn a dollar's worth of lesson."
~Jesse Robbins, Entrepreneur

OUTCOMES:

➤ Explain the importance of understanding accounting and financial information for a business professional.
➤ Describe the steps involved in the accounting cycle.
➤ Identify the difference between a balance sheet, income statement, and statement of cash flows.
➤ Discuss the types of financial ratios used to analyze financial data within an organization.
➤ Compare and contrast types of short-term and long-term financing options available for an organization.

ACCOUNTING

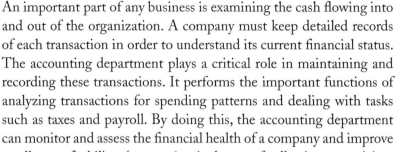

docstockmedia/Shutterstock.com

An important part of any business is examining the cash flowing into and out of the organization. A company must keep detailed records of each transaction in order to understand its current financial status. The accounting department plays a critical role in maintaining and recording these transactions. It performs the important functions of analyzing transactions for spending patterns and dealing with tasks such as taxes and payroll. By doing this, the accounting department can monitor and assess the financial health of a company and improve efficiency as well as profitability. **Accounting** is the act of collecting, organizing, and interpreting financial data. Another definition used by the American Accounting Association (AAA) is: "Accounting is the process of identifying, measuring and communicating economic information to permit informed judgment and decision by users of the information."[1]

Accounting: The act of collecting, organizing, and interpreting financial data.

ACCOUNTING VS. BOOKKEEPING

Bookkeeping: Keeping the financial records of a firm.

docstockmedia/Shutterstock.com

Every business needs a dependable and recognized record keeping system that is based on established accounting principles. **Bookkeeping** (also called record-keeping) refers to the process of accumulating, organizing, storing, and accessing the financial information of a business. This information fulfills two basic purposes: (1) Expediting day-to-day transactions of the business; and (2) Preparing financial statements, tax returns, and management reports. A key component in every recordkeeping system is the need for internal controls, which are ways to check for accuracy and quality in reporting information. Accounting is a much more comprehensive concept than bookkeeping and accounting uses bookkeeping in much of its activities. The key difference between accounting and bookkeeping is that accounting includes bookkeeping but further extends it by analyzing information and using it in the decision-making.

concept check

Discuss the differences between bookkeeping and accounting.

TYPES OF ACCOUNTING

Creativa Images/Shutterstock.com

Accounting is a vast and dynamic profession that is constantly adapting itself to the specific and varying needs of its users. A Certified Public Accountant (CPA) is an individual who passes an exam and meets specific requirements in order to become an accountant. To become a CPA, individuals must earn a bachelor's degree, complete 150 hours of education, and spend two years working in the accounting field in addition to passing a certified exam. Over the past few decades, accountancy has branched out into different types of accounting based on how individuals in an organization use the information. **Table 5.1** provides information related to the various types of accounting and how information from these areas is used.[2]

Certified Public Accountant (CPA): An individual who passes an exam and meets specific requirements in order to become an accountant.

TYPE OF ACCOUNTING	USE
Financial accounting:	Used for external reporting
Management accounting:	Used by management for internal decision making
Governmental accounting:	Used in the public sector
Tax accounting:	Used for tax preparation
Project accounting:	Used to track the progress of a project

TABLE 5.1

Different Types of Accounting

Source: Types of Accounting, (n.d.). Retrieved on February 2, 2015, from: http://accounting-simplified.com/financial/types-of-accounting.html.

There are three main types of business activities involving accounting including financing, operating, and investing. Examining how money flows in and out of the organization as well as how it is utilized determines how transactions are categorized into these three areas. Each transaction needs to be identified and properly classified, so the accounting department can perform its duties and accurately prepare financial reports. These reports help decision-makers within the organization determine how the organization is run, which will be discussed in more detail later in the chapter.

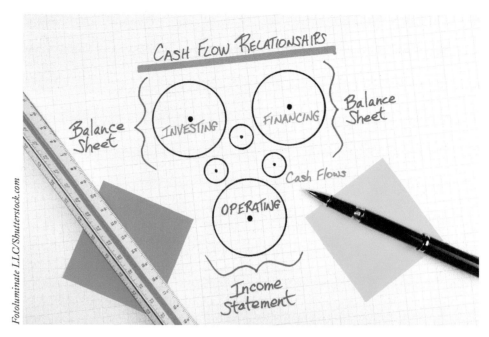

Financing activities:
Transactions directly involved with financing the company from startup to expansion.

Operating activities:
Day-to-day business operations of an organization.

Investing activities:
Transactions used for investing purposes.

Financing activities are those transactions directly involved with financing the company from startup to growth phases when expansion is necessary. A financial transaction would include anything purchased using credit such as a loan or credit card purchase. Money paid toward principal or interest on a loan would be considered a financing activity. Additional examples of financing activities are repurchasing company stock or paying dividends to shareholders.

Operating activities are day-to-day business transactions such as bill paying, operational and product delivery expenses, employee compensation, and other miscellaneous tasks. Anything related to operating the business on a daily basis is included in the operating section, and a company aims to have positive net cash flow from operating activities.

Investing activities, or investing transactions, are those used for investing purposes and are not considered part of the daily operations of a company. Loans made to customers or other parties and short-term investments would be considered an investing activity. Making money on investments, in the form of dividends or interest earned, or purchasing long-term investments such as equipment, land, or property are also classified as investments.

Once transactions are recorded, they are analyzed by internal and external users in order to make decisions about the financial health and direction of an organization.

USERS OF ACCOUNTING INFORMATION

Rawpixel/Shutterstock.com

Accounting information helps users make better financial decisions. Two categories of users who utilize accounting information are internal users and external users.

Internal users (*primary users*) are individuals inside the organization. Internal users utilize accounting information such as budgets and financial reports to share information within the organization. Internal users of accounting information include the following:

Internal users: Primary users within an organization.

- **Management:** Use information to examine the organization's performance and make decisions to improve company results.

- **Employees:** Use information to see how profitable the company is and how its performance might affect employees' future compensation and job security.

- **Owners:** Use information to analyze data and take action when profits or sustainability need to be adjusted.

External users:
Secondary users outside of
an organization.

External users (*secondary users*) are individuals outside of the firm. External users of accounting information include the following:

- **Creditors:** Use information to determine if a business is able to repay money borrowed from sources such as suppliers, banks or other lenders. Usually the credit terms set by creditors reflect the financial health of the business.

- **Tax authorities:** The Internal Revenue Service (IRS) uses this information to determine if tax returns filed on behalf of the company are trustworthy.

- **Investors:** Use information to determine if it makes financial sense to invest in a company.

- **Regulatory authorities:** Use information such as annual or government reports to be sure the organization complies with rules and regulations.[3]

concept check

Explain who uses accounting information and for what purposes they use it.

FASB AND GAAP

iQoncept/Shutterstock.com

FASB: Establishes accounting standards for financial reporting.

Many users rely on accounting information from organizations for decision-making purposes, so various boards and agencies have been established to create rules and regulations for companies to follow when reporting financial information. This helps maintain ethical and legal standards in reporting information and helps to ensure accuracy in preparing such information for both internal and external users.

The **Financial Accounting Standards Board (FASB)**, created in 1973, provides the private sector with established accounting standards for the preparation of all financial reports. The standards are utilized by all nongovernmental entities. The standards are officially recognized as reliable by the Securities and Exchange Commission (SEC), a governmental body designed to protect investors and help the market run efficiently, as well as the American Institute of Certified Public Accountants. The mission of the FASB is "*to establish and improve standards of financial accounting and reporting that foster financial reporting by non-*

governmental entities that provides decision-useful information to investors and other users of financial reports" (para. 3).[4]

Generally Accepted Accounting Principles (GAAP) are the expectations of how information should be reported by governmental and nongovernmental agencies. GAAP are set forth by the FASB and mandated by the U.S. Securities and Exchange Commission (SEC). The financial reporting process should provide information that is:

iQoncept/Shutterstock.com

- truthful and appropriate to potential investors and/or creditors who use such information for making sound investments or other financial decisions regarding the company;

- useful for determining and making financial and long-term decisions regarding various business strategies; and

- helpful in improving business performance and meeting financial goals.

To achieve basic objectives and implement fundamental qualities, GAAP requires full disclosure, or sharing specific information, within various financial reports at certain times. In addition, financial reporting must be consistent over time, relevant to the time period that is being reported, reliable, and comparable to other firms' financial reports.[5]

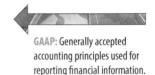
GAAP: Generally accepted accounting principles used for reporting financial information.

concept check

What is the relationship between FASB and GAAP?

ACCOUNTING CYCLE

In order to determine a company's financial health, a business must take information, record transactions, and then use that information to create financial statements. This process is known as the accounting cycle. The **accounting cycle** involves identifying, collecting, and analyzing documents and transactions to create financial statements such as the balance sheet, income statement, Statement of Owner's Equity, and Statement of Cash Flows. Today, many businesses use accounting software that processes multiple steps at once. The first step

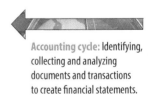
Accounting cycle: Identifying, collecting and analyzing documents and transactions to create financial statements.

nasirkhan/Shutterstock.com

in the accounting cycle is taking invoices, receipts, or other source documents and recording them into a journal. Once these data are entered, it moves the information to a ledger, which shows an increase or decrease in various accounts. From there, the information is entered into a trial balance to check for accuracy. Once the information has been verified as accurate, it is used to create financial statements, which we will discuss in detail below. The accounting cycle is continual in order to create new statements for each reporting cycle.

THE ACCOUNTING EQUATION

Assets: Valuable items that are owned by a business.

Liabilities: Debt that businesses owe to others.

Owner's equity: Amount owner has invested plus profits not distributed.

Accounting equation: Assets = Liabilities + Owner's Equity

Double-entry bookkeeping: Transactions are recorded in two areas that offset one another.

In order to create financial statements, an organization must assess what they own and what they owe others. Assets are items that are owned by, and are of value to, an organization. Cash, inventory, property, and machinery are all examples of assets. Trademarks and patents are also considered assets as they add value to a company. Liabilities include anything that is owed to others. For example, a loan to purchase an asset is considered a liability as money is owed to a creditor. Owner's equity is the amount of money that a person has invested in an organization and is another liability for the company as the owner has a claim on this debt. These three terms are used to create the basic accounting equation.

Ribah/Shutterstock.com

The **accounting equation** is: Assets = Liabilities + Owners Equity. This shows the financial position of a company at a given time. The most important thing to remember is that both sides of the accounting equation *must* be equal. If they do not balance, then there is an error in the recordkeeping of the organization. It is also called the balance sheet equation, which you will see as you examine the two sides of the balance sheet. It is the foundation for the **double-entry bookkeeping** system where two accounting entries are required to record each financial transaction. For each transaction, total debits equal total credits.

concept check

What is the purpose of the accounting equation?

FINANCIAL STATEMENTS

arka38/Shutterstock.com

A **balance sheet** is a financial statement that summarizes a company's assets, liabilities, and owners' equity at a specific point in time. This is what an investor utilizes to see what a company owns and owes to others. It is called a balance sheet because the two sides must be equal to one another. Accounts such as cash, inventory, and property are on the asset side of the balance sheet, whereas the liability side consists of accounts such as accounts payable or long-term debt. Current assets and liabilities include anything that is used up within the accounting period in which the statement is prepared. Fixed assets include items that are used for more than one accounting period. There are no standard templates to differentiate between industries so accounts will be different for each organization; however, the structure for creating a balance sheet is similar for all companies (shown in **Table 5.2**).

Balance sheet: Summarizes a company's assets, liabilities, and owner's equity.

TABLE 5.2

Structure for Balance Sheet

BALANCE SHEET	
ASSETS	**LIABILITIES**
Current Assets (cash, buildings, inventory, equipment, Accounts Receivable) **Fixed Assets** (land, buildings) *Minus Depreciation*	**Current Liabilities** (credit card debt, Accounts Payable, expenses, taxes) **Long-term Liabilities** (mortgages, bonds) **Owner's Equity** (Retained Earnings, outstanding stock)
Total Assets	**Total Liabilities**

mphotoz/Shutterstock.com

An **income statement** is a financial statement that measures a business's financial performance over a specific accounting period, typically a month, quarter, or year. The income statement is also known as a "profit and loss statement" or "statement of revenue and expenses," because it displays the net profit or loss incurred over a specific accounting period. The income statement is prepared using the accrual basis of accounting, which reports revenues that may not have been collected or expenses that not have been paid. It examines income and costs of an organization and helps determine how much will be owed in taxes. The more a company can reduce its income, the less it will pay in taxes. Taxes and expenses are deducted from revenue (income) collected, which shows a company its "net income after expenses and taxes." **Table 5.3** shows the basic structure of an income statement.

Income statement: Profit and loss statement.

TABLE 5.3

Structure for Income Statement

INCOME STATEMENT
Gross Income (Revenue or Sales)
Less Returns
Net Sales
Less Cost of Goods Sold
Less Expenses
Operating Profits
Plus Other Income Received
Gross Profits
Less Interest Expense
Income Before Taxes
Less Taxes
Net Income

Statement of Owner's Equity: Displays owner's equity in the firm.

Statement of Cash Flows: Reports cash generated and used in a specific time period.

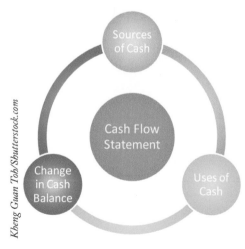

Kheng Guan Toh/Shutterstock.com

The **Statement of Owner's Equity** shows the owner's equity balance at the beginning and end of a given period plus any changes that occurred. This statement normally spans a 12-month period.

A **Statement of Cash Flows** reports the cash generated and used during a specific time period, which is denoted in the heading of the statement. For example, the heading may state, "For the Three Months Ended December 31, 2015" or "The Fiscal Year Ended July 31, 2015." The Statement of Cash Flows shows where cash is flowing in and out of a business, which helps determine how much cash is available to pay debts. It shows sources of cash, how cash is used within the organization, and any changes in the cash balance during the reporting period.

concept check

What financial statements are used in assessing a firm's financial situation?

ANALYSIS USING FINANCIAL RATIOS

Using financial statements is one way to determine the financial health of an organization; however, they do not create a complete picture of how a business is operating at a given time. In order to determine if an organization has the ability to pay debts, is profitable, and can turn over inventory efficiently, financial ratios are utilized through ratio analysis. Ratio analysis is used to calculate the financial health of an organization using data from financial statements. Calculating the results of the ratios helps an organization identify progress toward achieving performance objectives as well as compare performance levels with others in the same industry. Financial ratios are classified into four categories: liquidity, leverage, profitability, and activity ratios.

JPerez/Shutterstock.com

Ratio analysis: Using ratios to calculate the financial health of the organization.

Liquidity ratios: Ratios used to measure the ability of a firm to pay short-term debt.

LIQUIDITY RATIOS

Liquidity ratios are used to determine if a company has the ability to meet its short term debt and pay its short term liabilities. This tells analysts whether or not a company has the assets to pay liabilities or convert assets to cash in order to pay debt quickly. Two common types of liquidity ratios are the current ratio and acid test ratio (also known as quick ratio).[6]

Current Ratio

The current ratio measures a company's current assets against its current liabilities. In general, the higher the number the better. As with any liquidity ratio, the higher the amount of current assets compared to current liabilities the better an organization's ability to pay off debt. The formula used to calculate the current ratio is as follows:

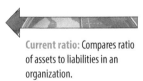

Current ratio: Compares ratio of assets to liabilities in an organization.

$$\text{Current Ratio} = \text{Current Assets} \div \text{Current Liabilities}$$

For example, if Company X's current assets are $1,900,000 and its current liabilities are $1,100,000, the current ratio would equal 1.73 (rounded). This indicates that the company has $1.73 of assets for every $1.00 of liabilities the firm owes. Lenders typically consider results that are two or higher safe; however, it is important to compare this number to industry standards and past ratios as large discrepancies may signal a warning for lenders.

Quick Ratio (Acid-Test)

Acid test (quick ratio): Measures ability to convert assets into cash.

Leverage ratios: Ratios used to measure how much a firm relies on debt to operate the business.

Debt ratio: Measures how much debt a company has for each dollar in assets.

Another liquidity ratio is the **quick ratio**, also referred to as the *acid-test ratio*. This ratio shows a firm's ability to pay short-term debt using *liquid assets* (assets that can be converted into cash quickly). Because liquid assets are used, inventory is excluded from the calculation because it may be difficult to liquidate quickly. The formula is as follows:

$$\text{Quick Ratio} = (\text{Current Assets} - \text{Inventory}) \div \text{Current Liabilities}$$

If current assets equal $4.6 million, inventory equals $1.9 million and current liabilities equal $3.1 million, we can calculate the quick ratio using the formula listed above, which is equal to 0.87. Any result less than one indicates that a firm may face difficulty paying debts in the short term.

LEVERAGE RATIOS

Leverage ratios are used to measure how much a firm relies on debt to operate the business. Two types of leverage ratios will be discussed including the debt ratio and debt-to-equity ratio. A high debt ratio shows that a company relies heavily on debt to operate and may not have enough cash flow to pay its debts. However, a low debt-to-equity ratio may reveal that a company may be able to use debt to expand or grow the business to increase profits.[7]

Debt Ratio

Tang Yan Song/Shutterstock.com

The **debt ratio** is calculated by dividing a company's total debt by its total assets and measures how many assets the firm has compared to each dollar in debt. A ratio of one or more means that a firm has more debt than assets, which is shown in the following calculation:

$$\text{Debt Ratio} = \text{Total Debt} \div \text{Total Assets}$$

If Company X had $20 million of debt on its balance sheet and $25 million of assets, the debt ratio calculation would be: $20,000,000 ÷ $25,000,000 = 0.80 or 80%. The results show that for every dollar in assets, Company X had $0.80 of debt.

Debt-to-Equity Ratio

The debt-to-equity ratio shows the relationship between liabilities and the owners' capital. The ratio shows who is contributing money to the organization and also gives shareholders an indication of whether or not they will be repaid if the company liquidates. The formula for the debt-to-equity ratio is shown below:

Debt-to-Equity Ratio = Total Liabilities ÷ Total Shareholder's Equity

If Company X had $10 million of debt on its balance sheet and $10 million of total equity, then Company X's debt ratio is: $10,000,000/$10,000,000 = 1.0 or $1.00. This means that for each dollar of Company X owned by the shareholders, Company X owes $1 to creditors. Higher numbers indicate a higher level of risk to lenders. Some industries may allow more debt than others so this ratio is compared with others in the industry to determine acceptability.

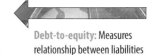

PROFITABILITY RATIOS

A profitability ratio is a measure of how well managers use available resources to make a profit. Profit is income that remains after all costs and expenses to produce a product or service are deducted from sales revenue. Typical profitability ratios used in analyzing a company's performance include: earnings per share, gross profit margin, return on sales or operating margin, return on equity, and return on investment.[8] We will examine three profitability ratios below.

iQoncept/Shutterstock.com

Gross profit margin reveals what percentage of each dollar results in profit after expenses are paid (related to production and distribution) and is calculated using numbers from the income statement. Gross profit margin is calculated by dividing gross profit (GP) by net sales (NS):

Gross Margin = Gross Profit ÷ Net Sales

OR

Gross Margin = (Net Sales-Cost of Goods Sold) ÷ Net Sales

Example: Imagine that a business sold $500,000 in long boards last year and had a gross profit of $70,000. Calculate the company's gross margin for the year as show below:

a. GM = $70,000 ÷ $500,000
b. GM = 0.14 or 14%

The results show that for each dollar of long board sales, the company has 14 cents left over to cover all other costs and expenses as well as profits. In this case, the company would need to work on lowering production costs as $0.86 of each dollar is going toward production and distribution.

Return on sales (operating margin): Shows how well a firm generates income from sales.

Return on Sales (Operating Margin) helps firms compare profitability to other firms in the same industry. A company determines if it is profitable by examining how much profit it makes after all expenses (production and operational) have been paid. This formula is often referred to as EBIT, or "earnings before interest and taxes". The formula to calculate return on sales is shown below:

Return on Sales OR Operating Margin = Operating Income ÷ Net Sales

Example: Company X produces computer parts. In 2015, the company had operating income of $14,000,000 and net sales of $100,000,000. What was the company operating margin?

a. ROS = OI / Revenue
b. ROS = $14,000,000 ÷ $100,000,000
c. ROS = 0.14 = 14%

A return on sales (operating margin) of 14 percent means that a profit of 14 cents was earned on each dollar of computer parts sales before interest and taxes are paid.

Return on equity: Shows how much a company earns on each dollar invested by shareholders of the company.

Return on equity (ROE) shows how much net income a company earns on each dollar invested by shareholders of the company. Profits help a company grow, so the results of this ratio are monitored closely by investors to determine the growth potential and performance of the organization. Many investors believe 15–20 percent returns are attractive; however, this may not be realistic during downturns in the economy. One caution in using ROE is that large debt can translate into higher returns, so it is wise for an investor to also review the leverage ratios before investing in an organization.[9] ROE is calculated using the formula below:

Return on Equity = Net Income ÷ Shareholder Investment

Example: Your new business went public last year, which resulted in a total investment of $100,000,000 by stockholders and produced net income of $10,000,000. What is the return on equity?

a. ROE = $10,000,000 ÷ 100,000,000
b. ROE = 0.10 = 10%

The results of this example show that your new business is generating a $0.10 profit for each dollar invested by investors.

ACTIVITY RATIOS

Activity ratios measure how well management turns over organizational assets, such as inventories and accounts receivables. The most common activity ratios include: average collection period, inventory turnover rate, fixed assets turnover, and total assets turnover.[10] For this discussion, we will examine average collection period and inventory turnover rate ratios.

Average collection period results show how long a company waits, on average, to collect money owed by its customers. The longer the collection period takes the larger investment in assets the company endures. The average collection period is calculated using two steps: (1) calculating the average daily sales (annual net sales ÷ 365 days), and (2) dividing accounts receivable by average daily sales. For instance, if a company's net sales equal $1,500,000, average daily sales would equal $4,110 ($1,500,000 ÷ 365). If accounts receivable equal $200,000, then the XYZ Company's average collection period would be calculated as follows:

$$\frac{\text{Accounts receivable}}{\text{Average daily sales}} = \frac{\$200,000}{\$4,110} = 49 \text{ days}$$

It takes 49 days, on average, to collect money that is owed to the company by customers. If the company were able to collect its receivables within 30 days, the company would reduce its accounts receivables by $78,090 ($4,110 × 19 days), which would allow the company to use their assets in more productive ways.

Inventory sitting in a warehouse costs money due to storage costs and potential damage to inventory, not to mention the fact that no profit is earned as it sits there. When inventory moves quickly, a company makes more revenue. Inventory turnover measures how quickly inventory is converted into sales, or turned over, in a year. Higher numbers indicate more turnover, which signals an increase in sales and revenues. The main point for any business is to keep inventory at a level where they are meeting sales without having too much inventory stored in warehouses.

XYZ Company has inventory of $188,000 and the cost of goods sold is $1,200,000. Inventory turnover is calculated below:

$$\frac{\text{Cost of goods sold}}{\text{Inventory}} = \frac{\$1,200,000}{\$188,000} = 6.4 \text{ times}$$

Activity ratios: Measure how effectively management uses organizational assets.

Average collection period: Shows how long a company waits to collect money from customers.

Inventory turnover rate: Measures how long it takes to convert inventory into sales.

XYZ Company turns over its inventory 6.4 times during the year on average. The results of the inventory turnover ratio depend on the industry, the product or the service. For instance, in the transportation industry, acceptable rates of turnover might be 30 or higher, whereas retail may be 7. Chipotle Mexican Grill has inventory turnover rates of 193.47 times, whereas Apple is 62.1 times and Coca-Cola is 12 times.[11]

concept check

Explain the types of financial ratios and what they show about a business.

INTERNATIONAL ACCOUNTING

seastika/Shutterstock.com

Accounting is affected by global markets and economic conditions. Because businesses and investors desire transparency in financial information, international organizations are working to standardize financial statements and reports around the globe.

IASB: Board developed to promote consistent financial reporting around the globe.

IFRS: International reporting standards.

In 1973, the International Accounting Standards Committee (IASC) was established to promote consistency in how financial information was reported globally. In 2001, this committee became the International Accounting Standards Board (IASB), an independent, accounting standard-setting body. The main mission was to develop a primary set of high-quality, reporting standards known as the International Financial Reporting Standards (IFRS). Besides developing these standards, the board is also responsible for promoting the use and application of these standards. In January 2009, the board announced the creation of a Monitoring Board and the expansion of the IASB to 16 members, which gave consideration to the geographical composition of the IASB. Today, over 100 countries use IFRS, which is similar to GAAP in the United States. The United States has been slow to convert financial reporting to IFRS as many do not see IFRS as a better system. While criticisms exist, IFRS is thought by many experts to be more transparent and less complicated than GAAP.[12]

ScandanavianStock/Shutterstock.com

concept check

Discuss why IFRS are being implemented worldwide.

IMPORTANCE OF FINANCE

pedrosek/Shutterstock.com

Once accounting statements are created and verified, the finance department uses them to create a financial plan to specify funding needs in both the short- and long-term. Companies have to consider their finances for numerous reasons, from survival during a down-turn in the economy to supporting success during prosperous periods. Company financing can affect a company's ability to hire employees, purchase goods and services, acquire licenses, or expand in the future.

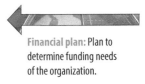

Financial plan: Plan to determine funding needs of the organization.

Pressmaster/Shutterstock.com

Financial manager:
Individual who examines, plans, assesses, and manages financial functions of the organization.

A **financial manager** implements the financial plan and takes care of all important financial functions of a business. This individual is responsible for examining, planning, assessing, and managing tasks that affect profitability, growth, and goodwill of the company. The main functions of a financial manager include raising capital, allocating funds, forecasting profits, and understanding capital markets (see **Table 5.4**).[5]

TABLE 5.4

The Role of a Financial Manager

Raising capital	A financial manager must decide the proper debt to equity ratio and maintain a good balance between the two.
Allocating funds	The proper allocation of funds is one of the most important activities as it directly influences all management decisions.
Forecasting profits	Forecasting profits is important to ensure that current funds are used properly to increase and sustain profits in the future.
Understanding capital markets	Knowledge and understanding of the capital markets and deciding where the profits are distributed are important tasks.

concept check

What role does a financial manager play in an organization?

SHORT-TERM AND LONG-TERM FINANCING

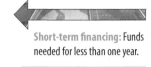

Short-term financing: Funds needed for less than one year.

Most businesses need short-term working capital at some point in their operations. Short-term financing is funding needed for less than one year. For example, if a business wants to increase its seasonal inventory during the Christmas holiday, the owner might need short-term funds to do so. Inventory buildup usually occurs within the months of September through November and requires cash payments for the products, which many retailers do not have on hand. A financial manager must determine how to borrow funds for a short period of time in order to have inventory on hand during the busy holiday season. The five most common sources of short-term financing are included in **Table 5.5**.[14]

Zerbor/Shutterstock.com

TYPE OF FINANCING	SOURCE OF FUNDS
Personal equity	Funds come from personal resources, friends, family members, or an interested third party.
Trade creditors	Funds come from suppliers that provide the inventory to the business by delaying the terms of payment (from 30 to 45 days, for example). This is particularly helpful during busy seasons or slow turn-around in inventories.
Factoring	Selling off accounts receivable at a discount in order to receive cash quickly versus waiting for others to pay your firm. This is a trade-off between quick cash and waiting for payments from your customers.
Line of credit	Funds come from a credit card, a business, or a bank and typically have higher interest charges than other forms of short-term credit.
Short-term loan	Funds from a banker that most often are paid back within one year. It is important to establish good relationships with bankers who can help with these types of situations.

TABLE 5.5

Sources of Short-Term Financing

An additional source of capital available for large, financially stable companies is called commercial paper. It is an unsecured, short-term debt instrument issued by a corporation to raise money. It is a form of an IOU that usually matures within 270 days and is normally offered at a discount rate compared to what banks would offer. Commercial paper is offered for amounts ranging from $100,000 to $1 million.

Commercial paper: Short-term debt issued by a corporation to raise money.

Northfoto/Shutterstock.com

Long-term financing is required when funds are needed for more than a year. The two main types of long-term financing available to small business owners are debt and equity financing, which can be obtained through banks, the sale of stock or bonds, or from other investors.

Debt financing relates to bank or lender loans for various types of business needs that must be repaid. An example of this is securing debt financing from a bank for startup costs or other business needs. This type of debt is repaid over a long period of time and interest is paid on the loan.

Long-term financing: Funds needed for more than one year.

Debt financing: Borrowing money that must be repaid.

Equity financing: Investments by others for an exchange of ownership in the business.

Equity financing involves direct capital investments from venture capitalists, private investment firms, or the sale of stocks or bonds in exchange for ownership in the company. With venture capitalists and private investment firms, contracts are drawn up to outline the amount and length of investment.

Corporations can sell stocks or bonds to help fund operational needs. Other options for financing include *private placements*, where some new stock or new bonds are sold to a small group of major investors such as pension funds and insurance companies. *Private equity funds* are investment companies that raise and use funds to make large investments in either private or publicly held companies. *Hedge funds* are private investment companies open only to qualified large investors. They raise capital from investors and then hire a manager to administer investments matching the fund's stated goals.

concept check

What types of short-term and long-term financing options are available for an organization?

UNDERCAPITALIZATION

Although it is possible for any business to suffer during an economic downturn, not having enough capital to operate a business typically comes from ineffective planning. Undercapitalization refers to a situation where a business does not have enough capital to conduct daily operations and/or pay its creditors. It is better to project on the high side for expenses and low side for revenue. This allows a company to set up a contingency fund to cover unexpected expenses. It is better to underestimate funds required to operate than to not have enough.

Undercapitalization:
Not having enough capital to operate or expand a business.

Undercapitalization is a major problem for new businesses and is the number-one reason that startup companies fail. It is important for a business to obtain sufficient financing up front in order to increase the chances for success.[15]

Effects of undercapitalization may result in a company not being able to operate due to the inability to pay its operational expenses or the inability to expand due to the failure to obtain necessary financing. Not having enough capital can lead an organization to bankruptcy, so it is important for financial managers to review the financial plan and determine current and future funding needs for an organization.

concept check

What are the effects of undercapitalization?

WRAPPING UP...

In this chapter, accounting and financial information have been introduced to help you understand this complex and ever-changing area. Most individuals rely on experts within, and outside of, their organizations to help wade through the myriad tenants of accounting and finance; however, having a basic level of understanding about the subject will serve you well in your career.

In Chapter 6, we will examine how marketing functions work within an organization and help you understand its importance to business success.

BUSINESS TERMINOLOGY

Accounting
Bookkeeping
Certified Public Accountant (CPA)
Financing activities
Operating activities
Investing activities
Internal users
External users
Financial Accounting Standards
    Board (FASB)
Generally Accepted Accounting
    Principles (GAAP)
Accounting cycle
Assets
Liabilities
Owner's equity
Accounting equation
Double-entry bookkeeping
    system
Balance sheet
Income statement
Statement of Owner's Equity
Statement of Cash Flows
Ratio analysis
Liquidity ratios

Current ratio
Quick ratio
Leverage ratios
Debt ratio
Debt-to-equity ratio
Profitability ratio
Profit
Gross profit margin
Return on Sales
Return on equity (ROE)
Activity ratios
Average collection period
Inventory turnover
International Accounting
    Standards Board (IASB)
International Financial Reporting
    Standards (IFRS)
Financial plan
Financial manager
Short-term financing
Commercial paper
Long-term financing
Debt financing
Equity financing
Undercapitalization

DISCUSSION QUESTIONS

1. How are accounting and financial information used in decision-making?

2. How can data, such as wages or personnel evaluations, be kept confidential yet available to managers who need this information? What type of information must be protected legally?

3. Why should financial statements be audited by a CPA? What purpose would this serve to the public looking at these statements?

4. How can negative owner's equity occur, and what does it mean to a company?

5. You are interested in investing in a company that has been in operation for ten years. What other information would you want to examine beyond the company's balance sheet, income statement and statement of cash flows before investing? Explain.

LEARNING ACTIVITIES

1. Visit the U.S. Securities and Exchange Commission web site (www.sec.gov) and search for the Spotlight section related to the Foreign Corrupt Practices Act (FCPA). Select a violation cited in the past five years and review the article. Prepare a short summary of how the company specifically violated the FCPA and the consequences the company faced for its violation(s). Discuss in a closing paragraph if you believe the consequences will deter the company from future violations of the FCPA.

2. Visit a public company's web site and locate their most recent annual report. Examine the income statement, balance sheet, and other financial information as well as comments related to the company's financial situation. Select three financial ratios listed in Chapter 5 and calculate them using information from the annual report. Be prepared to share your results as well as briefly discuss what the results show about the organization.

3. Research information about challenges facing organizations as they share financial information globally. Based on your research, support or reject the notion that worldwide consistency in financial and accounting reporting should be mandatory for all countries.

4. Select one area of accounting (managerial, financial, tax, auditing, or non-profit/governmental) and locate, using personal contacts, social media, or a search engine, an accountant who works in that area to interview. As you interview the accountant, discuss his/her path to the current position, what types of activities or responsibilities are encountered on a daily basis, and the type of information needed to complete those activities. Also, ask about challenges and rewards of the position and for advice to an individual starting in this position. Report your findings in a summary report that includes the individual's name, company, and title as well as the questions asked and response given in the interview.

Note: *Because web sites often change, use a search engine to find alternative web sites to access required information when necessary.*

CASE STUDY: A LITTLE OFF THE TOP

Lynn Campbell serves as a senior partner for a local CPA firm. Her company provides auditing and other accounting services to small and medium size clients, in addition to auditing clients' books. A new client, Benny Blanco, owner of Paradise Imports, requested preparation of financial statements and tax returns for his business. Susan Carpenter is the part-time bookkeeper for Paradise Imports and is also an accounting student enrolled at a local university.

During their initial meeting, Susan recognized Lynn as a potential mentor and confidant. She openly discussed a situation currently happening at Paradise Imports and asked for Lynn's opinion. Susan's concerns related to the handling of sales revenue. Every sale is recorded into a category based on the type of payment received such as cash, checks or credit card. Sandy creates records and after each weekly deposit, the owner, Benny Blanco, returns the records with his own, handwritten total of the amount deposited.

Upon review of the weekly deposits, Susan noticed $400 missing from each deposit. After further inspection of monthly tax documents, she noticed that the reported gross income was $1,600 less than actually counted. Susan addressed the owner regarding this discrepancy and was assured that every dollar of reported income was accounted for and also mentioned that, since Susan did not sign the forms, she should not be concerned.

CASE STUDY ANALYSIS

Based on the information provided, answer the following questions:

(1) What ethical considerations are involved for each of the following in this scenario?

    a. Lynn Campbell
    b. Susan Carpenter
    c. Benny Blanco

(2) How should Lynn Campbell proceed with this client?

(3) Are any laws being violated in this scenario?

CHAPTER 6

UNDERSTANDING MARKETING

OUTCOMES:

- ➤ Discuss the role of marketing in an organization.
- ➤ Distinguish between business-to-business and consumer markets.
- ➤ Analyze how a business utilizes the marketing mix to sell a product or service.
- ➤ Evaluate the use of marketing research and segmentation in meeting the needs of consumers.
- ➤ Explain the product life cycle and strategies used at various stages to increase sales and/or profits.

WHAT IS MARKETING?

Peter Bernik/Shutterstock.com

Marketing: The process of creating, communicating, delivering, and exchanging goods and services that have value.

Utility: How products and services satisfy the needs and wants of those who use them.

Many people see marketing as selling or advertising but that is only a portion of marketing. According to the American Marketing Association (AMA) Board of Directors, marketing is the process of creating, communicating, delivering, and exchanging goods and services that have value to customers, suppliers, and organizations. Dr. Philip Kotler defines marketing as identifying the unmet needs and desires of customers while making a profit.[1]

UTILITY

Goncharuk Maksim/Shutterstock.com

In the marketplace, products and services must be useful to consumers or they have no incentive to purchase them. The concept of utility refers to how products and services satisfy the needs and wants of those who use them. Utility is typically defined using five areas including: form, task, time, place, and ownership.

Form utility refers to how raw materials are converted into finished products. A producer creates form utility when a dress is created from fabric, which allows customers to purchase the dress instead of making it on their own.

Task utility relates to a service or task such as cutting one's hair or changing the oil in a car. This form of utility requires quality communication to assure that the task being completed meets customer expectations.

Time utility is created when a product is available for customers to purchase in a timely fashion. For instance, when ordering fast food, customers expect to receive all food items fairly quickly. To help satisfy customers, McDonald's designed thinner French fries than Wendy's to allow for faster cooking, which means they can get food to customers more quickly.

Place utility ensures a product is conveniently available and accessible for customers to purchase. If a product is advertised, consumers should be able to locate the product or service without much effort. Too much effort to find a particular product will prompt a search for more convenient products or services, which means loss of revenue to a company.

Rido/Shutterstock.com

Ownership (possession) utility allows the customer to physically take "possession" of a given product. A business needs to make it easy for consumers to pay for and take possession of products, which has increased the use of debit and credit cards as well as online services such as PayPal.[2] Car dealerships want customers to immediately take possession of cars so they feel good about their purchase.

Firms work to create multiple forms of utility for their customers. Technology has helped a great deal in this effort as is evidenced by the ability of consumers to get products and services from multiple sources in relatively quick timeframes.[3]

concept check

Contrast the five forms of utility.

FIVE ERAS IN MARKETING HISTORY

Over time, the marketing efforts of organizations have changed based on what the company and consumers want and/or need. Many of the changes in marketing align with business eras discussed in Chapter 1. Marketing eras have been classified as follows: the production era, selling era, marketing era, relationship era, and holistic era. These five eras do not have distinct beginning or ending dates as the practices of each are still in use; however, their order demonstrates the evolution of marketing as a discipline.[4]

Everett Collection/Shutterstock.com

- **Production Era:** One of earliest eras was the production era where businesses believed that a product should be inexpensive and available everywhere for consumers to purchase. Not much focus was placed on what the customer wanted as it was believed that a product should "sell itself." This meant mass production, low costs, and production efficiencies were the focus.

- **Selling Era:** The selling era featured aggressive product promotion and pushy sales efforts. A company's goal was to produce products efficiently and then convince customers that they needed what was produced. Henry Ford is famous for saying that he would make a car in any color the customer wanted—as long as it was black!

- **Marketing Era:** During the mid-1950s, companies made a major shift and started creating products that customers wanted to buy. Marketing research became prominent during this era to determine what consumers needed and wanted. This effort, often referred to as the marketing concept, helped businesses focus on producing products and services that would provide customers with what they wanted, provide excellent customer service, and create profit for the organization.

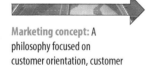

Marketing concept: A philosophy focused on customer orientation, customer satisfaction, and profit.

- **Relationship Era:** In the 1990s, businesses realized the value in creating relationships with customers in order to develop life-long customers. The focus on relationships and high levels of customer satisfaction is a continued focus to develop loyal users of products and services available in the market.

bokan/Shutterstock.com

- **Holistic Era:** Today, marketing has evolved into the notion that "everything matters." Marketing is aligned to companies' goals and the strategies for attaining them. The main goal of holistic marketing is making sure the company is socially responsible and meeting customer needs. Within this era, social media and the power of the Internet have been recognized for their major impact on marketing efforts and strategies. For this reason, it has also been deemed the *social era*.

concept check

How have the marketing efforts of businesses changed over time?

B2B VERSUS B2C MARKETING

Marketing generally has two areas of focus which include **business-to-business (B2B)** and **business-to-consumer (B2C)** marketing. B2B marketing refers to businesses selling products or services to other businesses, which in turn creates another product or service or uses it to operate their business. This type of marketing is much higher in sales volume than B2C marketing purchases as it is organizationally versus individually based.

B2C marketing refers to businesses selling products or services to end-users (consumers) for consumption. Most individuals understand B2C because we purchase products on a daily basis and are most familiar with it.

B2B: Businesses selling products or services to other businesses.

B2C: Businesses selling products or services to end-users (consumers).

Marketing initiatives feature different motivators in B2B and B2C transactions. **Table 6.1** displays three factors that differentiate B2B and B2C marketing strategies.[5]

TABLE 6.1

B2B and B2C
Motivational Factors

MOTIVATORS/ FACTORS	B2B	B2C
PURCHASING MOTIVATION (*MOST IMPORTANT FACTOR)	• Focus on the practical benefits of products. • The purchaser needs approval to purchase products.	• Purchases based largely on emotional connections with the products. • Consumers do not need approval to purchase.
MARKETING TIME PERIOD	• Long term in nature. • Customer decisions may take considerable time before finalizing a purchase.	• Limited time period. • Customers "act now" so they do not miss out on something great.
DELIVERY METHODS	• Relationship selling is important. • It is essential to maintain direct one-on-one contact with perspective customers.	• Communication channels are directed at consumers through print ads, billboards, social media or TV commercials. • Typically one-way communication (with the exception of social media having interactive capabilities).

Source: Templeman, M., (2014). Three Key Differences in Strategy of B2B Marketing vs. B2C Marketing. Retrieved on February 12, 2015, from: http://foxtailmarketing.com/3-key-differences-strategy-b2b-marketing-vs-b2c-marketing/.

concept check

What distinguishes B2B from B2C marketing?

NON-PROFIT MARKETING

Non-profit marketing:
Marketing related to non-profit business activities.

As a reminder, non-profit businesses are those who do not make a profit but rather operate to help a specific cause or event. Therefore, non-profit marketing includes activities and strategies intended to broaden an organization's message, to solicit donations, or search for volunteers to help with the cause. Non-profit marketing involves the development of a media campaign, the creation of logos or slogans, and the creation of clear objectives to expose the organization to an outside audience. During difficult economic times, non-profit organizations, such as the Salvation Army and UNICEF, suffer because donations are typically reduced by the general public. At the same time, the amount of need for their services increases. During such times, advertising costs increase due to the need to create awareness of organizational needs, which is challenging as consumers have fewer dollars to donate to non-profits. Marketing efforts are vital to their ability to provide services and obtain necessary donations.

Leonard Zhukovsky/Shutterstock.com

DEVELOPING A MARKETING PLAN

Regardless of the type of organization, a marketing plan and strategy must be developed that aligns with the goals of the company. A **marketing plan** is a written document that shows how a business will use its resources, establish objectives, develop a marketing strategy, and implement and control the plan. The key to the marketing plan is to make it as complete as possible. The development of a marketing plan is crucial because it provides a written path of how a company will utilize its resources to sell its products. **Figure 6.1** displays various components of the market planning process and **Table 6.2** includes elements included within the plan.[6]

Marketing plan: A written document that shows how a business will use its resources, establish objectives, develop marketing strategy, and implement and control the plan.

FIGURE 6.1

Market Planning

TABLE 6.2

Elements of the
Marketing Plan

Executive summary	Include a brief overview of the proposed marketing plan (one–two pages).
Marketing objectives	Set measureable objectives and goals that will guide your plan.
Environmental analysis	Examine the internal and external environment market.
SWOT analysis	Determine the company's strengths, weaknesses, opportunities, threats, and trends.
Marketing strategies	Develop strategies that will help a company complete the objectives.
Marketing budget	Determine how much money, time, and resources will be devoted to marketing efforts.
Marketing implementation	Decide how and when the plan will be implemented and how much time will be allowed for each phase of the plan.
Evaluation and control	Provide guidelines on how often the plan will be evaluated, how success will be measured, and how revisions to the plan will be made.

Source: Source: Templeman, M., (2014). Three Key Differences in Strategy of B2B Marketing vs. B2C Marketing. Retrieved on February 12, 2015, from: http://foxtailmarketing.com/3-key-differences-strategy-b2b-marketing-vs-b2c-marketing/.

Within the marketing plan, it is important to determine the target customers, competition, goals, the budget, and how the company will measure success. A company should review the marketing plan each quarter and make adjustments as necessary; however, some firms review the plan only once a year.[7] Today, with the influence and use of social media and the Internet, marketing is changing rapidly, so businesses need to monitor their marketing efforts carefully.

concept check

What elements are included in a marketing plan?

MARKETING STRATEGY DEVELOPMENT

Marketing strategies function as the basis of a marketing plan. A **marketing strategy** is a plan to determine the target market and proper marketing mix needed to increase sales and create a competitive advantage in the market. A marketing strategy includes all of the marketing activities that align with the company's strategic plan as well as the marketing plan discussed previously. **Figure 6.2** shows the cycle used to create a marketing strategy.

Marketing strategy: A plan to determine the target market and proper marketing mix.

FIGURE 6.2

Marketing Strategy Cycle

arka38/Shutterstock.com

Normally, marketing strategies are established as multiyear plans; however, companies use **tactical plans** (steps or tactics needed to achieve the goals defined in a strategic plan) to determine what will be accomplished in the current year.

Tactical plan: Steps or tactics needed to achieve the goals defined in a strategic plan.

After a comprehensive environmental scan is complete, a strategic plan can be created to identify business alternatives, establish inspiring goals, determine the ideal marketing mix to accomplish the goals, and develop a detailed implementation plan. The final step is creating a plan to monitor progress and a set of options to fall back on if problems arise in the implementation of the plan.

MARKETING PLANNING TERMINOLOGY

In order to develop the marketing plan and strategy, it is important to understand key concepts and terminology that will help facilitate the creation of such plans. Some of these terms include segmentation, target markets, and marketing research—all of which are included in the plan.

Market Segmentation is subdividing a large market into identifiable segments that have similar needs, wants, or characteristics. The objective in segmenting the market is to determine a company's target market as well as to design a marketing mix that meets the needs of customers and the organization. One of the most popular methods for dividing customers into segments is using demographics.

Demographics are the study of a population that analyzes factors such as race, age, sex, socioeconomic status, education level, employment status, or other factors. Demographics can be used by companies to learn more about a population's characteristics in order to determine who the target population will be for their products. Demographic trends are significant as the size and needs of demographic groups change over time. Segmenting a population into demographics permits companies to measure the size of a potential market and see if its products and services are reaching the company's target market. For instance, a company that sells high-end travel trailer homes wants to determine approximately how many people are at or nearing retirement age and how many of those individuals could afford their product. This helps the company determine their target market and how much money to allocate to production and advertising of their trailer homes to those individuals.

Once groups are segmented by various characteristics, companies study the behavior of consumers to determine how they decide what goods and services to purchase. **Consumer behavior** is the study of buyers and the processes they use to select products or services that satisfy their needs and wants. The study of consumers helps develop marketing strategies by understanding what determines buying behaviors (see **Figure 6.3**)[8]:

Marketing segmentation: Subdividing a large market into identifiable segments that have similar needs, wants, or characteristics.

Demographics: The study of a population that analyzes factors such as race, age, sex, etc.

Consumer behavior: The study of buyers and the processes they use to select products or services that satisfy their needs and wants.

FIGURE 6.3

The Psychology of
Consumer Decisions

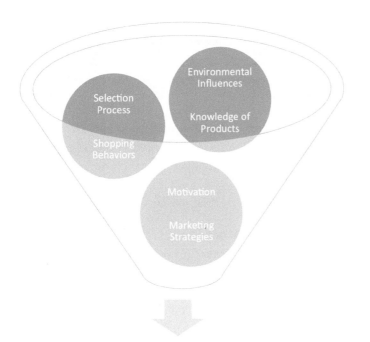

Purchasing Decision

Source: Perner, L. (2010). Consumer behavior: The psychology of marketing. Retrieved on January 11, 2015 from: http://www.consumerpsychologist.com/.

Once segmentation occurs and the population is studied, a company must determine which of the segments it will target. A **target market** is a specific consumer group that a company has identified through segmentation and to whom it will direct its marketing efforts. A business cannot sell to everyone so defining a target market helps focus efforts and resources. A **target audience** is a specific cluster of people within the target market. For example, if a business sells nutritional programs for women with diabetes (target market), the message may be directed at a spouse or family member (target audience) who manages the nutritional plan of the person with diabetes. Either way, a company should describe the target market and audience in detail based on what it knows about the needs and wants of those groups.

Oez/Shutterstock.com

Target market: A specific consumer group that a company focuses its marketing efforts toward.

Target audience: A specific cluster of people within the target market.

concept check

How are segmentation and target markets related?

THE MARKETING RESEARCH PROCESS

After segmentation has been completed and a target market selected, companies research the needs and wants of those individuals who will purchase their products or services. **Marketing research** is the process of gathering, analyzing, and interpreting data about a market, product or service, and consumers. In particular, marketing research looks at consumers' characteristics, spending habits, location, and needs. The research should also examine the industry and competition.

Marketing research: the process of gathering, analyzing, and interpreting data about a market, product or service, and consumers.

Conducting marketing research requires a set process in order to make informed decisions. Marketing research uses a similar research process to the Scientific Method known as the marketing research process. For marketing and science, defined steps are used. **Figure 6.4** displays the steps used in the marketing research process.

FIGURE 6.4

Marketing Research Process

My Life Graphic/Shutterstock.com

The first step is to identify the specific problem. Once it has been identified, hypotheses are developed as educated guesses about the solution to the problem. Identifying hypotheses allows the research team to determine the research design or how they will collect the data. Then, it is important to determine who will be surveyed and the type of data needed to address the objectives of the research. Data are collected and analyzed using specific tools, which helps interpret the meaning behind the data. This helps managers make sound conclusions and leads to proper implementation of the marketing plan.[9]

Market research is conducted using two types of data: primary data or secondary data. **Primary data** is collected first-hand by an organization, which is considered original data. The advantage of collecting primary data includes the ability to answer questions specifically related to your brand or marketing efforts; however, disadvantages include the time and cost of collecting the data. **Secondary data** is research that has been collected by another agency, which a company can use in making marketing decisions. Advantages in using secondary data include the availability of data and the low costs of gathering it. Disadvantages include the lack of knowledge in how information was gathered as well as the inability to personalize the data. Secondary data can come from sources such as government agencies, industry and trade associations, labor unions, media sources, or chambers of commerce. The information is typically published in pamphlets, newsletters, trade publications, websites, magazines, or newspapers. **Table 6.3** displays three types of secondary sources.[10]

Kheng Guan Toh/Shutterstock.com

Primary data: Data collected first-hand by the company.

Secondary data: Data collected by outside sources used to make internal decisions.

SECONDARY SOURCE	ACCESS AND FEES
Public sources	Generally free to the public, offers relevant information for researchers.
Commercial sources	Usually a fee associated with sources. Includes research and trade associations, such as Dun & Bradstreet and Robert Morris & Associates, banks, and publicly traded corporations.
Educational institutions	Research conducted in colleges, universities, and technical institutes. Fees depend on the type of information gathered (private or public).

TABLE 6.3

Types of Secondary Sources

Source: Market Research (2015). Retrieved on January 9, 2015 from: http://www.entrepreneur.com/encyclopedia/market-research.

DATA COLLECTION METHODS

Data can be collected using several methods. **Qualitative research** is inquiry research used to uncover trends in thoughts and opinions. Some common qualitative research methods include focus groups (group discussions), individual interviews, and observations. The sample size is typically small and respondents are often selected to fulfill a given quota. Qualitative research is costly and takes a tremendous amount of time; however, it can yield higher quality results based on its flexibility and in-depth nature.

Qualitative research: Inquiry research used to uncover trends in thoughts and opinions.

Franz Pfluegl/Shutterstock.com

Quantitative research uses numbers to formulate facts and uncover patterns in a set of data. Quantitative data collection methods include various forms of surveys (online, paper, mobile, and kiosk), face-to-face interviews, telephone interviews, longitudinal studies, website interceptors, online polls, and systematic observations. Advantages to using quantitative research include its ease of use, specific responses, and quick turn-around for analyzing. Disadvantages include the inability to understand the "why" behind the numbers and lack of flexibility to probe a respondent when a response is given.

mama_mia/Shutterstock.com

Sometimes, an organization must act quickly to research a particular issue without going through all of the formal stages of the marketing research process. When this happens, **action research** is initiated to solve an immediate problem. It can also be part of a reflective process to improve the way issues are addressed and solved. The sole purpose of action research is to solve a particular problem and produce "best practice" procedures.

concept check

Compare and contrast the types of data collection methods.

THE FOUR P'S OF MARKETING

Once plans have been created and research conducted, an organization must determine how they will market their products or services in relation to the Four P's of marketing: product, price, place, and promotion. It is important for an organization to bring the right product to the right people at the right time in order to find success. The four P's are known as the marketing mix, which is the strategic mix of controllable elements within a product's marketing plan. **Table 6.4** displays the definition of each of the four P's of the marketing mix.[11]

Four P's: Product, price, place, and promotion.

Marketing mix: The strategic mix of the controllable elements within a product's marketing plan.

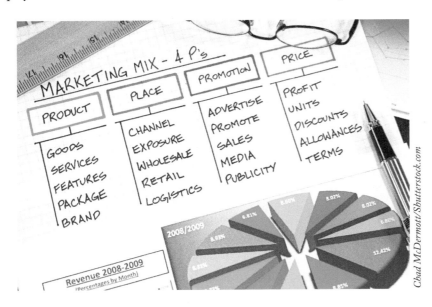

Chad McDermott/Shutterstock.com

TABLE 6.4

The Four P's of the Marketing Mix

FOUR P'S	DEFINITIONS
Product	The benefits and features of all goods and services that a business sells to the target market.
Price	The amount of money businesses must charge in order to make a profit and satisfy customers.
Place	The distribution, location, and method of getting products or services to the customer.
Promotion	How an organization communicates the benefits and value of products or services to consumers.

Source: The Marketing Mix and the 4Ps of Marketing (n.d.). Retrieved on January 14, 2015 from: http://www.mindtools.com/pages/article/newSTR_94.htm.

concept check

What is the importance of the 4 P's in marketing?

PRODUCT

Differentiating your product from the competition provides an advantage in the marketplace. This can only be done by understanding what the customer wants and needs from your product or service. Through this understanding, a company will produce items that fit the company brand as they provide features that consumers value. These decisions create a company's product lines and product mix.

Product line: A group of similar products aimed at the same target market.

Product mix: All the product lines that a company sells.

Although product mix and product lines are similar, each can have a drastic impact on the success of a company. A **product line** is a group of similar products aimed at the same target market. For instance, if a business creates a group of products that deal with personal hygiene (soap, shaving cream, and shampoo), this is known as a product line. The line of products typically shares the same logo, brand, and color scheme so customers can easily identify other products within the same product line. A **product mix** is comprised of all the product lines that a company sells. The product mix could include several lines of products or individual products sold by the larger company. For example, if a business owns a line of personal hygiene products and a product line of household cleaning products, all of the products together would represent the total product mix for the business.

Branding: Creating an exclusive name, image, or symbol for a company or product that differentiates it from its competition.

Branding is the process involved in creating an exclusive name, image, or symbol for a company or product that differentiates it from its competition. This is often accomplished through advertising campaigns with a consistent theme. Branding aims to establish a differentiated presence in the market that attracts and retains loyal customers. If a company is successful, individuals will identify product or company brands immediately. Brand examples that you can identify quickly are McDonald's, Nike, and Starbucks Coffee.

Images © Shutterstock, Inc.

Other companies might try to take advantage of a company's name or brand in the marketplace; therefore, a company is wise to use trademarks to protect their branding. A **trademark** is legal protection for a brand or product and is recognized by the symbol ™. A **service mark** is legal protection for a service rather than products. The trademark goes beyond just the brand name and includes colors, packaging, and slogans, as it is important for a company to retain control over how their product and brand is used. A "registered" trademark that is symbolized by ® indicates that the trademark has been filed with the United States Patent and Trademark Office (USPTO). This federal registration has several advantages including a public notice of the registrant's claim of ownership of the mark, a legal presumption of nationwide ownership, and the exclusive right to use the mark on or in connection with their goods or services.

esbeauda/Shutterstock.com

Often, a company develops an idea or product and wants to protect it prior to taking it to market. A **patent** is legal protection for an invention. Normally, there is a limited duration (usually 20 years) on all rights relating to an invention. The USPTO grants rights for a patent in exchange for public disclosure of the invention. A **copyright** legally protects an author's original works (for 50 years plus the author's life) on music, writings, and art work that has physically been documented or recorded.[12] It is common to hear about copyright infringement on music recordings, movies, books, or other artistic works. It is important to note that having a U.S. patent only protects that invention in the United States, not in the global market. This is why you often see knock-off (fake) products in other parts of the world.

Trademark: Legal protection for a brand or product.

Service mark: Legal protection for a service.

Patent: Legal protection for an invention.

Copyright: Legal protection for an author's original works.

concept check

Explain various legal protections available to businesses, authors, or inventors today.

Of course having these competitive advantages or distinguished products allows for a company to develop **brand loyalty** (consumers' faithfulness to a specific brand). Brand loyalty exists when a customer asks specifically for a product. For instance, a person might ask for Pepsi instead of Coke or a Big Mac (McDonald's) instead of a Whopper (Burger King). Brand loyalty leads to **brand equity**, which is the value that a company's name gives to a product or service. For instance, Apple or Sony products translate into higher sales volumes and higher profit margins against competing brands based on their quality and name recognition.

pichetw/Shutterstock.com

Brand loyalty: Consumers' faithfulness to a specific brand.

Brand equity: The value that a company's name gives to a product or service.

Product Classification

Consumer products are divided into classifications based on use in order to help marketers determine what marketing strategy to use. Four classifications of consumer goods include convenience, shopping, specialty, and unsought goods. **Table 6.5** provides examples of the types of product classification and how the four P's of the marketing mix are addressed in each category.[13]

TABLE 6.5

Types of Product Classifications

COMPARISON	CONVENIENCE	SHOPPING	SPECIALTY	UNSOUGHT
Product	Milk, bread, newspaper,	TVs, cars, cell phones	Rolex watches, high end cars	Burial insurance
Price	Inexpensive	Fairly inexpensive	Typically very expensive	Depends but typically higher prices in emergency situations
Place	Diverse, lots of outlets	Large number of selected outlets	Very limited	Limited in nature
Promotion	Price and availability important and stressed	Competitor differentiation is stressed	Brand uniqueness and status stressed	Needs awareness
Consumer brand loyalty	Brand awareness and substitutes acceptable	Brand specific but will use substitutes	Only brand loyal, no substitutes	Can use substitutes
Consumer behavior	Frequent buy, little effort spent	Infrequent buy, need comparisons	Infrequent buy, lots of decision time	Infrequent buy, potential for comparison shopping

Source: Types of Product Classification (2015). Retrieved on March 29, 2015, from: http://www.mbanetbook.co.in/2011/01/types-of-product-classification-product.html.

concept check

Describe the types of product classifications.

PRICE

A **price objective** is a marketing strategy that helps guide businesses in setting the selling price of products or services. Each pricing objective involves a different price-setting strategy in order to effectively achieve business goals, making price a critical component of the marketing mix. Pricing objectives should generate a return on investment (ROI) and help support the other marketing mix elements. Pricing objectives may include maximizing short run profits, increasing sales volume, or matching competitors' prices. **Table 6.6** presents four strategic pricing objectives.[14]

Price objective: A marketing strategy that helps guide businesses in setting the selling price of products or services.

TABLE 6.6

The Four Types of Pricing Objectives

TYPE OF PRICING OBJECTIVE	GOAL
Survival	Reduce prices to help a business remain operational.
Profit	Set price at a point to maximize sales and profits.
Sales	Price increases sales volume or market share.
Status quo	Encourages competition based on factors other than price (free baggage, better service, etc.).

Source: Uhlig, D. (2015). Four types of pricing objectives. Retrieved on March 29, 2015, from: http://smallbusiness.chron.com/four-types-pricing-objectives-33873.html.

Pricing Strategies

In a perfect world, supply and demand would determine prices for goods and services (as discussed in Chapter 3); however, due to a lack of information and an imperfect market, companies must use various strategies to determine the best pricing strategy for products or services in the market place.

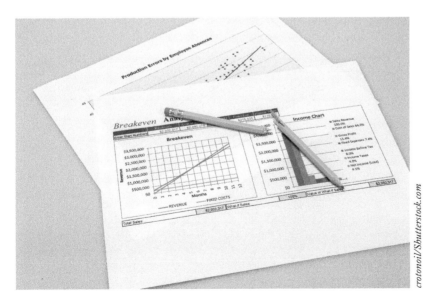

crotonoil/Shutterstock.com

Breakeven analysis: The point at which the number of units sold covers the cost of producing the products.

Fixed costs: Costs that do not fluctuate based on sales volume.

Variable costs: Costs that change directly with sales volume.

A **breakeven analysis** is one method used to establish prices. This type of analysis determines the point at which the number of units sold covers the cost of producing the products. The point where costs are covered by sales is referred to as the breakeven point. To calculate the breakeven point, all fixed and variable costs must be identified. **Fixed costs** are costs that do not fluctuate based on sales volume, such as rent or administrative salaries. These expenses must be paid regardless of the amount of sales. **Variable costs** change directly with sales volume, such as inventory, shipping, and raw materials used to produce goods. To determine the breakeven point, use the following equation:

BREAKEVEN POINT = FIXED COSTS ÷ (UNIT SELLING PRICE − VARIABLE COSTS)

Example: If a company has fixed costs of $25,000 with a selling price of $10 and variable costs of $5 per unit, then the breakeven point would be calculated as follows:

Breakeven Point (in units) = $25,000 ÷ ($10 − 5) = $25,000 ÷ $5 = 5,000 units

So, the company would have to sell 5,000 units in order to cover all costs to produce their product. Any units sold over 5,000 would produce a profit for the business.

Price skimming: Setting the initial price high to maximize profits.

When a product or service first arrives in the market, a company must decide on price—price low and gain a greater share of the market or price high and gain higher profits up front to recover costs. Several pricing strategies exist and choices should align with the company's marketing strategy. One strategy is price skimming. **Price skimming** is a pricing strategy used by companies entering a market with new products or services who wish to maximize profits from the beginning. When a product is released, it is offered at a high price and then lowered later in the product life cycle or when competition begins to enter the market. Different versions of gaming consoles like the PS3 or Xbox or Apple's iPhone are examples of using price skimming in the market.

Penetration pricing: Setting a low initial price to gain a greater percentage of the overall market.

EDLP: Continuous low prices.

Another strategy for entering the market is penetration pricing. **Penetration pricing** is a pricing strategy that sets a low initial price to gain a greater percentage of the overall market. The goal is to quickly attract new customers based on the low cost in order to increase market share and sales volume while at the same time discouraging competition.

CarmenKarin/Shutterstock.com

Everyday low pricing (EDLP) is a pricing strategy that maintains continuous low prices versus short-term price cuts to attract customers. Walmart and grocery stores such as Hy-Vee find great success in offering EDLP as customers do not have to wait for items to go on sale. Discount pricing is a pricing strategy that offers consumers a short-term price drop in order to increase sales. It is important to remove discounts after the time period has elapsed so that customers respond when price discounts are offered.

Competitive pricing is setting the price of a product or service based on competitors' prices. This type of pricing strategy is generally used when a product has been on the market for a long time and there are many substitutes for the product. Businesses match competitors' pricing in order to retain customers and market share.

Odd pricing/psychological pricing is a pricing method that uses odd numbers such as $9.95 or $9.99 to create the perception that individuals are receiving a better price. Fast-food restaurants, such as Wendy's, offer a $.99 menu, whereas Walmart rolls back prices, which often end in seven ($8.77). This type of pricing originally was designed to prevent pilfering of cash by cashiers as it forced the cashier to open the cash drawer, thus registering the transaction. Proponents of this type of pricing believe that individuals view a price such as $49.95 as closer to $40.00 than to $50.00 and therefore, feel as if they are receiving more value.[15] A study published in the *Marketing Bulletin* showed the frequency of odd digit pricing in advertising materials as shown in **Figure 6.5**.[16]

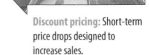

Discount pricing: Short-term price drops designed to increase sales.

Competitive pricing: Matching competitors' pricing.

Odd pricing: Using odd number to price products.

little Whale/Shutterstock.com

FIGURE 6.5

Frequency of Odd Digit Pricing

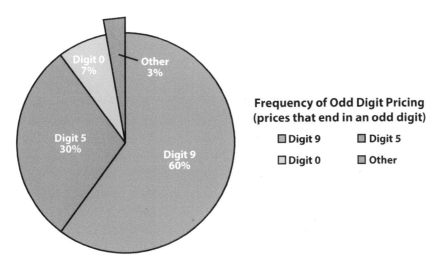

Frequency of Odd Digit Pricing (prices that end in an odd digit)

- Digit 9
- Digit 5
- Digit 0
- Other

Source: The ultimate list of psychological pricing strategies (n.d.). Retrieved on March 1, 2016, from: http://www.psychologicalpricing.net/odd-pricing.

concept check

What types of pricing strategies might a firm use?

PLACE (DISTRIBUTION STRATEGY)

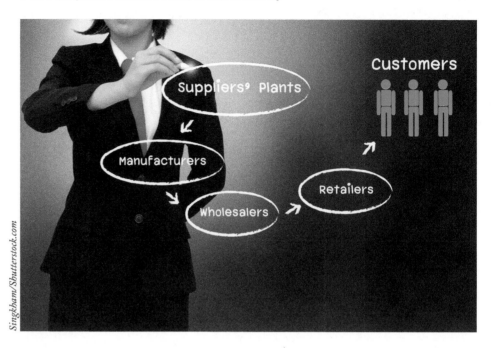

Singkham/Shutterstock.com

Distribution channel: The route a product travels between the producer and the consumer.

Place refers to the distribution of goods and services from its point of origin to the end-user. Businesses want to provide goods and services to customers where and when they need it, which makes distribution an important component in a firm's marketing plan. A **distribution channel** is the route a product travels between the producer and the consumer. A distribution channel can involve a direct transaction between the producer and the consumer or may include several interconnected intermediaries such as wholesalers, distributors, agents, or retailers. Every intermediary is a separate buyer because they pay a price for goods or services and then sell them to another buyer at a profit until it reaches the end user. This is called *mark-up* as it adds cost to the products or services being purchased. For example, farmers produce vegetables and sell them to a co-op for $.0.50, who sells to a grocery store for $0.75, who ultimately sells to the customer in the store for $1.00.[17]

There are a variety of intermediaries involved in getting products to the consumer. **Figure 6.6** shows the various options for moving goods or services through the distribution channel. The key players involved potentially include the *producer* or the company that makes products; the *agent/broker* who serves as the middle man that sells the product from the producer to the wholesaler; a *wholesaler* who sells products to businesses (not to consumers); the *retailer* who sells goods to the consumer; and finally, the *consumer* who purchases goods or services for direct use or ownership rather than for resale or use in production and manufacturing.

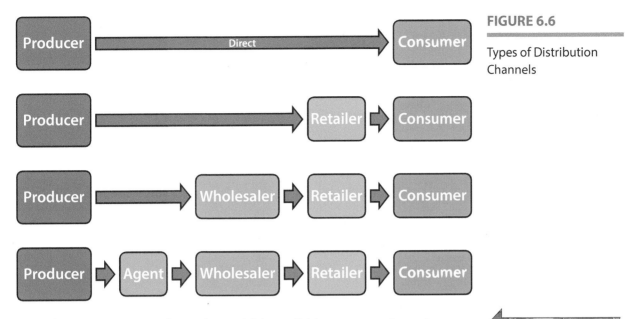

FIGURE 6.6

Types of Distribution
Channels

Distribution intensity refers to how widely available a company's products are distributed in the market place. Three levels exist for distribution including intensive, selective, and exclusive. **Table 6.7** displays the three levels of distribution, their definitions, and examples of each.[18]

Distribution intensity: How widely available a company's products are distributed in the market place.

TABLE 6.7

Levels of Distribution Intensity

INTENSIVE	SELECTIVE	EXCLUSIVE
Products are widely available at multiple locations. Examples: Snacks, milk, soft drinks, magazines, etc.	Products are available in a few selective areas of a geographic region. Examples: iPods, televisions, computers.	Products are available through one specialty or luxury distributor in a geographic area. Examples: Rolex watches, Rolls Royce, Vera Wang dresses.

Source: Perner, L. (2010). Level of distribution coverage (n.d.). Retrieved on February 3, 2015 from: http://www.knowthis.com/distribution-decisions/level-of-distribution-coverage.

Pushing versus Pulling Strategy

Creating demand can be done through the distribution channel intermediaries or through end-users. Two strategies used to create demand for products are pushing strategies and pulling strategies. A pushing strategy involves marketing products to individuals in the distribution channel, such as wholesalers or retailers, instead of end-users. Examples of pushing strategies include trade show promotions to encourage retailer demand, direct selling to retailers, pro-

Pushing strategy: Creating demand for products within the distribution channel.

Pulling strategy: Creating demand for products through customers.

viding incentives for retailers to carry a particular line of products, or point-of-purchase displays. A **pulling strategy** focuses on motivating customers to demand a company's products. Examples of pulling tactics include advertising and sales promotions such as coupons or free trials, which encourage customers to demand products from retailers and/or suppliers.[19] If a customer sees an advertisement for a new candy on a commercial and asks the convenience clerk if it is available, this is an example of a pulling strategy as the demand is pulled from the bottom of the distribution channel upward to the retailer who wants to please a customer.

concept check

How does the distribution channel affect marketing decisions in an organization?

Modes of Transportation

Digital Genetics/Shutterstock.com

Transportation is an important component of the distribution channel as it affects the overall pricing of products. The most dominant modes of urban transport are land transport, including road, rail, water, and air transport. Other modes exist, including pipelines, cable transport, and digital transport.[20] The differences in speed, accessibility, cost, and capacity of moving freight using various types of transportation is shown in **Table 6.8**.

TABLE 6.8

Types of Transportation

TYPE	SPEED	ACCESSIBILITY	COST	CAPACITY
Truck	Moderate	High	Moderate	Low
Railroad	Slow	Moderate	Low	Moderate
Air	Fast	Low	Very High	Very Low
Water	Very Slow	Moderate	Very Low	Very High
Pipeline	Very Slow	Low	Low	Very High
Digital	Very Fast	Very High	Very Low	Moderate

Source: Modes of transportation comparison (2015). Retrieved February 11, 2015, from: http://www.knowthis.com/managing-product-movement/modes-of-transportation-comparison.

PROMOTION

As a consumer, *you* are the main target of marketing companies because you decide whether or not to buy their products. Organizations use a variety of techniques to get you to notice and purchase their brands. Promotional efforts by top companies such as the Walt Disney Company, American Express, Verizon, General Motors, and Proctor and Gamble cost billions of dollars each year.[21] Promotion refers to creating consumer awareness of a product or brand, generating sales, and creating brand loyalty. Integrated marketing communications (IMC) is the process of coordinating all promotional activities within an organization to achieve the objectives set forth in the marketing plan. Promotional objectives are specific goals to be achieved through various marketing activities such as promotional items, sales events, advertising, news releases, media events, coupons, community involvement, on-line marketing, or trade shows. Potential objectives for marketing promotions may include building product awareness, providing information, stimulating demand, or reinforcing the brand.

nasirkhan/Shutterstock.com

Promotion: Creating consumer awareness of a product or brand, generating sales, and creating brand loyalty.

IMC: The process of coordinating all promotional activities within an organization.

Promotional objectives: Specific goals to be achieved through various marketing activities.

Advertising is the practice of calling public attention to a company's product or service through paid advertisements in newspapers, magazines, radio, television, the Internet, or other sources. There are many types of advertising that a company can utilize depending on their goals such as product, institutional, or cause advertising.

A company might use *product advertising* to sell its products to the public. This type of advertising focuses on the product or service directly. *Institutional advertising* uses public service announcements and community outreach programs to promote causes, ideas, or goodwill. *Cause advertising* or *cause-related marketing* involves the promotion of a specific viewpoint on a public issue in order to sway public opinion. A Cone Evolution Study noted that 79 percent of Americans would switch brands if the new brand was associated with a cause, given that pricing and quality are equal to comparable brands.[22] There are many examples of cause marketing used to attract and retain customers including the National Football League (NFL) working with the Susan G. Komen foundation or Meals from the Heartland feeding individuals locally and globally.

Joseph Sohm/Shutterstock.com

Monkey Business Images/Shutterstock.com

Food Donations

Cartoonresource/Shutterstock.com

SURE, I'D LOVE TO BUY THIRTY THOUSAND SUBSCRIPTIONS!

Personal selling occurs where a salesperson sells a product, service, or solution to a customer. You can think of it as the face-to-face selling method. Today, personal selling involves the development of long-standing customer relationships and can be costly to an organization due to the resources and time it takes to successfully develop relationships.

Keepsmiling4u/Shutterstock.com

Sales promotions include activities that attempt to provide added value or incentives to customers to encourage immediate purchases. Examples of commonly used sales promotions include discounts, coupons, samples, premiums, rebates, or sweepstakes.

Public relations includes actions by a business to create a strong and favorable public image. Public relations are conducted through the media, such as newspapers, television, or magazines and are paid endorsements by the company. Public relations advertising informs the public about the company and its products.

Publicity is a type of promotion that relies on public opinion about a company's products or services, usually from a mass media news story. Publicity is free; however, the company does not control publicity, which can be positive or negative. Publicity for a particular business can be extremely valuable in building credibility and awareness or extremely harmful if it is negative. Many companies have come under fire for promoting child labor in manufacturing plants that produce their products, which is negative publicity for the business and can hurt sales revenue.

Direct selling is the use of independent sales representatives who use person-to-person sales, typically within customers' homes or others hosting an event. Direct sellers are independent contractors who market and sell the products or services of a company in return for a commission on sales. Examples of direct selling include Avon, The Pampered Chef, and Cutco cutlery.

Sales promotion: Activities that attempt to provide added value or incentives to customers to encourage immediate purchase.

Public relations: Actions by a business to create a strong and favorable public image.

Publicity: Unpaid promotion of a company's products or services.

Direct selling: The use of independent sales representatives who use person-to-person sales directly to consumers.

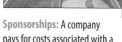

Sponsorships: A company pays for costs associated with a project or program in exchange for advertising or recognition.

Sponsorships exist when a company pays for costs associated with a project or program in exchange for advertising or recognition. Corporate sponsorships are commonly associated with non-profit groups, who could not fund the project without outside help. When this happens, the company is given credit through recognition such as the following statement on a program or advertisement, "Thanks to Burger King for their sponsorship." However, it is becoming more common to see corporate sponsorships in College Bowl games and Nascar races as mutual benefit comes to the sponsored event and the company providing the sponsorship.

ciapix/Shutterstock.com

concept check

Compare and contrast different advertising methods used by businesses.

PRODUCT LIFE CYCLE (PLC)

The product life cycle (PLC) is defined as the time a product enters the market through the time when it is withdrawn from the market. PLC is characterized by specific stages: research and development, introduction, growth, maturity, decline, and finally obsolescence as the product is discontinued. Every product or service in the marketplace goes through the product life cycle; however, each product or service exists within the life cycle for different amounts of time. Many businesses invest heavily in new product development to make sure that their businesses grow and continue to invest heavily once the product is in the market to produce future revenue. **Figure 6.7** illustrates each stage in the PLC from a product's introduction, growth, maturity, and through decline as well as shows sales forecasts within each stage.

Product life cycle (PLC): The four stages of a product's life in the marketplace.

FIGURE 6.7

Stages of the Product Life Cycle

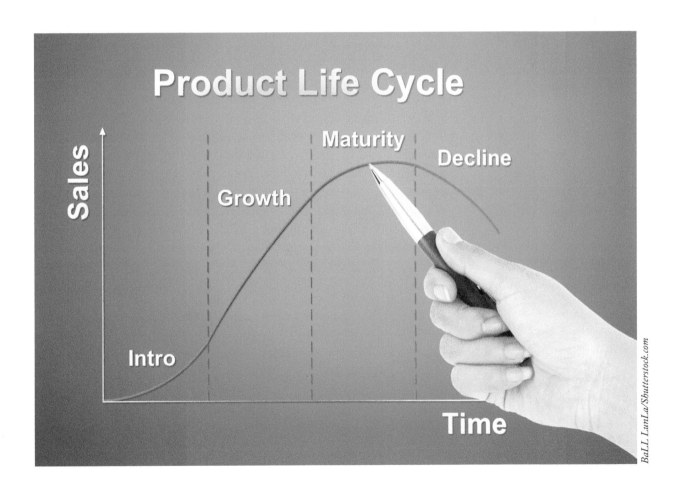

BaLL. LanLa/Shutterstock.com

STAGES

The product life cycle has four clearly defined stages, each with its own characteristics.[23]

- **Introduction Stage**—This stage primarily relates to the development of a new product, from the time it is initially conceptualized to the point it is introduced to the market. This stage is typically the most expensive as the cost of research and development, consumer testing, and marketing needed to launch the product are very high while sales are low.

- **Growth Stage**—The growth stage is characterized by strong sales growth as new competitors enter the market. This stage tends to be associated with high levels of profit as costs are recovered and sales increase rapidly. This makes it possible for businesses to invest more in promotional activities in an effort to maximize potential growth and profits during this stage.

- **Maturity Stage**—During this stage, the product is well-established and the goal is to maintain market share. This is typically the most competitive time for products so the investment in product promotion should be strategically planned. Furthermore, any product modifications or production process improvements should be considered to give the product a competitive advantage.

- **Decline Stage**—Sooner or later, the market for a product will start to shrink as the product becomes obsolete. During this stage, production takes place in low cost locations as volume slows tremendously. This shrinkage could be due to the market becoming saturated with similar products or because the consumers are switching to a different type of product. In the decline stage, it is still possible to make a profit by switching to less-expensive production methods and cheaper markets or by withdrawing the product slowly in order to phase out the line completely.

The product life cycle is a useful tool for any company to use as a guide in developing their marketing and strategic plans. Maintaining a product's life, as long as it is profitable, makes sense to many companies. **Table 6.9** depicts what happens to the four P's at each stage of the PLC and what a company can do to help the marketing campaign find the highest levels of success.[24]

TABLE 6.9

Marketing Implications at Each Stage

FOCUS:	INTRODUCTION	GROWTH	MATURITY	DECLINE
Marketing goal	Create product awareness	Emphasis on product differentiation	Continue brand loyalty	Picking up remaining customers
Product	One	More styles or varieties	Full product line	Keep best sellers
Price	Market penetration pricing or price skimming	Gain market share by granting deals	Defend market share, competitive pricing	Stay profitable, reduce pricing
Promotion	Educate about product	Stress important differences	Reminder based	Limited promotion
Place	Limited	More distribution channels	Maximum distribution channels	Few channels
Competition	Little to none	Increasing	High	Reduced

Source: Sharma, N., (2013). Market strategy on different stages PLC and its marketing implications on FMCG products. *International Journal of Marketing, Financial Services & Management Research*, 2(3). Retrieved on February 3, 2015, from: http://indianresearchjournals.com/pdf/IJMFSMR/2013/March/12.pdf

concept check

How do marketing needs change in each stage of the PLC?

WRAPPING UP...

Within Chapter 6, we have examined the role of marketing, the marketing process, and four elements that are vital to creating an effective marketing mix for an organization. Marketing is all around us and hopefully, this information will help you understand it from a rational business perspective along with your emotional consumer perspective.

In Chapter 7, we will focus on how management and leadership affect business operations. Various management theories and models will be examined to help you determine what type of leader and/or manager you most align with and the effect different leadership styles have in the work place.

BUSINESS TERMINOLOGY

Marketing

Utility

Marketing concept

Business-to-business (B2B)

Business-to-consumer (B2C)

Non-profit marketing

Marketing plan

Marketing strategy

Tactical plans

Consumer behavior

Market segmentation

Demographics

Target market

Target audience

Marketing research

Primary data

Secondary data

Qualitative research

Quantitative research

Action research

Four P's

Marketing mix

Product line

Product mix

Branding

Trademark

Service mark

Patent

Copyright

Brand loyalty

Brand equity

Product classification

Price objective

Breakeven analysis

Fixed costs

Variable costs

Price skimming

Penetration pricing

Everyday low pricing (EDLP)

Discount pricing

Competitive pricing

Odd pricing/psychological pricing

Distribution channel

Distribution intensity

Pushing strategy

Pulling strategy

Promotion

Integrated marketing
  communications (IMC)

Promotional objectives

Advertising

Personal selling

Sales promotions

Public relations

Publicity

Direct selling

Sponsorships

Product life cycle (PLC)

DISCUSSION QUESTIONS

1. How has the focus of marketing in organizations changed over time?

2. Why is it important for marketers to understand buying behaviors?

3. What relationship exists between market segmentation and target market selection?

4. What are the five major categories of pricing strategies? Provide an example of each.

5. Explain the stages of the product life cycle and the implications for marketers at each stage.

LEARNING ACTIVITIES

1. Find a celebrity who supports a charitable cause and write a summary of the cause they support, how/why the celebrity started with or is connected to the cause, and discuss the impact the celebrity has had on the cause.

2. Complete the VALS (Values, Attitudes, Lifestyles Survey) found at: http://www.strategicbusinessinsights.com/vals/presurvey.shtml. Once you have completed the survey, write a short summary of which segment you were categorized into, what parts of the segment are like (or not like) you, and how VALS information could be used to help market products or services to various segments.

3. Find an ad from a printed or online source and analyze it based on the following areas: target market, product or service promoted, effectiveness of ad, and your emotional reaction to the product or service based on the ad. Discuss each of the areas above as well as how you might change the ad to fit a different segment in the marketplace.

4. Explore the American Marketing Association web site. Be prepared to discuss what type of information is available on the site and what marketing mix variable the site exemplifies. Be sure to have concrete examples to show your knowledge of what the AMA is and information on the site.

Note: *Because web sites often change, use a search engine to find alternative web sites to access required information when necessary.*

CASE STUDY: PLAYING THE PRICE GAME

Betty's Bakery is owned by Betty Koschak, who has recently decided to enter the cupcake and cookie business. Currently, Betty's main business is bread and rolls but increased competition has forced her to look into other product lines. Her marketing research has shown that the cupcake and cookie business is a viable option. The local market has three competitors who specialize in selling these products. The competition includes the following: (1) Jensen's Food, a local market that sells cupcakes and cookies; (2) Daphne's Cupcakes, a small store that only sells cupcakes and cookies; and (3) Costco, a large discount warehouse that sells bulk cupcakes and cookies. Her research found that prices range from $1.99 to $2.69 per cupcake and from $0.99 to $1.99 per cookie.

CASE STUDY ANALYSIS

Based on the information provided, answer the following questions:

(1) What pricing strategy would you recommend to Betty? Explain your answer.

(2) Looking at the competition, how would you suggest Betty carve her niche into this type of market?

(3) What types of advertising could Betty use to differentiate herself from the competition?

CHAPTER 7

MANAGEMENT VS. LEADERSHIP

"The courage of leadership is giving others the chance to succeed even though you bear the responsibility for getting things done."

~Simon Sinek, Author

OUTCOMES:

> Describe the functions of management.
> Distinguish between management and leadership.
> Compare different leadership styles and their effect on employees within an organization.
> Illustrate the communication model and explain its importance in business.
> Identify organizational structures used within businesses.

WHAT IS MANAGEMENT?

Rawpixel/Shutterstock.com

Management: The organization and coordination of business activities, resources, and people in order to achieve strategic goals.

In today's fast-paced business environment, organizations are looking for individuals who are willing and able to help them meet strategic goals and prepare for future success. Individuals who help achieve these goals are often part of an organization's management team. Management is the organization and coordination of business activities, resources, and people in order to achieve strategic goals. According to management guru, Peter Drucker (1909–2005), the basic tasks of management include marketing and innovation.[1] Management works to develop corporate strategy through planning, organizing, leading, and controlling an organization's resources.

BASIC MANAGEMENT FUNCTIONS

The basic management functions are a set of core activities that managers perform in a business environment. The four functions of management include planning, organizing, leading, and controlling and their purposes are found in **Table 7.1**.[2]

FUNCTION	PURPOSE
Planning	Determining current and future business goals and how to achieve them.
Organizing	Allocating people, tasks, and resources.
Leading	Motivating employees to meet organizational goals.
Controlling	Measuring completed assignments against established objectives and goals.

Source: Norman, L. (2015). What are the four basic functions that make up the management process? Retrieved on March 1, 2015, from: http://smallbusiness.chron.com/four-basic-functions-make-up-management-process-23852.html.

TABLE 7.1

Four Functions of Management

concept check

What are the four functions of management?

In most organizations, there are three levels of management including first-level, middle-level, and top-level management. Each level is responsible for different functions and responsibilities, each vital to the success of the organization. The following information highlights the roles and responsibilities of each level of management.

Top-level management is the top source of authority and establishes strategies, manages objectives, and sets goals and policies for a company. This level can take many forms but typically consists of a board of directors and a chief executive or managing director. Individuals at this level devote the majority of their time planning and coordinating company functions from a broad perspective. The role of top-level management includes some of the following duties:

Top-level management: Upper management tasked with developing vision, goals, and objectives of the firm.

- Developing the company's strategic plans, objectives, and policies;
- Issuing instructions for planning budgets, procedures, and schedules;
- Developing and promoting positive public relations; and
- Monitoring the overall performance of the company.

iQoncept/Shutterstock.com

Middle-level management: Mid-level managers responsible for specific areas and who report to top managers.

Middle-level management encompasses positions such as a branch manager or department manager. They are responsible to top-level management for actions related to the operation of their area and devote their time to organizational and directional functions. In a small company, there may be only one layer of middle-level management and in large companies there may be senior and junior management. Their duties may include:

michaeljung/Shutterstock.com

- Executing company plans in conjunction with policies and top-level management directives;
- Hiring and training first-level management personnel;
- Communicating information from top-level to first-level;
- Coordinating division or departmental activities;
- Communicating key data to top-level management;
- Evaluating junior-level managers; and
- Motivating first-level managers.

First-level management: Supervisory managers responsible for employees and front-line tasks.

First-level management is also referred to as supervisory management. This level of management concerns itself with personnel oversight and direction of operational employees and basic controlling functions. Their duties might include the following:

Robert Kneschke/Shutterstock.com

- Assigning employee jobs and tasks;
- Overseeing day-to-day operations;
- Accountability for production control;
- Communicating goals and objectives to the workers;
- Relaying concerns of workers to higher levels;
- Providing employee training;
- Conducting employee performance reviews and reports;
- Ensuring company discipline; and
- Motivating employees.

A summary of the information listed above is shown in **Table 7.2**.[3]

LEVEL OF MANAGEMENT	TYPES OF POSITIONS	RESPONSIBILITIES
TOP-LEVEL	Chief Executive Officer (CEO), Chief Financial Officer (CFO), Chief Operating Officer (COO), Chief Information Officer (CIO), President, and VP positions	• Responsible for long term planning • Set vision and strategic objectives for the organization • Create plans for the long-term success of the organization
MIDDLE-LEVEL	Department Heads, Sales Managers, Plant Managers, and General Managers	• Report to top management, oversee first-level management • Develop and implement plans and procedures to meet strategic goals of the organization • Interpret plans and set actions related to products, customers, or operations
FIRST-LEVEL (SUPERVISORY)	Supervisors, Crew Leaders, Foremen, Shift Managers, Team Leaders, and Assistant Managers	• Responsible for day-to-day operations • Report to middle managers • Supervise employees and evaluate performance

Source: Levels of Management (2015). Retrieved on March 31, 2015 from: http://www.managementstudyguide.com/management_levels.htm.

TABLE 7.2

Levels of Management and Responsibilities

concept check

Compare and contrast the three levels of management.

MANAGEMENT SKILLS

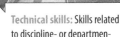

It is easy for employees to feel disconnected from a CEO if employees do not believe the CEO has the skill set to do their job on the sales or production floor. However, it is important to realize that there are different kinds of skills utilized at various levels of management to successfully complete their responsibilities including technical, human, and conceptual skills. **Technical skills** are discipline—or departmental—specific tasks, such as running a cash register or stocking inventory. **Human relation skills** are skills that enable managers to

Technical skills: Skills related to discipline- or departmental-specific tasks.

Human relation skills: Skills that enable managers to effectively communicate with and motivate people.

Conceptual skills: Skills that allow a manager to view the organization as a whole.

effectively communicate with and motivate people. Finally, conceptual skills allow a manager to view the organization as a whole and see the interconnectivity of all of the business functions. This ability helps create the vision for future growth and profitability. **Figure 7.1** displays the skills needed at each level of management.

FIGURE 7.1

Skills Needed at each Level of Management

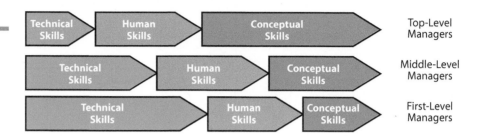

All successful managers must possess a variety of skills to be effective. All companies rely on good management to help with day-to-day operations. Good managers tend to move up within an organization, which helps employees and management plan for the future. **Table 7.3** depicts six essential management skills that employees should possess in order to move into higher-level management positions within an organization.[4]

TABLE 7.3

Essential Management Skills

ESSENTIAL MANAGEMENT SKILLS
Management and Leadership Skills: To establish priorities, delegate, motivate and develop employees, and communicate company objectives and goals.
Communication Skills: Ability to listen, dialog with employees, provide inspiration for others, and effectively demonstrate emotional intelligence.
Collaboration Skills: Possess an aptitude for appreciating differences, form rapport, effectively negotiate, and develop alliances.
Critical Thinking Skills: To approach problem-solving logically, possess the ability to be clear, open-minded, unbiased, and be informed using evidence.
Finance Skills: To weigh consequences of decisions on the bottom-line, possess the ability to construct a financially sound budget, and create sensible forecasts.
Project Management Skills: Understand a project's scope and goals, identify the responsibilities of others, use technology proficiently to track projects, and become a good cross-functional team member.

Source: AMA's list of must-have management skills (2015). Retrieved on March 22, 2015, from: http://www.amanet.org/training/promotions/six-skills-for-managers-and-leaders.aspx.

concept check

What skills should one possess in order to move to higher level positions within an organization?

VISION AND MISSION STATEMENTS

The planning function of management determines a company's vision, mission, goals, and objectives. These help lead an organization today and into the future as well as tells stakeholders what the company values. A **vision statement** is an explanation of what a business is and where it wants to go in the future. It serves as a clear guide for present and future courses of action and states the values of the organization. Amazon.com's vision statement is: *Our vision is to be earth's most customer centric company; to build a place where people can come to find and discover anything they might want to buy online.* While Habitat for Humanity's vision statement is: *A world where everyone has a decent place to live.*[5] Although each vision is different, examining them clearly tells stakeholders what the company's goals and mission are in the marketplace.

alexmillos/Shutterstock.com0

Vision statement: An explanation of what a business is currently and where it wants to go in the future.

Mission statement: A statement describing the reason a company exists.

Helga Esteb/Shutterstock.com

Mission statements are generally a one-sentence statement describing the reason a company exists and include the target market, the purpose of the business, and what it intends to accomplish. Mission statements are used to help guide the decision-making process and set the goals and objectives of a business. For example, the American Heart Association's mission statement is: *To build healthier lives, free of cardiovascular diseases and stroke,* which they promote though their "Go Red" campaign for women. The Human Society has a simple, yet effective, mission: *Celebrating Animals, Confronting Cruelty,* which goes right to the heart of those who support their cause.[6]

PLANNING

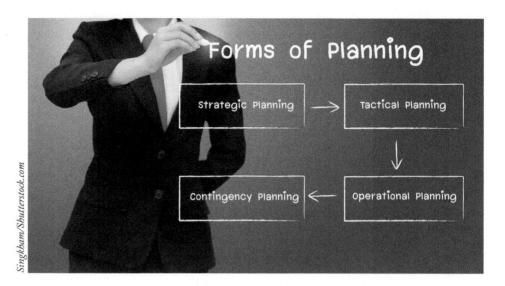

Once the vision and mission statements have been created, it is important to develop plans for implementing actions within the organization. Several types of managerial planning are involved in these phases including strategic, tactical, operational, and contingency planning.[7]

STRATEGIC PLANS

Strategic plan: A plan that defines the goals of the entire organization.

Tactical plan: A plan that specifies what must be done and how goals should be met, typically one year or less.

A **strategic plan** defines the goals of the entire organization, rather than the goals of specific divisions or departments. Strategic planning begins with top-level management, who develops the organization's vision and mission statements. Strategic plans help focus future plans of the organization and often span five or more years. Strategic planning becomes a framework for planning at other levels of the organization and helps determine how resources will be allocated to achieve goals.

TACTICAL PLANS

"Great plan. Could we get some more details?"

A **tactical plan** is directed at middle-level management and specifies who is responsible for completing the plan, what must be done, and how to complete tasks needed to achieve goals set by the organization. Tactical plans usually span one year or less as they are considered short-term goals. Typically, it is middle management's duty to take the comprehensive strategic plan and pinpoint tactical actions.

OPERATIONAL PLANS

Operational plans are used to support the tactical plans of middle-level management. Operational plans are very specific and outline the standards and schedules needed to achieve tactical objectives. These plans use goals that are quantitative in nature, which help measure and assess if objectives have been met. Examples of such goals are: "Process 50 sales calls per day" or "Produce 2000 cars per quarter." Results are adjusted as necessary.

Operational plans can be a single-use plan (a one-time occurrence) or an on-going (continuing) plan. A one-time occurrence, such as a budget or sales program, is a single-use plan because it is directly connected to a special project. Continuing or on-going plans, such as policies, procedures, or rules, are usually made once and reused over a period of years.

Operational plan: A plan that is very specific and outlines the standards and schedules needed to achieve tactical objectives.

Contingency plan: Alternative course of action that can be utilized if the original plan needs revision.

CONTINGENCY PLANS

Even with the best laid plans, things can go wrong. This creates a need for contingency plans in an organization. Contingency planning means developing alternative courses of action in the event that the original plan needs revision. This is similar to planning a picnic and hoping for nice weather. If it is sunny, you have your picnic as planned; however, if it rains, locating a shelter or finding a nearby restaurant would be viable contingency plans. In today's rapidly changing business environment, alternative actions are often required.

Thinglass/Shutterstock.com

concept check

What types of planning are necessary in an organization?

PROGRAMMED VERSUS NON-PROGRAMMED DECISIONS

Having plans in place provides direction for a business and makes it easier for managers to be decision-makers. The act of business decision-making is choosing an option from a list of alternatives that is most beneficial for the company.

Sometimes decisions are made easily and with a great deal of information and/or experience, while other times decisions are made without much information or experience in a given area.

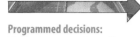

Programmed decisions: Simple, common, and typically frequent decisions where the outcome is fairly predictable.

Programmed decisions are simple, common, and typically frequent decisions where the outcome is fairly predictable based on past experience. A business decision becomes easier to make when a manager has encountered a similar situation before or the decision is routine. As a result, programmed decisions allow a manager to make rational and consistently effective choices. Common business practices may develop into standard operating procedures (SOP) that define how decisions are made in an organization. Successful management decisions and actions become routine over time and are used to develop a manual of SOPs that address areas such as technical issues, customer service problems, or disciplinary matters.

Non-programmed decisions: Decisions made in situations where no established policies or protocols have been determined.

Non-programmed decisions involve new or unusual circumstances that arise where no established policies or protocols have been determined. In this instance, a manager must make a decision without the luxury of previous information or standard policies. These decisions generally take longer to make due to the time it takes to collect all necessary information to make a decision. Fast-food companies make non-programmed decisions about consumer health concerns regarding high fat content and lack of healthy menu options. Uncertainty about customer preferences and changes in menu options to accommodate such changes are often non-programmed decisions.[8] Other times when non-programmed decisions are made include times of crisis or emergency situations.

MANAGEMENT VERSUS LEADERSHIP

As mentioned earlier, management involves four functions (planning, organizing, leading, and controlling). Often, leadership and management are lumped into the same category but they are different. It is fair to say that a leader can be a manager and that a manager can be a leader; however, they are different in nature. The key difference is in the decision employees make to follow an individual. Managers (bosses) often have people follow them because they hold power or authority over employees. Leaders are followed because they inspire employees and may or may not have an official title within the organization. **Figure 7.2** displays the differences between leaders and managers.

FIGURE 7.2

Leaders vs. Managers

Keepsmiling4u/Shutterstock.com

concept check

What makes a leader different than a manager?

LEADERSHIP

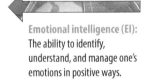

Emotional intelligence (EI):
The ability to identify, understand, and manage one's emotions in positive ways.

To identify exactly what traits make an effective leader is impossible as what works for one leader may not work for another leader. Leaders display different qualities and this section will discuss many leadership theories as well as abilities that successful leaders share. Leadership is more about employee and organizational needs as opposed to the needs of the leader. However, it is important for a leader to understand one's self in order to be effective in motivating and developing others. A successful leader possesses a high level of emotional intelligence (EI). EI is the ability to identify, understand, and manage one's emotions in positive ways in order to guide thinking and behavior in the workplace.

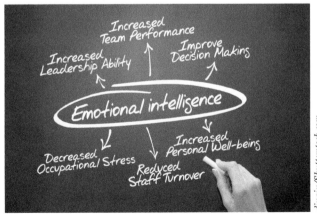

dizain/Shutterstock.com

Daniel Goleman, who popularized EI, discussed six styles of leadership that effective leaders utilize depending on the needs of the organization at a given moment. The benefits of possessing high levels of EI include increased leadership ability, team performance, and decision-making while decreasing stress and turn-over of employees. All styles should be developed and included in a leader's repertoire of leadership tools. **Table 7.4** displays Goleman's six leadership styles.[9]

TABLE 7.4

Six Leadership Styles (Goleman)

STYLE	HOW STYLE IS USED BY LEADERS
Visionary	Creating a "vision" for employees when a new direction is needed.
Coaching	Developing employees on a one-on-one basis by linking personal goals to company goals.
Affiliative	Creating group coherence through employee involvement and shared meaning of work.
Democratic	Using employees' knowledge and skills to refocus group commitment on organizational goals.
Pacesetting	Increasing performance by using high standards; however, this can reduce morale if standards are not met.
Commanding	Using a military model of leadership. Effective in a crisis but regular use can undercut morale and create dissatisfaction.

Source: Murray, A. (2009). Leadership styles. The Wall Street Journal. Retrieved on March 2, 2015, from: http://guides.wsj.com/management/developing-a-leadership-style/how-to-develop-a-leadership-style/.

TYPES OF LEADERSHIP

All leaders have a personal way to lead others, which forms the basis for a preferred leadership style. There are five primary leadership styles (shown in **Figure 7.3**), which include transactional, participative/democratic, authoritative, laissez-faire, and transformational. All five styles can be effectively used in the appropriate circumstances.

FIGURE 7.3

Types of Leadership

Autocratic

Transactional

Democratic

Leadership Styles

Laissez - Faire

Transformational

Kheng Guan Toh/Shutterstock.com

Source: Johnson, R. (n.d.). Five different types of leadership styles. Retrieved on April 1, 2015, from: http://smallbusiness.chron.com/5-different-types-leadership-styles-17584.html.

Autocratic leadership, also known as authoritarian leadership, is characterized by the manager having control over a majority of the decisions and obtaining little input from group members. Autocratic leadership involves absolute control over a group and can be successful in times of war, with new employees who need direction, or in emergency situations where only one person should take the lead in making decisions.

Autocratic leadership: Manager makes most decisions with little input from others.

Participative/democratic leadership: Employees are involved in the decision-making process.

Participative or democratic leadership involves a team directed by a leader where employees are involved in the decision-making process to determine what needs to be done organizationally. Although the leader still may make the ultimate decision, employees are usually more satisfied with their jobs when they are able to participate or have input.

gguy/Shutterstock.com

Laissez-faire or **free-rein leadership** is leading by setting objectives and allowing the group to choose its own path for achieving them. Employees determine policies and methods for achieving necessary goals. It is most effective when employees have the skills to work independently, are self-motivated, and are held accountable for results. Researchers, doctors, and college professors are examples of individuals who operate well under this type of leadership style.

Laissez-faire/Free-rein leadership: Employees determine policies and methods used to achieve goals.

Transformational leadership: Emphasizes employee motivation and morale to change behavior.

Transactional leadership: Provides rewards or punishments based on performance outcomes.

Transformational leadership emphasizes employee motivation and morale in order to change behaviors for the greater good. These leaders create a visionary pathway for others to follow and support individual transformation, often moving employees to new heights personally and professionally. Transformational leaders are encouraging, motivating, supportive, and inspire individuals to perform at their highest levels.

Transactional leadership provides rewards or punishments based on performance outcomes from predetermined goals. This type of leader establishes clear rules and procedures so expectations are clear and subordinates follow what the leader tells them to do. How well an employee performs determines the level of reward or punishment received.[10]

concept check

Compare and contrast various leadership styles.

LEADERSHIP THEORIES

Hersey and Blanchard's Situational Leadership Theory states that successful leaders should change their leadership styles based on employees' maturity and task readiness. Leaders analyze a given situation and decide where to stress importance of the task and employee relationships in order to get the job done efficiently. According to Hersey and Blanchard, there are four main leadership styles including telling, selling, participating, and delegating. A leader *tells* employees what goals to accomplish and specifically directs them on how to move forward. *Selling* the message to employees is an important task as it supports employees as they achieve goals. *Participating* focuses on relationships and support while *delegating* moves the responsibility of completing tasks to employees as the leader becomes less involved in decision-making.[11]

Douglas McGregor's theory was developed in the 1960's and suggests that there are two fundamental approaches to managing people: Theory X and Theory Y. Theory X managers believe that employees inherently dislike only work to provide security, and will do anything to avoid work. Employees are believed to be unmotivated and avoid responsibility; therefore, a manager must continually coerce and control employees in order to get work accomplished. This aligns with the commanding and authoritative leadership styles mentioned earlier.

Theory Y managers, on the other hand, believe that employees are happy to work, are motivated, and will assume and accept responsibility when it is given to them. Theory Y managers tend to be participative when making decisions and value trust, results, and relationships. These managers are inclined to delegate and empower employees as well as express regular recognition and appreciation. They feel that employees are worth developing and employees working for these managers tend to feel appreciated and respected.[12]

Situational leadership: Changing leadership styles based on employees' maturity and readiness to complete tasks.

Theory X: The belief that employees inherently dislike work and will avoid it when possible.

Theory Y: The belief that employees are motivated to work and accept responsibility.

OneO2/Shutterstock.com

Pressmaster/Shutterstock.com

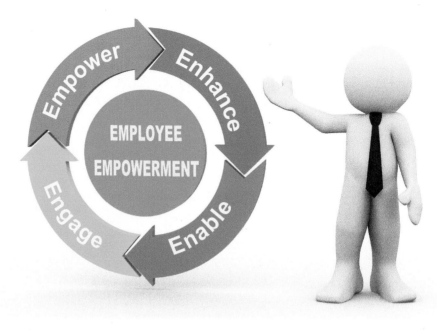

nasirkhan/Shutterstock.com

Theory Z: Japanese management style that focuses on empowerment and the team over the individual.

An extension of McGregor's work is William Ouchi's **Theory Z** or "Japanese management style" that developed in the 1980s. Theory Z management focuses on increasing employee loyalty through empowerment at all levels of the organization as well as focusing on the team over the individual. By encouraging employees at all levels to make decisions, the organization experiences increased employee morale and job satisfaction, cooperative employee relationships, and increased productivity.[13]

MANAGEMENT COMMUNICATION

Regardless which management style is selected, communication, or lack thereof, changes interactions within an organization. You can likely think of a time when communication failed with a boss or someone you know personally. When this happens, it is difficult to resolve the issue(s) without effective communication. Managers are the key communicators in a business so it is important for them to have excellent communication skills. This helps keep day-to-day information flowing properly and keeps all stakeholders informed. The ability to communicate effectively with superiors, colleagues, and staff is essential, regardless of what industry you work in.

The top 10 communication skills that managers should possess include: listening, nonverbal communication, clarity and conciseness, friendliness, confidence, empathy, open-mindedness, respect, feedback, and knowing which type of communication to use in various situations. Without proper communication, employees become frustrated, distanced from the organization, and dissatisfied with their work.[14]

"What if, and I know this sounds kooky, we communicated with the employees."

Cartoonresource/Shutterstock.com

Part of communicating well with employees and stakeholders is the ability to share information about the organization clearly and fully. Transparency exists when management makes financial information and documentation available for public review. Being transparent develops trust with stakeholders and helps reduce hidden agendas or secretive information. Transparency is critical through all levels of the organization from the executive management team to the employees. Some key points which help improve transparency in a company include:

Transparency: Making financial information and documentation available for public review.

1. *Leadership being present* and showing up for regularly scheduled meetings;

2. *Agreeing on the agenda* and making everyone aware of proposed topics and time allocated for each topic;

3. *Being proactive* and visible to others;

4. *Explaining the rationale behind a decision;*

5. *Allowing anonymous feedback* by providing multiple options for submitting feedback anonymously;

6. *Requesting a 360-feedback* evaluation to receive feedback about your effectiveness as a leader.[15]

It is important for leaders to utilize feedback and suggestions made by employees. Otherwise, employees feel as if their efforts have been wasted or ignored, which will lead to apathy and dissatisfaction in the work place. Good leaders understand that open communication, trust, and transparency create a more positive, creative, and productive working environment for everyone.

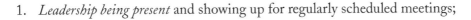

COMMUNICATION MODEL

The key to any successful business is communication between stakeholders. This process requires all levels to understand and utilize good communication skills. To help management understand the communication process, the SMCR model is often used. Using a model helps managers focus on how messages are received as well as understand what might interfere with successful communications between parties involved. The SMCR communication model is show in **Figure 7.4**.

FIGURE 7.4

SMCR Communication Model

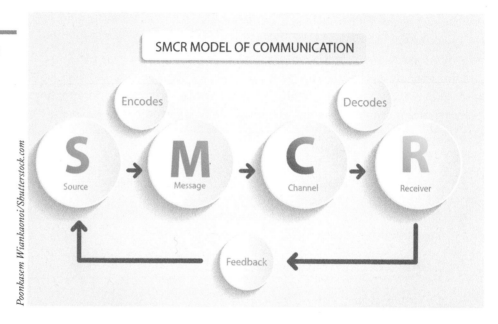

Poonkasem Wuankaomoi/Shutterstock.com

Key players include the sender of the message, the receiver of the message, the *channel* (or method of sending the message), and the *feedback* from the receiver which tells the sender that the message was received. However, many barriers to transmitting a clear message exist, which is called noise.

Noise: Anything that interferes with communicating a message properly.

"The goal of all communication is understanding. Anything that interferes with this understanding is called noise," stated Rosie Bunnow from the University of Wisconsin.[16] Noise can consist of mental and emotional noise, physical and environmental noise, or physiological and semantic noise. **Figure 7.5** displays the myriad noises that get in the way of a message being received properly from the sender. The importance of organizational communication is paramount as miscommunication, even what might appear to be minor, can be very costly to a company.

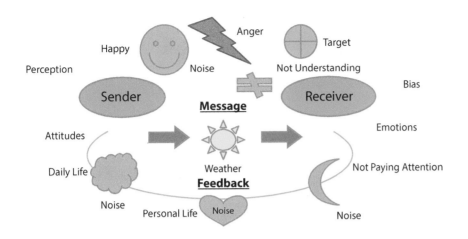

FIGURE 7.5

Barriers to Effective
Communication

concept check

Why is it important for organizational members to communicate well?

ORGANIZATIONAL STRUCTURES

Organizational structure refers to the organization of employees, jobs, and the way work gets done in a company. The reporting structure depends on the size and type of business; however, there is typically an identifiable method of reporting within the organization. An organization may be structured based on the company's goals and objectives, its size, the type of product or service it offers, or by the use of technology within the firm. The more people in the organization, typically the more complex the organizational structure.

In any size company, employees' responsibilities are defined by what they do, who they report to, and for managers, who reports to them. These responsibilities are assigned to positions rather than to specific employees. An **organizational chart** illustrates the various reporting relationships within a hierarchical structure (see **Figure 7.6**); however, it is important to note that each company's reporting structure will vary according to their needs.

A company can further divide itself into more manageable units. **Departmentalization** is dividing a company by functional units or other criteria. This is done so that employees

Organizational structure:
The organization of employees, jobs, and the way work will get done.

Organizational chart:
Illustrates reporting relationships within an organization.

Departmentalization: Dividing a company by functional units or other criteria.

FIGURE 7.6

Sample Hierarchy
Within a Company

MapensStudio/Shutterstock.com

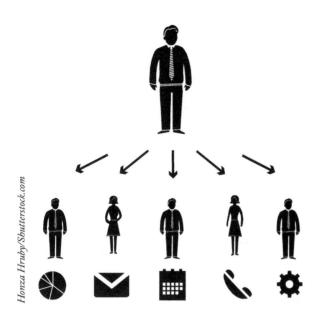

Honza Hruby/Shutterstock.com

and managers can specialize in a particular function, such as finance, marketing, or sales. Most companies, including restaurants, are likely to use two or more types of departmentalization simultaneously. Standard departmentalization methods might include job alignment by functional activities, product or services types, customer groups, geographical location, or processes.[17]

A manager can empower employees through the **delegation** of duties, which refers to the assignment of responsibility or authority to an employee to accomplish a task. However, the manager who delegated the work remains accountable for the outcome of the delegated work, so a manager may not delegate if he feels employees are not ready to take on the tasks independently or do not have the skills or knowledge to complete tasks well. Delegation can create trust within a company as employees feel empowered and respected. The opposite of effective delegation is **micromanagement**, when a manager provides too much oversight and direction after delegating work to employees. Although it is important to be supportive, micromanagers make employees fearful of making mistakes or step in to complete tasks themselves, which creates a lack of trust and disempowerment in the organization. In general, delegation is a good tool for building skills and motivating employees.

Span of control is the number of employees, sometimes called direct reports, who report to one manager in a company's hierarchy. The more employees under the control of one manager, the wider the span of control; less employees means a narrower span of control. The advantages of a narrow span of control include quick access to employees and more effective feedback. In recent years, many organizations have widened the span of control due to restricted budgets and economic challenges. The advantages of wider spans of control include less layers of management which result in cost savings for the organization as fewer managers exist in the hierarchy.[18]

Another area of consideration in structuring organizations relates to how decisions are typically made. **Centralization** occurs when decision-making is maintained at the top-levels of management. **Decentralization** occurs when decision-making is delegated to lower-level managers and employees who are more familiar with local conditions and tasks than corporate management. **Table 7.5** summarizes the advantages and disadvantages of centralized versus decentralized management.[19]

Delegation: Assigning responsibility and authority to employees to accomplish tasks.

Micromanagement: Providing too much oversight or control over employees after delegating.

Span of control: The number of employees who report to a manager.

Centralization: Decisions are made from the top-down in an organization.

Decentralization: Decisions are made from the bottom-up in an organization.

TABLE 7.5

Centralization Versus Decentralization

MANAGEMENT	ADVANTAGES	DISADVANTAGES
Centralization	• Greater upper-management control • Improved efficiency • Better brand/corporate reputation • Simple delivery structure	• Reduced customer responsiveness • Decreased employee empowerment • Inter-organizational conflict • Lower workplace morale
Decentralization	• Better response to customer wants and demands • More employee empowerment or delegation • Quicker changes at lower levels • Increased workplace morale	• Decreased proficiency • Decreased top-management control • Complex delivery structure • Weaker corporate reputation

Source: Centralization versus decentralization of authority (n.d.). Retrieved on April 1, 2015, from: http://business-basics.org/centralization-versus-decentralization-of-authority/.

concept check

Discuss the advantages and disadvantages of centralization and decentralization.

TYPES OF ORGANIZATIONAL STRUCTURES

Once the organizational design has been determined, the company must determine how it will be structured. There are four basic structures used in businesses today including: line, line-and-staff, committee, and matrix structures.

A line organization is the simplest form of organizational structure (see **Figure 7.7**). The chain of command flows from top-level management to employees and is effective in providing a clear chain of command where everyone understands who they report to and how decisions are made. This is a great structure for an emergency situation or a small company with few individuals.

Line organization: The chain of command flows from top-level management to employees.

FIGURE 7.7

Line Organization
Structure

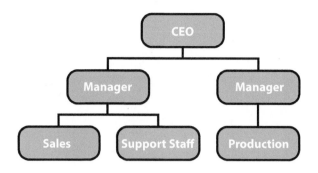

Line-and-staff organizations display two types of managerial authority within the organizational structure: line and staff. Line managers are responsible for overseeing subordinates and reporting directly to their own managers. Staff managers, function outside of the official hierarchy and are tasked with independently overseeing a particular function, such as Human Resources or Accounting. Staff managers perform specific job functions and share information with line managers, who help make broader organizational decisions. Staff managers do not make decisions outside of their functional area, where line managers can and do have the authority to make cross-departmental or organizational decisions. Most mid- to large companies operate using this type of organizational structure (**Figure 7.8**).

FIGURE 7.8

Line-and-Staff
Organization

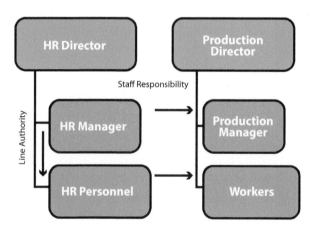

Committee organization: Utilizes a group or committee for authority and oversight instead of a single manager.

A **committee organization** utilizes a group or committee for authority and oversight instead of a single manager. These committees typically function within the line-and-staff organization. A committee organization is a group with different perspectives or areas of expertise that is set up to arrive at solutions to a problem. Often a committee organizational structure is utilized when a new product or campaign is created or when all departments need to be included in the decision-making process.

For instance, a Finance Committee will include all functional managers (Marketing, Production, Human Resources, and Sales) as members, and the General

Manager as the Chairman. The committee will decide the financial requirements of each department. A competent top manager can handle conflicts during meetings to get the maximum benefit out of committee organization. However, a weak or submissive manager may cause conflict, in-fighting, or poor decision-making. Other drawbacks of using committees are the increased time it takes to find a solution due to various viewpoints being taken into consideration and developing solutions through consensus instead of finding and using optimal solutions.[20]

A matrix organization is the practice of managing employees with more than one reporting line and is commonly associated with cross-functional teams. This type of organization is used mainly in the management of large projects or product development processes. Employees in a matrix organization report the day-to-day performance to a project manager whose authority flows sideways (horizontally) across departmental boundaries (see **Figure 7.9**). At the same time, employees continue to report overall performance to the head of their department whose authority flows downward (vertically) within his or her department. Because of its flexibility in adapting to change and focusing resources on specific problems, matrix organizations are commonly used in technology, healthcare, and consulting firms. However, drawbacks of using matrix organizations revolve around adjustments to regular workloads of those serving two areas as well as potential confusion in answering to more than one manager.[21]

Matrix organization: Managing employees with more than one reporting line.

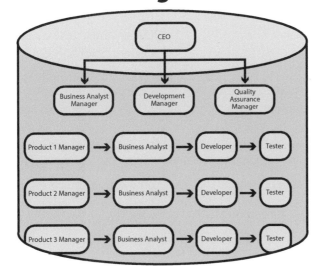

FIGURE 7.9

Matrix Organization

concept check

What organizational structures are utilized in businesses today?

WRAPPING UP...

Managing and leading an organization is challenging. However, solid planning, effective communication, and utilizing appropriate organizational structures help organizations find success. As you move from one workplace to another, hopefully, you will better observe and understand the organizational structure and leadership styles of management.

In Chapter 8, we will be examining the role of Human Resources in an organization as the department works to recruit, train, motivate, and retain a high-quality workforce.

BUSINESS TERMINOLOGY

Management	Transformational leadership
Top-level management	Transactional leadership
Middle-level management	Situational Leadership
First-level management	Theory X
Technical skills	Theory Y
Human relation skills	Theory Z
Conceptual skills	Transparency
Vision statement	Noise
Mission statements	Organizational structure
Strategic plan	Organizational chart
Tactical plan	Departmentalization
Operational plan	Delegation
Contingency plan	Micromanagement
Programmed decisions	Span of control
Non-programmed decisions	Centralization
Emotional intelligence (EI)	Decentralization
Autocratic leadership	Line organization
Participative or democratic leadership	Line-and-staff organization
	Committee organization
Laissez-faire or free-rein leadership	Matrix organization

DISCUSSION QUESTIONS

1. Does a prospering company have to worry about effective management? Why or why not?

2. Explain the type of leadership style you most closely align with and the implications that style has for you as a manager.

3. Explain the importance of effective communication in the workplace.

4. Explain which leadership function (planning, organizing, leading, or controlling) is most important for: an entry-level manager, a district manager, and a CEO.

5. Looking at page 163 regarding the Top 10 Communication Skills, discuss which skills are strongest for you personally as well as professionally and what you need to do to improve upon weak areas.

LEARNING ACTIVITIES

1. Identify one nonprofit organization and one for-profit business. Review the vision and/or mission statement of each company and compare and contrast similarities and differences.

2. Conduct an Internet search for "Leadership Style Assessment" and select an assessment that determines your preference for autocratic, democratic (participative), or laissez-faire leadership. Take the test and be prepared to share your results and their implications for you as a manager.

3. Select one individual who you believe is a good leader and describe the traits that you believe make him/her a great leader. Are the traits discussed in the chapter similar to those you have listed?

4. Using your current company, or one you have experience working with, diagram their organizational structure. Discuss the pros and cons of this type of structure and what effect(s) the structure has on communication and decision-making.

Note: *Because web sites often change, use a search engine to find alternative web sites to access required information when necessary.*

CASE STUDY: THE COMMUNICATION TRAP

Patrick is the front line manager of a local pizzeria and recently added the duties of marketing manager to his job description. Patrick noticed confusion among employees regarding their individual job responsibilities. Although Patrick believes each was trained appropriately, there seem to be questions or lack of knowledge about what each employee should be doing.

Patrick has always been a good communicator and has observed miscommunication at all levels of the organization. He believes his best chance for being successful as a marketing manager is to determine how to resolve poor communication within the workplace.

CASE STUDY ANALYSIS

Based on the information provided, answer the following questions:

(1) Is Patrick correct in his assessment that he will be successful if he solves communication issues within the company? Why or why not?

(2) Do you feel it will help if Patrick approaches the owners about his concerns? Why or why not?

(3) If the owners do not respond, what else might Patrick do to improve the issues within the company?

CHAPTER 8

HUMAN RESOURCES AND EMPLOYEE MANAGEMENT

HIRING — PEOPLE — STRATEGIC — HUMAN RESOURCES — FIRING — CORPORATE — ORGANIZATION — ECONOMY — MANAGEMENT — WORKPLACE — DIVERSITY

"Hire character. Train skill."
~ Peter Schutz, former President & CEO of Porsche

OUTCOMES:

➤ Describe the role of human resources in an organization.
➤ Identify employee recruitment, selection, and training processes commonly used in organizations today.
➤ Compare and contrast motivational theories.
➤ Evaluate the use of various performance appraisals in organizations.
➤ Outline the evolution of management–labor relations in the United States.

HUMAN RESOURCE MANAGEMENT

Asfia/Shutterstock.com

Human Resources (HR): Department that attracts, trains, develops, and retains employees who help the organization reach its goals and objectives.

Finding and retaining quality workers is important for every organization. It is costly to recruit and train new employees, so it is important to put forth the effort to find the right employees the first time. This is the job of the **Human Resources (HR)** department. Having qualified and satisfied workers helps an organization remain profitable in the marketplace; therefore, the job of HR is to attract, train, develop, and retain employees who will help the organization reach its goals and objectives. Additional functions of HR departments are to forecast future employment needs and provide attractive compensation packages to employees. The tasks involved in this process are called human resource management. Mid- to large organizations typically have a human resource manager to oversee these functions.

In this chapter, we will discuss the process HR departments use to hire and retain workers, types of compensation, laws that affect the hiring process, and how labor–management relationships affect the work environment.

ROLE OF HR IN ORGANIZATIONS

As mentioned, human resources plays a large role in the success of any business. Without effective systems in place, companies lose money, resources, and time as employees seek better places to work and higher levels of compensation. This can be seen in the amount of employee turnover an organization experiences, which indicates how employees feel about the work environment as well as the compensation received.

Today companies closely examine the costs of employee turnover or the number of employees who leave an organization after initial training is completed. Employee turnover costs include advertising, pre-employment interviewing, paperwork, administrative time, benefits enrollment, employee orientation, training, and the loss of production until the open position is filled. There is a simple formula used to calculate a company's employee turnover rate, which is shown below.[1]

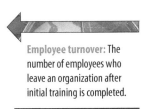

Employee turnover: The number of employees who leave an organization after initial training is completed.

CALCULATING EMPLOYEE TURNOVER RATE

Over a 12-month period, a company must determine the number of voluntary resignations. Next, a company divides this number by the total number of employees within the organization at the end of the same 12-month period.

Resignations = _____
Number of Employees = _____
Formula: (Resignations ÷ Total number of employees)
Employee Turnover rate = _____%

Example: Suppose Company XYZ has 45 volunteer resignations during the year and 500 total employees. The employee turnover rate is calculated as follows:

Resignations = 45
Number of employees = 500
Turnover Rate = 45 ÷ 500 = 0.09 or 9%

As noted above, there are costs associated with each employee loss, which can be significant if employee turnover rates are high. The example below extends the exercise by examining the rate of employee turnover to include the cost to an organization when employees leave.

COST OF EMPLOYEE TURNOVER

Using Company XYZ with 500 employees and a 9 percent turnover rate, we can calculate the annual cost of losing employees by multiplying the average turnover cost by the number of employees they lose each year. See the following:

Number of employees	500
Annual turnover	9%
Number of employees turning over (= 500 × 0.09)	45
Average turnover cost per employee	$2,000*
Total annual cost ($2000 × 45)	$90,000

*Note: Every company will differ

If a company can reduce its turnover rate by a small percentage, it can save them a great deal of money. Again, using Company XYZ, assume that the company reduced its employee turnover rate from 9 to 6 percent. The cost savings of the lower turnover rate can be seen in the following calculations.

Turnover reduced to 6%	$500 \times 0.06 = 30$ employees
Reduced employee turnover (from 45 at 9%)	$45 - 30 = 15$
Turnover cost at 6%	$30 \times \$2000 = \$60,000$
Savings from reducing turnover by 3% ($90,000 – 60,000$)	$30,000

By reducing employee turnover by 3 percent, Company XYZ can reduce costs by $30,000. This money can be used to incentivize current employees or expand recruitment efforts in order to attract highly qualified candidates. As you can see, turnover expenses are costly to any company. Reducing the turnover rate by a small percentage affects the bottom line of the company in a positive way, which is why human resource management is so important.

concept check

Why is employee turnover important to organizations today?

EMPLOYEE RECRUITMENT

In order to reduce the level of employee turnover and costs, high-quality recruitment and training efforts must be in place. Recruiting employees is an ongoing process and should be incorporated into a company's strategic plan as hiring high-quality talent is important to an organization's future development. **Table 8.1** offers five areas a company should focus on when creating a recruitment program.[2]

TABLE 8.1

Five Areas of a Good Recruitment Program

AREA	ACTION(S)
Identify key positional skills and establish a continuous recruitment program	Be proactive with hiring, needs change over time but HR should always be on the lookout for potentially great employees.
Establish and maintain long-term employee relationships	Get to know employees and show them that they are appreciated and valued.

(Continued)

Develop positive employer branding and public relations	Building a reputation as a company that everyone wants to work for helps quality workers search for your organization, which reduces recruitment efforts.
Offer employee referral programs	Good employees are great resources for finding other talented individuals. They can help HR do their job!
Use Social Media Recruiting	Engagement through social media attracts followers and potential job candidates (Facebook, Twitter, and LinkedIn).

Source: Morgan, R. (2014). Five key elements to hiring a first class team. Retrieved on March 18, 2015, from: http://realbusiness.co.uk/article/26678-5-key-elements-to-hiring-a-first-class-team.

RECRUITMENT

Rawpixel/Shutterstock.com

Every company has a hiring process that starts with recruiting or the process of attracting qualified candidates to fill open positions in an organization. As mentioned earlier, this is a time-consuming and costly process, so a proven hiring system should be established. Sometimes, there are many available candidates available in the market, whereas other times, few candidates exist. In the past, the more specialized the skill set and educational level, the fewer the candidates, which means higher levels of compensation as well as recruitment efforts. However, in today's market, many employers are having difficulty finding enough workers at lower-wage positions as the incentive to work in those positions is low and turnover rates are high.

Two types of recruitment efforts that a company can use for finding qualified candidates are internal and external recruiting. Internal recruiting looks at employees within the company as candidates for open positions. Many refer to this as "promoting from within," which is a good motivational and retention tool as

Recruiting: The process of attracting qualified candidates to fill open positions in an organization.

Internal recruiting: Hiring employees from within the organization to fill open positions.

employees see opportunities to grow within the organization. Of course, this process also brings concerns such as hiring costs for the vacant position left open due to advancement.

External recruiting is hiring job candidates from outside the company. There are many avenues of external recruiting such as newspapers, social media, employment agencies, college campuses, headhunting firms, and the Internet. Hiring from outside of the organization may cause workplace resentment and cause individuals within the company to seek advancement opportunities elsewhere. However, many organizations feel that there is value in having fresh ideas and perspectives brought into the company from outsiders. It is important to understand which type of recruiting is utilized in your current organization as it may help you to plan your future.

External recruiting: Hiring employees from outside of the organization.

concept check

What is the difference between internal and external recruiting?

SELECTION

Selection process: Gathering applicants' information and basing hiring decisions on qualifications and education.

The **selection process** includes gathering applicants' information and basing hiring decisions on the qualifications and education necessary to fill the position. The human resource department must consider which employees will be most appropriate for the position as well as who will fit within the organizational structure and culture. In order for a candidate to be considered a good hire, he or she should fit well into the corporate culture; however, this does not mean that everyone in the organization should be the same.

There is usually a standard process during the selection period. *First*, many companies have job candidates fill out employment applications and submit resumes in order to gather information. Online applications and resume submissions allow companies to easily scan materials for key words or information that help them screen available candidates.

Second, some companies may require that an applicant take an employment, aptitude, or drug test prior to being interviewed or hired. These tests look at areas such as computer literacy, aptitude, predictive behavior, general intelligence, or personality. Any test given must measure what the company says it will measure, meaning no trick tests. Drug tests may be required for positions dealing with safety or medical fields; however, the results over time have been unreliable and are often disputed, which makes their use rather ineffective.

Third is the interview process, which may include an initial phone interview, a virtual interview, or a face-to-face interview. Every company has its own interview process but be aware that you may have to interview in a variety of ways and with a number of different people. We will examine various types of interviews in Chapter 13, but it is important to understand that there are certain questions that should never be discussed in an interview including those related to your marital status, religion, mental illness, or children. An employer can ask questions related to **bona fide occupational qualifications (BFOQ)** or qualifications that an employee must hold in order to fulfill the duties of a given job. For example, if a firefighter must be able to carry a 300-pound person down two flights of stairs, then it is not discriminatory to reject an applicant who could not do this as it could endanger the lives of others.

Bona fide occupational qualifications (BFOQ): Qualifications that an employee must hold in order to fulfill the duties of a given job.

Fourth, it is common for an organization to complete a reference check for which the candidate provides names of people who can verify work history, accomplishments, or background information. Companies today can also readily look up information about potential candidates on Internet accounts, such as Twitter, Facebook, or LinkedIn. So be extremely careful what pictures and other information you post about yourself as it could prevent you from getting hired.

Orientation: Process to help new employees become acquainted with the company, employees, and policies.

Upon acceptance of an offer by the candidate, the final step includes an **orientation**. The orientation helps new employees become acquainted with the company, employees, and policies in addition to providing training to help them find success in their new position.

TRAINING

Employee training is set up to allow new employees the opportunity to become productive members of an organization. Training is different for different positions within an organization and between organizations; however, the company should at a minimum have a standard training process that explains the company, its code of ethics, expectations of the position, and the code of conduct. If done properly, employee training adds value to an organization by reducing the need to recruit outside employees, reducing turnover, and helping prepare future leaders within the organization. **Table 8.2** displays common types of training human resource departments may utilize when training new employees.

TABLE 8.2

Types of Training for New Employees

TYPE OF TRAINING	DEFINITION
On-the-job (OJT) training	Employees learn while they work with a mentor in the actual job.
Simulations	Employees learn the job online or using technology where they can make decisions in remote settings.
Classroom training	Employees are taught in a classroom setting (seminars, workshops, etc.)
Role playing	Employees participate in real-life scenarios with others to learn how to respond in various situations.
Online or computer-based training	Employees take classes on the computer with or without an instructor, typically coursework is self-paced.

concept check

What types of training are commonly used to guide new employees?

RETENTION

Employee retention is the ability of a company to retain its employees. As previously referenced in the cost of employee turnover, focusing on retention can produce a more motivated workforce. A solid on-boarding program helps new hires acquire the necessary knowledge, skills, and behaviors to become effective employees. Other tools used to retain employees include: mentoring programs, a strong corporate culture, employee compensation, an employee recognition and reward system, quality of work-life balance, training and development, and workplace communication. Human Resource departments continually develop methods for retaining employees. However, it is natural for some level of employee turnover to exist due to retirements, advancement, or personal reasons, so organizations must do their best to monitor factors within their control in order to keep the best workforce possible.

mary416/Shutterstock.com

Employee retention: A company's ability to retain employees.

Job enlargement: Adding to the number of tasks associated with a certain job.

Job enrichment: Empowering employees to make the job more challenging by adding new skills, knowledge, and decision-making ability.

There are different strategies utilized by companies to retain employees, such as job enlargement, job enrichment, or job rotation. Restructuring jobs increases the likelihood that employees will be challenged, more productive, and more engaged, which creates a work environment that is responsive to employees' needs.

Job enlargement increases employee responsibilities by adding to the number of tasks associated with a certain job. The purpose is to increase workforce utility while allowing for employees' growth and eliminating job monotony. There must be appropriate training associated with job enlargement in order to be successful. Also, HR must be careful not to add too many tasks, which would reduce productivity. A common example of job enlargement is allowing a worker on an assembly line to assemble several parts of the finished product versus completing only one task all day long.

Dmitry Kalinovsky/Shutterstock.com

Job enrichment is a management concept that involves empowering employees to make a job more challenging by adding new skills and knowledge and allowing employees to make decisions about work themselves. The goal is to increase employee satisfaction by giving their work more meaning and demonstrating their importance to the company. An insurance salesman might decide to expand into financial services with the parent company, so after he passes the exams, he adds a new product to

Dragon Images/Shutterstock.com

offer his current clients. In addition, the salesman can determine his schedule and how much or little he wants to work. Although this is a great way to expand employee knowledge and skills, it can decrease productivity or effectiveness if the employee is spread too thin or loses interest and/or motivation.[3]

Job rotation: Learning several jobs within an organization.

Job rotation refers to the process by which an employee learns several jobs within an organization. This allows for a better understanding of what employees in other departments do while giving employees a chance to broaden their skills. Proper training and guidance are important when utilizing job rotation. An individual training to become a store manager may rotate to various departments within the store in order to gain a better understanding of the responsibilities and inventory in each area. This helps her become more effective when she leads the store as she has knowledge of each area and can communicate with employees in each department.

concept check

Compare job enlargement, job enrichment, and job rotation.

EVALUATION

alexskopje/Shutterstock.com

Performance appraisals: A formal evaluation of employees' skills and productivity.

Each employee must be evaluated by a supervisor or peers to determine if he or she is reaching the goals set forth by the organization. **Performance appraisals** are a formal evaluation of employees' skills and productivity. They allow managers to measure how employees are doing in their role and document what necessary improvements the employee needs to make to find greater levels of success. It also provides a basis for giving rewards, such as pay increases, bonuses, and promotions. Finally, appraisals help a company monitor its hiring process, training, and employee development programs. Typical performance appraisals include objective methods, such as units of output, sales volume, or defective products, which are all measurable goals. The other types, known as judgmental methods, often use a rating scale to "judge" an employee's work performance. When you study human resources or management more in-depth, you will learn about the advantages and disadvantages of using such systems, but for now, suffice to say that it is important for an organization to have objective ways to measure employee growth and contributions. Managers need effective appraisal systems so that their own judgment and biases don't interfere with properly evaluating an employee's contributions to the company.

An evaluation tool that is commonly used to gain a broader picture of an employee's contributions is a 360-degree feedback evaluation. A **360-degree feedback** evaluation is a comprehensive tool that collects reviews from peers, supervisors, and subordinates and combines them into one feedback report. This process helps eliminate individual management bias and gives a well-rounded view of how an employee interacts within individuals throughout the organization. Regardless of the feedback collected, a manager should always provide feedback by starting with something positive and then discussing areas of improvement with the employee.[4]

"Your evaluation is based on the next 30 seconds. Go!"

Cartoonresource/Shutterstock.com

360-degree feedback: A comprehensive evaluation tool that gathers information from multiple sources.

360 feedback

madpixblue/Shutterstock.com

concept check

Explain the pros and cons of a 360-degree evaluation.

COMPENSATION AND BENEFITS

Compensation is the total of all wages and benefits paid to employees by employers. Typical monetary compensation comes in the form of wages or salaries and is based on a 40-hour work week. Wages can include an hourly wage, salary, commission, incentives, lump–sum increases, or profit sharing. Different types of monetary compensation and an explanation of what each means is located in **Table 8.3**.[5]

iQoncept/Shutterstock.com

Compensation: The total of all wages and benefits paid to employees.

TABLE 8.3

Types of Compensation

COMPENSATION TYPE	EXPLANATION
Hourly wage	A set amount paid per hour. This amount is paid for the first 40 hours worked, and time beyond 40 hours is called *overtime* and is paid at one and one half times the hourly wage. Construction, fast-food, and retail positions are often paid hourly wages.
Salary (weekly, monthly, or annually)	Specific compensation paid regardless of hours worked, no overtime pay is given for hours worked over 40 hours. Professional positions are often paid salaries.
Commissions	Pay awarded strictly as a percentage of sales. No hourly wage or salary is provided, so employees must be motivated to sell as much as possible to earn a living. Real estate and insurance sales positions are commonly paid this way.
Incentive payments (bonus)	Pay given in addition to normal wages as a reward for outstanding job performance. Commonly used as an employee motivator in a variety of industries.
Lump-sum salary increases	A one-time bonus or right to purchase company stocks based on performance. Often included as part of a pay-reward system.
Profit sharing	Bonuses paid to employees that come from the company's profits. This creates a team environment where all employees are rewarded based on the group's success.

Source: The different forms of compensation (2013). Retrieved on March 20, 2015, from: http://businessecon.org/2013/01/the-different-forms-of-compensation/.

Different industries pay employees differently, so it is important to research what is common in a given industry. This will help you negotiate your wages more effectively as well as help you determine whether or not a job offer is fair. Whatever a company decides to do, it should remain competitive in the market place to help attract high-quality employees.

concept check

What types of compensation are available?

iQoncept/Shutterstock.com

Beyond wages and salaries, employers provide additional benefits to employees, which in recent years have become equally as important in attracting qualified workers. **Fringe benefits** or *employee benefits* are indirect compensation in addition to the regular salary or wages that an employee receives from a company. Benefits can include vacation time, insurance packages (health, dental, or life), college tuition reimbursement, child care, health club memberships, or retirement or pension plans. According to the U.S. Department of Labor, the value of employee benefits can equal up to 30 percent of an employee's total compensation.[6] For example, if an employee earned a salary of $30,000/year and the benefits were worth $10,000, the total compensation package for the employee would be $40,000/year. This demonstrates the importance of individuals examining the total compensation package when determining which job offer is best, not simply using salary.

Some companies offer **flexible benefit plans**, sometimes called *cafeteria plans*, where employees are allocated a specific amount of money to pick and choose which benefits best fit their needs. This type of plan provides flexibility and choice for employees at different stages of their lives and careers, which is beneficial as companies and employees pay for only what they need.

Additional nonwage benefits offered by some companies include paid time off, flextime, compressed work weeks, job sharing, or remote offices. **Paid time off (PTO)** works much like vacation time in organizations; however, many employees use it to participate in school events for their children or for doctor appointments. Companies that use PTO give employees a set number of hours to use during a year versus offering separate vacation, sick, or holiday pay. Many employees like this as it provides them the flexibility to decide how and when they use their time. **Flextime** allows workers to determine their start time versus every employee starting at 8:00 a.m. Workers are able to start at 7:00 a.m., 8:30 a.m., or 10:00 a.m. to accommodate their needs. Core hours for the business must be covered; however, employees have flexibility in selecting which shift works best for them. **Compressed work weeks** allow workers to work 40 hours in three or four days

Fringe benefits: Indirect compensation paid to employees.

Flexible benefits: The ability to select benefits that best fit an employee's needs.

Paid time off (PTO): Flexible time given to employees to use for vacation, sick, or holiday time.

Flextime: Offering a variety of shifts for employees to select from in an organization.

Compressed work week: Shifting a 40-hour work week into less than five days.

Photographee.eu/Shutterstock.com

Job sharing: Two employees sharing one full-time position.

Remote offices: Working from home to complete job responsibilities.

instead of five days. Nurses commonly work three, 12-hour shifts to be considered full time versus working five, 8-hour days. **Job sharing** allows two employees to split one full-time position within the organization. Finally, **remote offices**, or telecommuting, allow individuals to work from home to complete their job responsibilities. While individuals must have the ability to work independently and be self-disciplined, it is a great option for individuals with disabilities, parents, or individuals who travel long distances to work. Technology has made remote work more appealing and more cost effective for many organizations.

concept check

Discuss various fringe benefits available to employees.

LABOR LAWS

In the past, and sometimes today, hiring practices have favored individuals who look and act like those hiring within an organization. This has made it difficult for many women, minorities, individuals with disabilities, and older workers to obtain employment. Concern about fairness in hiring practices has led to a series of laws, created by state and federal agencies, to protect individuals who are under-represented in the workforce or have become protected classes. Laws have also been established to protect employers in their hiring practices, who may be victims of a wrongful lawsuit. **Table 8.4** shows key employment laws that have been passed and what they were established to protect.[7] An individual or company should seek legal advice when confronted with lawsuits related to any of these issues.

kentoh/Shutterstock.com

TABLE 8.4

Federal Employment Laws

LAW	YEAR	AREA OF PROTECTION
National Labor Relations Act	1935	National Labor Relations Board (NLRB) established; created a collective bargaining for labor/management relations
Fair Labor Standards Act	1938	Created the minimum wage and the overtime pay rate for over 40 hours/week
Labor-Management Relations Act	1947	Known as the Taft-Hartley Act, allows for a balance of power between unions and management
Equal Pay Act	1963	Requires that the same wage be paid to men and women who have equal skills, experience, and education if the job is the same
Title VII of the Civil Rights Act	1964	Forbids discriminatory employment practices based on race, sex, color, religion, or national origin
Age Discrimination in Employment Act	1967, 1986	Established the 40 years or older age discrimination guideline; 1986 elimination of the mandatory retirement age
Occupational Safety and Health Act	1970	Known as OSHA, protects workers' safety in the workplace
Employment Retirement Income Security Act	1974	Sets up a federal insurance program for retirement plans that go bankrupt and regulates businesses' retirement programs
Worker Adjustment and Retraining Notification (WARN)	1988	Employers must provide 60-day notice if they are closing down a plant or will have a layoff of 50 or more employees
Americans with Disabilities Act	1990	Prohibits discriminatory hiring practices against qualified individuals with disabilities
Civil Rights Act	1991	Employees are allowed to sue employers for sexual discrimination and collect punitive damages
Family and Medical Leave Act	1993	Requires employers with 50 or more employees to provide up to 12 weeks of leave without pay on the birth or adoption of an employee's child or illness of a family member
Affordable Care Act	2010	Requires a company with 50 or more employees to provide insurance to employees or gives employees the right to buy alternative health insurance if employer's is too expensive

Source: Summary of Labor Laws (n.d.). Retrieved on March 17, 2015, from: http://www.dol.gov/opa/aboutdol/lawsprog.htm

A few of these laws you might already be familiar with as they are regularly outlined in workplace hiring practices. These laws become part of many companies' written human resource policies; however, a few laws are so important in the hiring process that they deserve additional discussion in the text. Although many of these laws have been on record for many years, they are still some of the most commonly violated laws today.

Title VII of the Civil Rights Act of 1964 was created to make sure that employers make hiring decisions based on qualifications only. This act prohibits employers with 15 or more employees from discriminating on the basis of race, sex, religion, color, or national origin. A person who feels they have been discriminated against can contact the Equal Employment Opportunity Commission (EEOC), who will inquire on behalf of the employee. If warranted, the commission can take legal action on behalf of the employee. This law was expanded under the Civil Rights Act of 1991 to include a jury trial and the right to receive punitive and emotional distress damages for victims, which had not been included previously.

Affirmative action: Programs designed to hire under-represented individuals in the workplace.

Reverse discrimination: Discrimination against majority groups in hiring practices.

In an effort to increase job opportunities for women, minorities, and individuals with disabilities, the EEOC developed affirmative action programs. These programs were designed to have underrepresented individuals in organizations be hired when equal qualifications existed among applicants. However, many employers implemented the programs ineffectively by hiring candidates that were not equally qualified, which lead to claims of reverse discrimination and increased tension between some groups in the workforce.

Becky Stares/Shutterstock.com

As businesses noticed that they could hire younger individuals less expensively than older workers with more experience (and often education), laws were passed to protect individuals over the age of 40 to help curtail age discrimination. The **Age Discrimination in Employment Act** was passed in 1967 to set 40 years as the target age for discriminatory hiring practices. This was expanded in 1986 to eliminate age 65 as the mandatory age at which employees had to retire. This, combined with the fact that individuals are living longer, is why so many older workers stay in the workforce without fear of being fired for simply reaching a certain age.

Alexandr IIV/Shutterstock.com

The **Americans with Disabilities Act (ADA)** was established in 1990 and prohibits discrimination against qualified individuals with disabilities. This includes all employment practices, such as the job application process, hiring, training, advancement, compensation, and termination. This law also allows for reasonable accommodations to be expected of employers (at the employer's expense) so an employee with a disability can complete the work required by the organization.[8]

The **Family and Medical Leave Act (FMLA)** was signed in 1993 during former President Bill Clinton's first term in office. The intent of the legislation was to allow employees who are having or adopting a baby up to 12 weeks of unpaid leave in order to balance personal and professional responsibilities. This act also allows an employee the same time off if they or their spouse, child, or parent is seriously ill. Another goal in this legislation was "to accommodate the legitimate interests of employers and promote equal employment opportunity for men and women."[9] This is a requirement of companies with 50 or more employees; however you will find that many smaller companies follow this act as well. In order to receive this benefit, an employee must work for at least 1250 hours and for one year with an organization. Employees are protected to some degree as they are guaranteed employment once the leave is over; however, the employee may return to a comparable job and not the job they left. It is important to discuss with your employer what position you will be returning to before taking leave under this law.

It is important for HR personnel to understand employment laws in order to avoid costly lawsuits and negative perceptions of the organization, but it is equally important for employers to understand how to retain good employees once they hire them. Understanding motivational theories is another aspect of keeping good employees and maintaining the long-term success of the organization.

concept check

Explain why various employment laws exist.

MOTIVATIONAL THEORIES

Productivity in the workplace is driven by employee motivation, so it is important for a company to understand how to motivate employees to be more productive and satisfied, which in turn makes the company more profitable. Motivational theories help explain workforce motivation but also help managers recognize that employees are motivated by different needs. Below is a brief overview of several motivational theories.

MASLOW'S HIERARCHY OF NEEDS

In 1943, America psychologist, Abraham Maslow, suggested that people work to satisfy their needs based on a hierarchy. Employees move to higher-level needs after satisfying the level directly below it. Individuals can move back and forth through the levels depending on their circumstances; however, it is most common for an individual to continue movement toward a higher level. For instance, if an individual does not have money for food or shelter, it is hard to have positive self-esteem. Once basic needs are met and an individual feels safe, it is easier to move to higher levels of the hierarchy. A manager can help motivate employees by understanding where employees are on Maslow's Hierarchy of Needs. See **Figure 8.1** for the levels in Maslow's Hierarchy.

FIGURE 8.1

Maslow's Hierarchy
of Needs

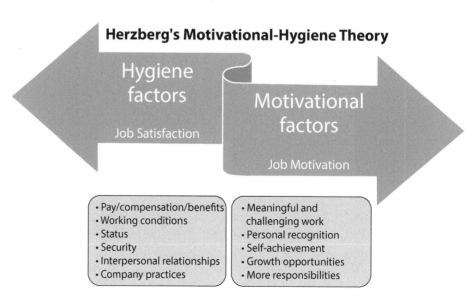

SELF-ACTUALIZA-TION
morality, creativity, spontaneity, acceptance, experience purpose, meaning and inner potential

SELF-ESTEEM
confidence, achievement, respect of others, the need to be a unique individual

LOVE AND BELONGING
friendship, family, intimacy, sense of connection

SAFETY AND SECURITY
health, employment, property, family and social abilty

PHYSIOLOGICAL NEEDS
breathing, food, water, shelter, clothing, sleep

Elenarts/Shutterstock.com

Herzberg's Two-Factor Model was developed by American psychologist, Frederick Herzberg, in the 1950s. Herzberg found that certain job factors are related to job satisfaction, whereas other factors are associated with job motivation. This research helped management understand that motivation and satisfaction require more than simply the tasks employees complete in their daily routine. Herzberg found two types of factors that influence motivation: motivational and hygiene factors. Motivational factors are factors specifically related to the job itself, such as responsibilities, recognition, and growth opportunities. Motivational factors increase motivation but, if not present, do not necessarily result in dissatisfaction. Hygiene factors are job factors that reduce dissatisfaction when present but do not necessarily result in high levels of motivation. Pay, working conditions, or relationships with coworkers are all factors that increase employees' satisfaction at work but do not have a direct impact on their motivation.[10]

Motivational factors: Factors related to the job itself that affect motivation.

Hygiene factors: Factors related to the work environment that affect satisfaction.

FIGURE 8.2

Herzberg's Two-Factor Model of Motivation

Herzberg's Motivational-Hygiene Theory

Hygiene factors

Job Satisfaction

Motivational factors

Job Motivation

- Pay/compensation/benefits
- Working conditions
- Status
- Security
- Interpersonal relationships
- Company practices

- Meaningful and challenging work
- Personal recognition
- Self-achievement
- Growth opportunities
- More responsibilities

VROOM'S EXPECTANCY THEORY

Victor Vroom's (1964) expectancy theory relates to the idea that employees will only invest time and energy on tasks where rewards equal expected outcomes. For instance, if an employee does not feel that learning a new computer software program will benefit him in his current position, then he will not take the time to learn it. However, if he will lose his job if he does not learn it, then there is greater motivation for learning the new software. Three factors influence motivation, according to Vroom's research. The first factor is how much an employee wants a reward or places value on it, called valence. The next factor is expectancy, which relates to an individual's belief that effort will lead to an expected performance. The third factor is instrumentality or the belief that an employee's effort will lead to the desired reward.[11] **Figure 8.3** demonstrates the connection between these three factors and motivation.

Valence: Value given to a reward.

Expectancy: A person's belief that effort leads to an expected performance.

Instrumentality: Belief that the company will deliver promised rewards.

FIGURE 8.3

Vroom's Expectancy Theory

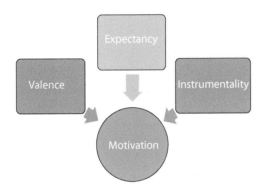

MANAGEMENT BY OBJECTIVE (MBO)

In the 1950s, Peter Drucker offered his Management by Objective (MBO) model, which utilizes clearly defined and measurable goals and objectives based on available organizational resources. This theory aims to help employees align personal and professional goals with those of the organization in order to increase motivation and performance. Goals are created using a collaborative process between employees and management. This process improves motivation as employees have a say in the goal setting process and, therefore, greater levels of commitment in achieving them. Major benefits of using this model are improved communication and employee motivation as well as an effective evaluation process to determine if goals have been met.[12]

Yabresse/Shutterstock.com

LOCKE'S GOAL-SETTING THEORY

Locke's Goal Setting Theory states that employees will be motivated if they are given challenging goals, provided appropriate tools to help accomplish goals, and presented with positive performance feedback. Goals must be specific, significantly challenging (without being too difficult), and acceptable to employees. Feedback about performance must be provided until the goals have been met. Employee motivation in goal setting is realized by setting clear goals, energizing employees, and providing appropriate feedback.[13]

A tool used by many to create effective goals is the SMART goal setting technique. It helps management and employees create goals that are specific, measurable, achievable, realistic, and timely. It is easy to set generic goals that are not SMART goals; however, using this tool helps managers and employees create goals that are measurable and productive. If an individual wants to stop smoking, a generic goal is to say, "I will stop smoking." A SMART goal would be stated as follows: "I will reduce my cigarette use by three cigarettes each day in the first week." It is specific, achievable, realistic, fits a given timeline, and is measurable for the individual wishing to stop smoking. By accomplishing smaller, more manageable goals, individuals can reach the larger end goals more quickly and successfully.

concept check

How might managers use different motivational theories in the workplace?

LABOR–MANAGEMENT RELATIONS

Labor union: A group of workers who join forces to improve working conditions and pay.

In a perfect world, employees and management teams would get along well; however, employees and management often have different views about the goals of work, the levels of productivity that should be achieved, and the pay for and treatment of employees in the workplace. These disagreements led to the development of labor unions in the United States. A labor union is a group of workers who join forces to improve working conditions and pay. Labor unions can be found locally, nationally or internationally.

The evolution of labor–management relations in the United States started in the mid-1860s with the Industrial Revolution when a surplus of labor and tough competition among factories existed. It was common to have unsafe working environments and work weeks that nearly doubled today's 40-hour work week. The first national union, known as the Knights of Labor, conducted and dominated arbitration meetings with companies on behalf of workers.

The development of labor unions in the United States started in response to the need to protect workers' rights and has become a part of American culture. Initial efforts were directed toward issues such as demands for an 8-hour work/day and the opposition to child labor. In 1886, the most famous union, the American Federation of Labor (AFL) was founded by Samuel Gompers. The AFL was responsible for member wage increases and enhancing workplace safety standards. Many other unions have since organized in the United States and globally. "According to a 2010 Bureau of Labor Statistic report, union membership is over 14 million in the United States and in the public sector has grown to over 37 percent."[14]

LAWS RELATED TO LABOR–MANAGEMENT ISSUES

Over the years, several laws have been passed to protect employees and management. Some of the landmark laws are included below:

- **Wagner Act of 1935**, also known as the National Labor Relations Act of 1935, established employee rights to organize and join labor unions and participate in the collective bargaining process. The act is the most important piece of labor legislation enacted in U.S. history because it involved the federal government in employee-employer relationships through the creation of the National Labor Relations Board (NLRB) and established the right of workers to organize and bargain with employers.[15]

- **Fair Labor Standards Act of 1938** created the federal minimum wage (25 cents per hour), a set number of hours per week in certain industries, and overtime pay of 1.5-times the regular rate of pay. It also restricted the work hours of those under the age of 16 and prohibits employment of those under age 18 in certain dangerous jobs.[16]

- **Taft-Hartley Act of 1947** limited unions' ability to force employees to join unions or discriminate against employees who were not a part of the union. It restricted unions from coercing employers to only hire union members. It also included provisions for improving unions' disclosure of financial and political transactions and worked to protect members from undesirable actions by some of the controlling union members.[17]

- **Landrum-Griffin Act of 1959**, commonly known as **The Labor–Management Reporting and Disclosure Act**, amended the Taft-Hartley Act and was designed to stop abuse and promote honesty in how unions were operated. Unions were required to have a constitution and bylaws as well as formal elections of union officials through the use of secret ballots. Financial reports were required to be sent to the U.S. Secretary of Labor.[18]

concept check

What legislation has been passed to support or refine labor unions?

Firma V/Shutterstock.com

Collective bargaining is the process by which union representation negotiates employee contracts with employers. Negotiated items include pay, health care, terms of employment, pensions, and other benefits. Priorities in any bargaining process are jointly decided by the employees and presented to the employer through the collective bargaining process. It is called this as each side must bargain for what they believe is fair and equitable. When the two sides agree, they negotiate the settlement agreements or terms which both parties will fulfill and the process moves forward amicably.

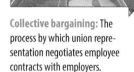

Collective bargaining: The process by which union representation negotiates employee contracts with employers.

Sometimes, the collective bargaining process does not go well and disputes arise between the negotiating parties. If the contracts cannot be agreed upon, labor and management tactics are used to help persuade the other side to come to an agreement. Settling disputes between labor and management can come in the form of arbitration, mediation by third parties, or through settlement negotiations between attorneys. Other times, labor or management may use more severe tactics to persuade the other party to come to an agreement.

Employees striking to increase wages at a local McDonalds.

Wal-Mart employees picketing to gain support for a wage increase.

Labor tactics are various actions used by employees against management or the company when collective bargaining does not work or employees feel their rights have been violated. Labor tactics can include strikes, picketing or boycotts. Strikes are the most frequently employed technique used by labor or non-labor union workers. Strikes occur when employees stop working in order to inflict financial hardship on an organization. Picketing involves standing or walking in front of a business with signs or posters in order to discourage customer patronage. A boycott is when employees or customers stop buying or using goods or services of a company as a protest to a particular cause or action.

Management tactics can also be used in disputes and include lockouts, hiring strikebreakers, and outsourcing. These tactics protect the company against potential employee strikes, boycotts, or pickets. A lockout is a when a company's management orders a temporary work stoppage or denies employment during a labor dispute. It is used to enforce employment agreements or to force the union to back down with certain demands. You have seen this in professional sports when management and players don't agree on the terms of contracts.

Hiring strikebreakers (scabs) to help resolve labor disputes is another alternative used by management to get employees to settle a dispute. In this case, a strikebreaker is any individual who will work when the regular workforce is on strike. "Crossing the line" can result in physical or emotional abuse to strikebreakers. Outsourcing is used by companies to reduce costs by utilizing outside suppliers to complete work rather than completing it internally. This saves the company labor costs, material costs, and frees up production processes, which can come at a great cost to employees.

Strikes: Employees stop working to inflict financial hardship on an organization.

Picketing: Standing or walking in front of a business in order to discourage customer patronage.

Boycott: Completely stopping the use or purchase of a company's goods or services.

Lockout: Ordering a temporary stop to work to force compliance in negotiations.

Strikebreaker: An individual who works for the company when employees are on strike.

Outsourcing: Utilizing outside suppliers to complete work.

concept check

Discuss various labor–management tactics that affect the bargaining process.

THE FUTURE OF LABOR UNIONS

U.S. labor unions have been declining in membership for decades as occupations have shifted from manufacturing to service and technological industries. "After reaching an all-time high of approximately 35 percent unionization of private sector employees in the 1950s, labor unions represent just 6.6 percent of private sector employees according to the National Labor Relations Board."[19] Public sector unions for teachers, nurses, and government employees have active union representation today but have witnessed a decline in membership as employee–management relations have improved over time.

Unions are aware of this decline and must be more flexible in the future in adapting to workers' needs and global economic changes. Unions have sought alternative means to expand their membership and have started working with nonunion workers and other organizations to try and gain political influence in recent years. Another option for unions is to work with management proactively to build collaborative relationships and avoid major conflicts. Although union membership in other countries remains strong, trends show that unions would be best served by creating global unions and building strength for the future.

WRAPPING UP...

As you can see, finding, hiring, and retaining employees is a much bigger process than one might initially understand. Productivity and long-term growth are major reasons that the human resource functions of a business are vital to an organization's success. Motivating and developing employees is an on-going process to help management avoid some of the labor-management issues discussed at the end of the chapter.

Chapter 9 moves into a different phase of business as we begin to analyze how the production process and layout of a business affects profitability and processes. Operations management and quality control are growing areas of study and focus for businesses, which is why they will provide many job possibilities in the future.

BUSINESS TERMINOLOGY

Human Resource (HR)
Employee turnover
Recruitment
Internal recruiting
External recruiting
Selection process
Bona fide occupational
   qualifications (BFOQ)
On-the-job (OJT) training
Simulations
Classroom training
Role playing
Computer-based training
Employee Retention
Job enlargement
Job enrichment
Job rotation
Performance appraisal
360-degree feedback
Compensation
Hourly wage
Salary
Commission
Incentive Payment
Lump-Sum salary increase
Profit Sharing

Fringe Benefits
Flexible benefit plan
Paid time off (PTO)
Flextime
Compressed work week
Job sharing
Remote office
Affirmative action program
Reverse discrimination
Maslow's Hierarchy of Needs
Herzberg's Two-Factor Model
Motivational factors
Hygiene factors
Vroom's Expectancy Theory
Management by Objective (MBO)
Locke's Goal-Setting Theory
Labor union
Collective bargaining
Strike
Picketing
Boycott
Lockout
Strikebreaker
Outsourcing

DISCUSSION QUESTIONS

1. Why is it important to establish labor–management laws?

2. Discuss how or why an individual could move from a higher-level to a lower-level on Maslow's Hierarchy of Needs in his or her life.

3. Based on expectancy theory, how might an employee determine if they are being treated fairly?

4. How does employee participation increase motivation?

5. Which motivational theory would be the most effective for you as an employee? A manager? Why?

LEARNING ACTIVITIES

1. Research an article related to a current labor–management dispute in the marketplace. Discuss what issues are being debated and what affects the dispute is having (or has had) on the organization.

2. Research the effect unions have had on today's workforce. Be prepared to share what benefits employees have received that stemmed from union-management legislation previously passed.

3. Locate an article that discusses the pros and cons of using a 360-degree evaluation or other performance evaluation tool. Prepare a brief presentation to share the type of evaluation you selected as well as the pros/cons of using it in the workplace.

4. Interview a local HR manager to determine the biggest challenges he/she faces in filling available positions or retaining employees in the organization. Ascertain what is being done to address those challenges, and discuss how compensation and training are affected by those challenges.

Note: *Because web sites often change, use a search engine to find alternative web sites to access required information when necessary.*

CASE STUDY: TO UNIONIZE OR NOT TO UNIONIZE?

Yellow Fin Logistics is a transportation company that serves the seafood industry. Currently, Yellow Fin employs 175 dock and loading employees, 35 truck drivers, and 15 office staff. The past 10 years have been very lucrative for Yellow Fin as they have seen substantial growth throughout the western United Sates. There are currently no labor issues as management and employees work well together.

In the past few months, some of the dock employees have been approached by a union representative about joining the local union. There has been talk that other transportation companies with unions are paying up to $3.00 more per hour than Yellow Fin as well as contributing to a 401K retirement account; however union fees amount to $1.27 per hour.

Over the past month, a spouse of one dock worker shared this information with the wife of one of the management team. The news has caused tension between the management team and dock workers. Ownership is unhappy as unionizing would cut into profits and, therefore, reduce future expansion opportunities; however, several employees have discussed leaving Yellow Fin in search of higher paying positions at local union-based businesses.

CASE STUDY ANALYSIS

Based on the information provided, answer the following questions:

(1) If you were in a management position at Yellow Fin Logistics, how would you approach the dock workers about this issue?

(2) What might ownership offer to employees to reduce the likelihood of union organization?

(3) What incentives do you feel workers would get by unionizing? What potential harm might it cause?

CHAPTER 9

PRODUCTION AND OPERATIONS MANAGEMENT

"Sound strategy starts with having the right goal."
~Michael E. Porter, Economist

OUTCOMES:

➢ Explain various production methods.
➢ Discuss strategic decisions made in the production process.
➢ Analyze different categories of production processes.
➢ Describe the steps taken in the production control process.
➢ Evaluate the use of quality control mechanisms in organizations.

WHAT IS PRODUCTION?

In this chapter, we will focus on the production process for creating goods and services and the importance of this process to organizational success. All companies are involved in production at some level and every company has a production process. There is a difference between manufacturing organizations and service organizations in the transformation process as manufacturing companies produce physical products like cell phones, televisions, computers, and other durable goods whereas service companies produce intangible products like health care, taxi cab rides, vacations, or education. All of these companies transform inputs into useable products or services. **Table 9.1** illustrates a variety of production systems for different industries.[1]

MOLPIX/Shutterstock.com

TABLE 9.1

Classic Production Systems

INDUSTRY	INPUTS	TRANSFORMATION	OUTPUTS
Retail Store	Building, displays, merchandise, employees, scanners	Inventory, attracts consumers, sells goods	Merchandise sold
Restaurant	Food, employees, building, hungry customers	Chef, waitress, atmosphere, service provided, good food	Satisfied customer
Fire Department	Personnel, fire equipment, fire trucks, building, utilities	Detects and monitors societal hazards such as fires and accidents	Protects society and reduces property damage

Images © Shutterstock, Inc.

Source: The various types of production systems and their importance (n.d.). Retrieved on March 26, 2015, from: http://www.scribd.com/doc/28207305/The-Various-Types-of-Production-Systems-and-their-Importance#scribd.

Production: The process of utilizing resources to transform raw materials into finished products and services.

Inputs: Raw materials or ideas used to create another product or service.

Production is the process of utilizing resources such as labor and machinery to transform raw materials into finished products and services. A company uses raw materials (wood, steel, oil, ideas) and transforms them into useable products or services for the consumer. Inputs are raw materials used to create products or services or ideas, while **outputs** are the finished products created by processing inputs. This process creates *form utility*, which is the value that producers add to raw materials, as discussed in Chapter 6. **Figure 9.1** shows the process of transforming raw materials into something new.

FIGURE 9.1

Transformation of Inputs to Outputs

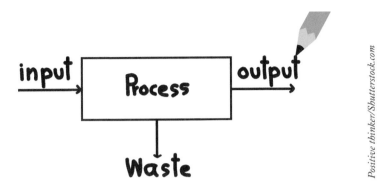

A prime example of this process is filling a car with gas. First, oil must be extracted from oil wells and transported to a refining facility through a pipeline. Once it is at the refining facility, it is processed using various production methods and the end product (gasoline) is transported by railways or highways to the consumer for consumption. As you can see, there is quite a production process that takes place in order for us to be able to pull up to a gas station and fill our tanks.

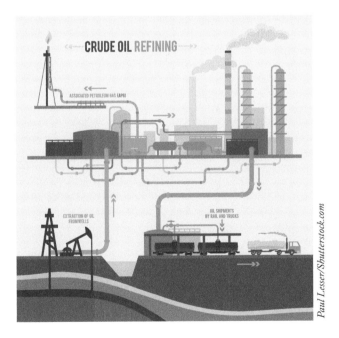

One seldom thinks about where or how the products we use are derived-only that you have access when you need them. The process of getting products to consumers when and where they want them is a dynamic system that demands a great deal of control. This control comes from an area of management called operations management.

Operations management oversees the entire production process by effectively managing people and processes to transform raw materials into finished products and services. Functions of operations managers include decision-making related to business operations, inventory control, production scheduling, quality control, or any task related to the production process. Operations managers must control five major areas: quality, process, capacity, inventory, and the workforce. From the start of a process through completion, a manager must balance the design, manufacturing, assembly, testing, and quality control of a product or service. An operations manager's goal is to provide the best product, at the highest quality, for the lowest price. That makes the choice of which production process to use in an organization an important decision.

concept check

Why is it important for an organization to manage its operations effectively?

TYPES OF PRODUCTION

Operations management: The process of managing people and processes to transform raw materials into finished products and services.

Mass production: The production of large quantities, typically on an assembly line.

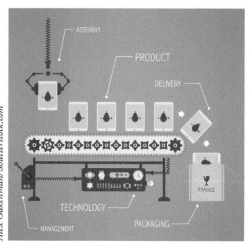

In the manufacturing world, different production methods are used to create products. Four common types of basic production systems are mass production, flexible production, project, and customer-driven production.

Mass production is commonly the production of large quantities of products which are sold at lower prices than if they are produced in smaller batches. This process allows us to have cars, televisions, or any product produced using this production method. Popularized by Henry Ford in the automobile industry, companies often have employees specialize in various areas so they can focus on one specific task and reduce assembly time. This increases productivity and helps create standardized products. Machines and robots have taken the place of many tasks that can be automated in mass production processes, which has affected the number of manufacturing jobs in the United States and globally. Mass production has great advantages for producing large quantities of similar products in a low-cost, efficient manner; however, it is neither effective for small batch production runs nor allows for flexibility in the production of goods. In addition, employees may become bored completing the same, repetitive task on a daily basis, which affects productivity.

Flexible manufacturing is a process that produces smaller quantities through the use of computer-based systems. This allows a company to customize orders using the same machinery it uses to mass produce items. This is done largely online or through the use of technology, which reduces labor costs and makes smaller batches more cost-effective. Special orders are sent to factory machines that communicate with other machines in order to create customized goods, which are sent to customers in a timely fashion.[2] Ironically, automobile manufacturers have started to use this process to create customized cars with a variety of features and colors in order to meet customer demand for unique cars. It is possible to order a new car online and have it shipped directly to the dealer with the features, options, and colors you demand. This is a far cry from Henry Ford's production of only black cars.

aGinger/Shutterstock.com

Flexible manufacturing: A process that produces smaller quantities through the use of computer-based systems.

A third production system is known as a **project system**. This system is used for a project-based product or "one-time use" system, such as the construction of a building, the development of an airplane, or creating a prototype car seen at annual car shows. Because these are project-based systems, management must use special controls in order to keep costs under control.[3]

Project system: A one-time-use system to develop a product or project.

Finally, **customer-driven production** is a process where products are produced by linking directly to customer demand. Scanners are used to determine how much inventory is needed. This inventory method is tied directly back to the manufacturer, who monitors products purchased. Another approach is making the product when a customer orders it, such as restaurant food or computers. Dell Computers, for example, makes computers when consumers order them directly from the company, which helps improve satisfaction and eliminates customer complaints about paying for unnecessary features.

Customer-driven production: A process where products are produced by linking directly to customer demand.

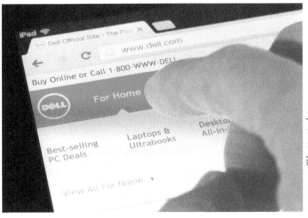

ymgerman/Shutterstock.com

concept check

Compare and contrast the various types of production.

CONTINUOUS VERSUS INTERMITTENT PRODUCTION

As the name implies, **continuous production** is the continuous physical flow of material through the product manufacturing process, commonly known as the assembly line. To achieve production cost savings, specially designed equipment or methods are operated on a continuous basis in order to produce as much of a given product as possible. Common continuous production assembly line systems are found in automobile, computer, soft drink, or appliance industries.

Continuous production:
Assembly line production where there is a continuous flow of products.

Intermittent production:
A system with interrupted intervals in the material flow process.

Intermittent production systems contain interrupted intervals in the material flow process. Unlike the continuous process, an intermittent production system operates with breaks in the production process. The same production machines are used but at varying times and with adjustments to the machines based on customer specifications. This type of production is similar to batch or job production as it relates to specific customer needs. Intermittent production is commonly used in maintenance shops, custom wedding dress boutiques, and welding shops.

ANALYTIC VERSUS SYNTHETIC SYSTEMS

Analytic production:
Breaking down raw materials into one or more products.

Synthetic production:
Combining two or more raw materials to create another product.

Beyond how a product is manufactured, it is important for a company to determine what it will do with raw materials—use them in other products or break them down into multiple products. **Analytic production** processes condense raw materials into parts in order to remove one or more marketable products. This process can be thought of as taking a raw material and breaking it down to get other products. An example is using crude oil to create both gasoline and heating oil. Soy beans are another example as they can be used as food products in soy milk, as seed for the following year, or in dog food. **Synthetic production systems** are the opposite of analytic production in that two or more raw materials are combined to make another product. This type of process puts together or assembles component parts such as meat, noodles, sauce, and spices in order to make a frozen lasagna dinner.

concept check

Provide examples of analytic and synthetic production products.

ADDITIONAL MANUFACTURING PROCESSES

The manufacturing environment can take many forms and it is up to a business to decide which production processes best serve its needs. **Figure 9.2** shows various types of manufacturing processes.

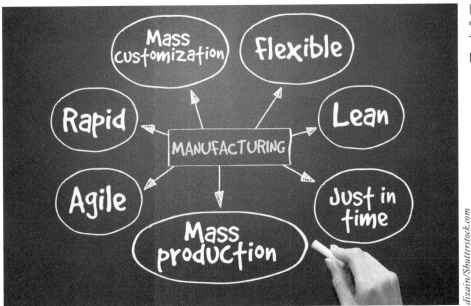

dizain/Shutterstock.com

FIGURE 9.2

Types of Manufacturing Processes

We have already discussed mass production, flexible manufacturing, and customer-driven production and will continue by focusing on additional processes used in manufacturing including lean manufacturing, just-in-time manufacturing, agile, and rapid manufacturing.

Lean manufacturing: A business philosophy that aims to reduce waste while still providing on-time, high-quality, cost-effective products to customers. The idea of creating more for less while keeping customer value high is at the heart of this philosophy.[4] Lean manufacturing is being used across manufacturing and service sectors in the United States to create a competitive advantage in industries such as health care, aerospace, furniture production, and electronics.[5]

Just-in-time manufacturing (JIT): An inventory strategy a business uses to reduce inventory costs by only producing products based on customer demands. The goal of JIT is to increase efficiency and decrease waste. Inventory and production are ordered only when there is a need for production versus having excess inventory and/or product stored in a warehouse waiting to be used.

Lean manufacturing: Aims to reduce waste while providing high-quality products.

JIT manufacturing: Reducing inventory and production costs by producing and ordering on demand.

Welf Aaron/Shutterstock.com

Agile manufacturing:
Using flexibility and speed as a competitive advantage.

Rapid manufacturing:
A process used to design, create, and manufacture products rapidly.

Computer-Aided Design (CAD): System that uses a computer to design and test products before producing them.

Computer-Aided Manufacturing (CAM): Uses technology to analyze each machine in the production process.

Computer-Integrated Manufacturing (CIM): Unifies all processes in manufacturing and with workers to effectively manage operations.

Agile manufacturing: A business strategy that helps an organization manage production processes quickly, efficiently, and cost effectively in order to respond to customer needs and market changes, which gives them a competitive advantage.

Rapid manufacturing: A new area of manufacturin g, sometimes called additive fabrication, that extensively uses "machines that can rapidly be redesigned or retooled to make subsequent batches of new products" (para. 4).[6]

TECHNOLOGICAL DEVELOPMENTS

As with any industry, technology helps a company be more productive and profitable. Companies utilize computers to assist in the development process and create more effective production systems. There are various types of technological advancements used in manufacturing and production including computer-aided design, computer-aided manufacturing, and computer-integrated manufacturing.

Computer-Aided Design (CAD) is a type of computer drafting system that allows design engineers the ability to design and test components of (or entire) products on the computer before actually producing them. Traditional drafting systems utilized manual drawings, which leads to more mistakes, so CAD systems bring technology into the design process and help minimize errors, costs, and time.

Computer-Aided Manufacturing (CAM) is an extension of CAD and allows the manufacturer to use the latest computer tools to analyze each machine in the production process. This system enables a manufacturer to evaluate the necessary steps that a particular piece of equipment must take to produce a product or part. Most organizations use CAD and CAM together to increase efficiency and save time.

FERNANDO BLANCO CALZADA/Shutterstock.com

Computer-Integrated Manufacturing (CIM) is used in the production process to analyze the design of products, machine control, material handling, and production control in a unified or integrated manner. It combines the efforts of workers with the use of technology to have seamless integration between the two. This helps companies organize the whole process and effectively manage operations.

concept check

How is technology used in the production process?

GREEN MANUFACTURING

Green manufacturing is incorporating environmentally-friendly operating processes for the benefit of sustainability and profitability. Sustainable manufacturing works to meet present-day needs without compromising the needs of future generations by reducing waste, air pollution, and energy consumption.[7] These efforts are a priority in many businesses today, not only because it saves them money, but it improves a company's goodwill and helps them fulfill socially responsible efforts as discussed in Chapter 2. Companies can receive a green certification is known as **Leadership in Energy and Environmental Design (LEED)**, which is well known in the building industry and recognizes only the best in sustainable new construction strategies and practices. A company must meet certain rigorous standards in order to earn LEED certification.[8]

Ismagilov/Shutterstock.com

Green manufacturing: Incorporating environmentally-friendly operating processes within an organization.

Sustainable manufacturing: Recognizing present and future needs of the environment in manufacturing practices.

LEED: Certification that recognizes sustainability in the construction of new buildings.

FACILITY LAYOUTS

The facility layout is how a business physically arranges machines, workers, and resources to produce its goods or services. Creating facility layouts involves determining how variables, such as material flow, handling, output needs, space utilization, and shipping and receiving impacts employee morale, the design of the space, and safety. It is very costly to redesign a facility, so it is important to analyze criteria and set it up efficiently the first time. However, keep in mind that each business is unique and should maximize its own facility to suit their needs. Below are examples of typical layout designs.

- **Product** or **assembly line layouts** are developed using workstations to produce large quantities of a few products. Each workstation specializes in one task and then the product is moved to another workstation to add to the product until it is completed.

Pavel L Photo and Video/Shutterstock.com

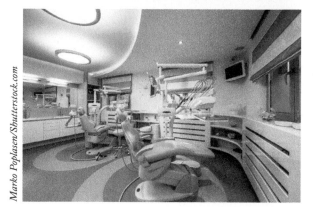

- **Modular layouts** involve teams combining several tasks from an assembly line into one complex unit instead of continually moving through various workstations.

- **Process layout** is designed by grouping machines or workers by function to make products. This allows for movement in the facility as well as flexibility to create products in smaller batches.

- **Fixed-position layout** is a production method that brings all materials, labor, and equipment to a site where products will be assembled versus moving through phases of an assembly line. This is typically done with large, bulky products that are not easily moved or transported. Building a new home or airplane are a few examples of using a fixed-position layout.

- **Customer-oriented (service industries) layouts** arrange facilities to help customers interact most effectively and efficiently with the service desired. A medical clinic and its patient greeting area or check-in process is designed to provide service quickly and easily to patients.

Production control is the list of activities used in any production process and can include materials handling, obtaining supplies or parts, and assembling the product from the beginning through completion. **Figure 9.3** displays the five-step production control process, which includes planning, routing, scheduling, dispatching, and follow-up. The first step is *planning*. Next, is *routing* which refers to the path for producing products and sequencing operations to produce them. Creating a time-table for completion is accomplished in the *scheduling* phase and *dispatching* is where the actual production begins to take place. Once production starts, it is important for an organization to *follow-up* and control production through the use of quality controls to ensure high-quality, efficient operations. With proper coordination, high production efficiency and low production costs result from thoughtful production control.

Production control: The list of activities used in any production process.

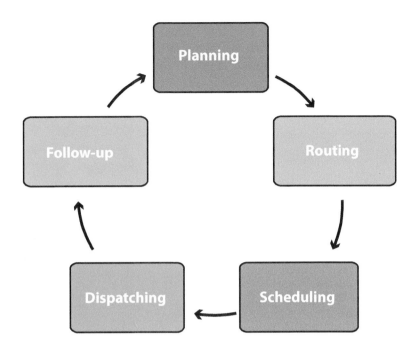

FIGURE 9.3

Production Control
Process

Two charts that help managers oversee the scheduling stage of production include the GANTT chart and Program Evaluation and Review Technique (PERT) chart. Both tools are used to help determine the amount of time spent on each phase of the production process as well as highlight areas that may be slowing down the process.

A **Gantt chart**, named after developer Henry Gantt, is a bar graph that is used to show what is currently being worked on, how long each task should take, and what has been completed. This gives an estimate of the total completion time as well as identifies areas that overlap in the production process and may potentially cause delays. **Figure 9.4** shows a Gantt chart and how many days each task should take to complete.

Gantt chart: A bar graph to show what task is being worked on and how long it will take to complete each task.

FIGURE 9.4

Gantt Chart

nasirkhan/Shutterstock.com

A **Program Evaluation and Review Technique (PERT) chart** is a project management tool utilized for scheduling, organizing, and coordinating project tasks. It is preferred over the Gantt chart as it provides greater detail; however, it can be hard to interpret. A PERT chart analyzes the numbers of days to complete each task and then develops a **critical path** to determine the highest number of days a project will require for completion (see the red line in **Figure 9.5**). This gives a more realistic view of the amount of time to complete a project and is often done using sophisticated software. A similar project management tool called the Critical Path Method (CPM) was developed about the same time as the PERT chart and is used in the private sector.[9]

FIGURE 9.5

PERT Chart

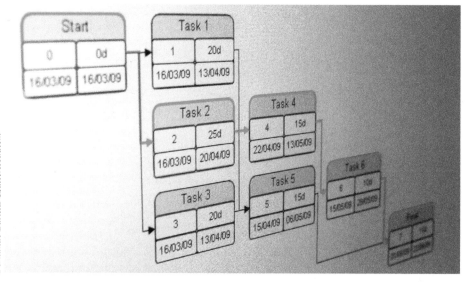

Fernando Batista/Shutterstock.com

QUALITY CONTROL

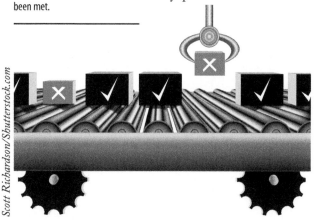

Scott Richardson/Shutterstock.com

Quality control is an important aspect of any organization. If ABC Company produced one million watches each year and had a 1 percent defect rate, 10,000 watches would be defective every year. At a cost of $10 per watch, that would result in a loss of $100,000/year in defective merchandise for the organization. **Quality control** is the careful monitoring of the production process to determine if company and customer standards have been met. Mistakes in production are costly to companies and may result in customer lawsuits or dissatisfaction, waste, or defective products that must be replaced. Common strategies for improving quality control include total quality management, Six Sigma, and ISO certifications.

TOTAL QUALITY MANAGEMENT (TQM)

Product and service quality is a goal that many organizations strive for because it provides a competitive advantage while meeting customers' needs. William Deming introduced TQM as a management philosophy in the 1950s in Japan, and it became more prominent in the United States in the 1980s. Total Quality Management (TQM) is an organization-wide philosophy that seeks to continuously improve its capacity to deliver the highest quality goods to customers. Individuals at all levels contribute to the betterment of the production process and organization.

"We need someone to get us beyond PQM, Partial Quality Management."

Cartoonresource/Shutterstock.com

Six Sigma is a way for a business to measure and achieve quality at the highest levels, with an end result of near perfection—only 3.4 defects per million items produced. It is a data-driven approach designed to eliminate defects in organizational processes from manufacturing to service industries.[10] Professionals involved in Six Sigma earn certifications in belt colors, similar to Karate. **Figure 9.6** defines the DMAIC fundamentals of Six Sigma.

Fundamentals of Six Sigma

D Define — Determine Project Goals, Identify Problem Areas, Understand Customer Concerns

M Measure — Identify Products and/or Services, Map Business Process, Baseline System Capacity, Collect all Relevant Data

A Analyze — Perform Detailed Data Analysis to Determine Root-Cause Relationships, Understand the Effects of Product or Service Variability to pave the way for Process Improvement

Improve — Optimization of Busines Processes, Creation of New and Improved Business Processes, Establish Operating Tolerances utilizing Key Performance Indicators

C Control — Implement Control Systems to Ensure newly Improved Business Processes do NOT Deviate from Target Key Performance Indicators

Committed to Quality Management

Fotoluminate LLC/Shutterstock.com

FIGURE 9.6

Fundamentals of Six Sigma

Total quality management (TQM): An organization-wide philosophy that seeks to continuously improve its capacity to deliver the highest quality goods to customers.

Six Sigma: A data-driven approach designed to eliminate defects.

ISO CERTIFICATION (9000 AND 14000)

The International Organization of Standardization, developed in 1947, created international standards for businesses that trade goods and services in the global marketplace. There are a variety of standard families that a company may pursue

Kae Deezign/Shutterstock.com

depending on the industry they service including ISO 9000 and ISO 14000. Many organizations only conduct business with other organizations that hold ISO certifications as they want assurance that their products are high-quality and that organizations strive to maintain a certain level of standards. These types of certifications provide a distinct competitive advantage while allowing a company to focus on quality management.[11]

The ISO 9000 principles exist to show that businesses have achieved certain levels of customer satisfaction and work toward continual quality improvement as organizations. This certification provides assurance of standards such as product testing, process controls, and storage, which translates into higher-quality goods being traded. ISO 9001 refers to the requirements that must be met by organizations who wish to achieve the certification.

ISO 9000: Principles to demonstrate work toward customer satisfaction and continual quality improvement as an organization.

ISO 14000: Standards to support companies who work to minimize environmental harm.

The ISO 14000 standards highlight companies who work to minimize environmental harm. In order to receive this standard, companies must have an environmental policy, list areas of improvement, and have audits of their programs conducted by independent agencies as well as top-level management. ISO 14001 relates to the criteria that must be met in order to prove an organization has an environmental management system.

concept check

Explain various methods utilized to ensure quality control in an organization.

WRAPPING UP...

The production of products and services is an area that most individuals don't spend a great deal of time thinking about as we simply take end-products and consume them. Hopefully, after reviewing the information in this chapter, you have a greater appreciation for the work involved in getting products and services to market in a cost-efficient and timely manner.

In Chapter 10, we will analyze the need for and effects of global trade in our personal and professional lives. The global economy has become a major force in how businesses interact with employees, customers, and suppliers, which makes this information vital to your understanding of the world of business.

BUSINESS TERMINOLOGY

Production
Inputs
Outputs
Operations management
Mass production
Flexible manufacturing
Project system
Customer-driven production
Continuous production
Intermittent production
Analytic production
Synthetic production
Lean manufacturing
Just-in-time manufacturing (JIT)
Agile manufacturing
Rapid manufacturing
Computer-Aided Design (CAD)
Computer-Aided Manufacturing
   (CAM)

Computer-Integrated
   Manufacturing (CIM)
Green manufacturing
Sustainable manufacturing
Leadership in Energy and
   Environmental Design (LEED)
Product or assembly line layout
Modular layout
Process layout
Fixed-position layout
Customer-oriented layout
Production control
Gantt chart
PERT Chart
Critical path
Quality Control
Total Quality Management (TQM)
Six Sigma
ISO 9000
ISO 14000

DISCUSSION QUESTIONS

1. Compare and contrast the various methods of production.

2. Do you feel it is necessary for service businesses to engage in TQM? Explain.

3. How does the production process create value for customers and the organization?

4. Describe how operations management is relevant to businesses like colleges or hospitals.

5. Discuss how technology has affected the production and manufacturing side of business. Discuss how it has affected the service side of business.

LEARNING ACTIVITIES

1. In small groups, discuss which production method is best suited for a new business entering the following industries: (a) a nursing home; (b) an electronics manufacturing firm; (c) a farm in Iowa; and (d) a CPA firm.

2. Conduct a search to determine what actions companies are taking that are considered green. Which companies rank highest in the United States and globally for their green efforts? In addition, conduct a search for those companies who are not utilizing green practices. Be prepared to discuss the link between green efforts and sustainability as well as the consequences for not incorporating green initiatives into a company's operations.

3. Off-shoring and reshoring are two concepts used in organizations today. Divide into two groups, one in favor of off-shoring and the other in favor of reshoring, and debate the advantages of each. Develop arguments to support your position using current, research-supported information (not opinions).

4. Find and examine job postings for project managers. Determine what project managers do within an organization specifically and the types of skills, certifications, and/or education a project manager must possess. Be prepared to discuss what industries use project managers and if being a project manager interests you personally.

Note: *Because web sites often change, use a search engine to find alternative web sites to access required information when necessary.*

INTRODUCTION TO THE WORLD OF BUSINESS

CASE STUDY: THE PRODUCTION BLUES!

Mark and Candy are colleagues who have recently invented a new product and are considering selling it to retailers. However, neither person knows how to get the process started in order to actually produce the products as their backgrounds are in education, not in production or operations management.

After conducting some research, Mark and Candy decided to purchase a small facility where they can produce their product. They have heard that obtaining ISO9000 certification might be good for their business; however, they have not done much research on the topic. They discovered that they need three pieces of large equipment, storage/warehouse space, an area for shipping/receiving, a materials handling area, and an assembly area. The building selected will provide plenty of space to satisfy all of their current needs.

CASE STUDY ANALYSIS

Based on the information provided, answer the following questions:

(1) What questions should Mark and Candy ask in order to create an appropriate production layout for their operations?

(2) Knowing that Mark and Candy will start with small production runs until sales develop, what type of project management tools might you suggest they use?

(3) Do you think the ISO 9000 certification will be of value to Mark and Candy as they begin the business? Why or why not?

CHAPTER 10

INTERNATIONAL TRADE

"The international business, instead of detracting from our business, is now additive to our business."
~Michael Casey, Chief Financial Officer, Starbucks

OUTCOMES:

- ➤ Explain the difference between importing and exporting.
- ➤ Distinguish between comparative and absolute advantage.
- ➤ Discuss various strategies used to enter global markets.
- ➤ Identify various barriers to global trade.
- ➤ Debate the advantages and disadvantages of global trade.

GLOBAL TRADE

khuconi/Shutterstock.com

As you examine the clothes you wear, the car you drive, or the products you use, it does not take long to figure out that much of what you consume is manufactured in other countries. The global market is expanding, and it is important to recognize the interdependence the United States has on other nations for products and services.

In this chapter, we will discuss the advantages and disadvantages of global trade, barriers that stifle or prevent trade, and how companies can enter foreign markets. We will also examine various organizations that work to promote free trade. As the world becomes smaller in relation to trade, we must learn to appreciate and value each nation's contributions to the global economy.

Many people wonder about the need for global trade, believing that each country should be able to produce what they want and need. The problem with this belief is that every country is limited by the finite resources and capital that they possess, such as infrastructure, human resources, and innovation. That being the case, expansion of global business becomes the logical move in creating wealth for an organization and country. Companies that have been in operation for a long time have likely maximized their reach in their own country and want to move into new territories. For instance, the United States has roughly 8 percent of the world's total population, so companies looking to expand their market share would increase their potential for growth by focusing on the other 92 percent. With over 7.3 billion people in the world, there is a lot of room for businesses to grow. **Figure 10.1** shows the percentages of the world's population by continent, which helps us understand why businesses are seeking growth opportunities in highly populated, developing nations.[1]

FIGURE 10.1

Population Around the Globe

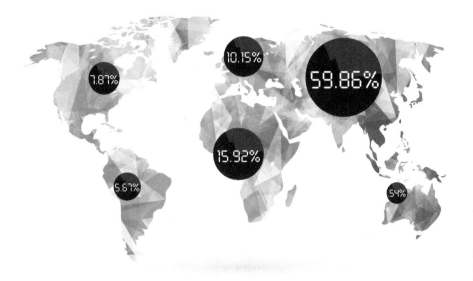

Merfin/Shutterstock.com

Source: The most populous continents in the world 2015 (2015). Retrieved on May 21, 2015, from: http://www.blatantworld.com/data/the-most-populous-continents-in-the-world-2015/.

Each country's economic success is built on the ability to trade goods and services with other countries. **Globalization** refers to the integration of world-wide economics, trade, financial systems, and communications. If a country is economically strong, it will engage in higher levels of trade, which benefits all parties. If a country is not economically strong, it negatively impacts all parties involved.

Globalization: The integration of world-wide economics, trade, financial systems, and communications.

EXPORTS AND IMPORTS

In Chapter 3, we discussed importing and exporting in relation to macroeconomics. As a reminder, exports are goods and services sold to another country, whereas imports are goods and services purchased from another country. Exporting and importing goods and services are common ways that countries conduct business. If France wants wheat from the United States, they import it as the United States exports it. If the United States wants wine from France, we will import it and France will export it. The two countries engage in global trade.

iQoncept/Shutterstock.com

In the United States, the top exporting states are Texas, California, Washington, Illinois, and Michigan. Products that are exported include machinery, electronics, oil, automobiles, and aircrafts.[2] **Table 10.1** shows the top five countries with whom the United States trades.[3]

TABLE 10.1

Top Five United States Trading Partners (2016) ($ in Billions)

RANK	COUNTRY	EXPORTS	IMPORTS
1	Canada	63.6	67.2
2	China	25.2	103.2
3	Mexico	55.6	70.3
4	Japan	15.1	32.0
5	Germany	12.3	27.8

Source: Top Trading Partners (2016). Retrieved on May 20, 2016, from: http://www.census.gov/foreign-trade/statistics/highlights/toppartners.html#total.

concept check

Explain the importance and challenges of international trade.

BALANCE OF TRADE VERSUS BALANCE OF PAYMENTS

Balance of trade: A nation's total exports minus the total imports over a given time period.

Trade deficit: When imports are greater than exports.

Trade surplus: When exports are greater than imports.

Due to active trade, methods for measuring global activity have been developed. One measure is the balance of trade, which is a nation's total exports minus the total imports over a given time period (monthly, quarterly, or annually). **Figure 10.2** displays the balance of trade in the United States from 2004 to 2014.[4] You can see that imports exceed exports as the graph displays negative numbers (in billions) over the 10-year period.

The United States has always been a world leader of exports; however, current trends have shown a trade deficit or net exports, where imports are greater than exports. According to the U.S. government, in March of 2016, the trade deficit was –$40.4 billion.[5] This means that the United States purchases more from other countries than others do from us. The opposite holds true if exports are greater than imports, which is known as a trade surplus or net imports.

FIGURE 10.2

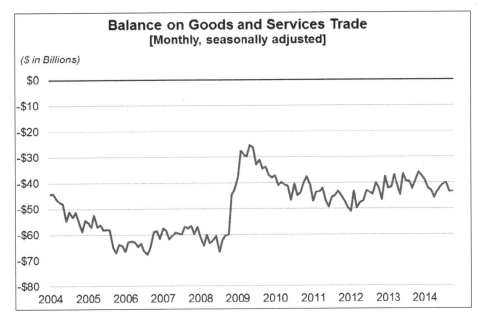

Balance on Goods and Services Trade
[Monthly, seasonally adjusted]

($ in Billions)

Source: U.S. international trade in goods and services (2016). Retrieved on May 20, 2016, from: http://www.bea.gov/newsreleases/international/trade /tradnewsrelease.htm.

The **balance of payments** is the flow of money in and out of a country in a given year. It is directly related to the balance of trade as that is how transactions occur. Money comes into and goes out of a country based on imports and exports, so the same principles of deficit and surplus exist with the balance of payments.

Balance of payments: The flow of money in and out of a country in a given year.

GDP per capita: A country's total output (GDP) divided by the number of people in the country, used to determine standard of living.

GDP PER CAPITA

You might recall from Chapter 3 that GDP represents the total amount of goods and services produced within a country's borders in a given year. GDP per capita is a measurement of a country's total output (GDP) divided by the number of people in the country. This is a useful tool for comparing countries as it shows the economic strength of a country as well as the relative standard of living.[6]

If the GDP per capita rises, it indicates an increase in production and economic growth. Countries such as Luxembourg, Norway, and Qatar have extremely high GDP and GDP per capita, which indicates that most individuals in those countries live well. Countries with low GDP per capita typically experience poverty among their people and often have less stable economies than those with higher GDPs per capita.[7] It is important to note that countries

Vlada Z/Shutterstock.com

Matyas Rebak/Shutterstock.com

with large populations might have high GDP, but may not have high GDP per capita, which indicates a lower standard of living. So, although it is attractive for businesses to want to expand in countries with large or growing populations, it is important to understand whether or not the individuals in those countries can afford the products and services the company offers. **Figures 10.3** and **10.4** show the wealthiest and poorest countries in the world based on GDP per capita.

FIGURE 10.3

Wealthiest Countries by GDP per Capita

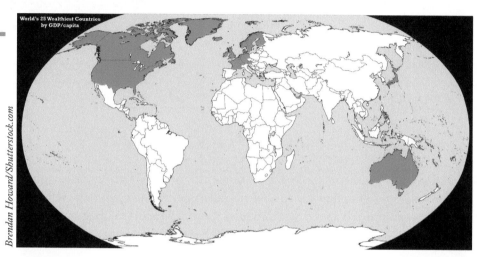
Brendan Howard/Shutterstock.com

FIGURE 10.4

Poorest Countries by GDP per Capita

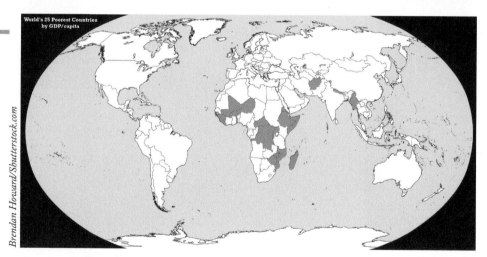
Brendan Howard/Shutterstock.com

concept check

How is GDP per capita related to trade?

ABSOLUTE VERSUS COMPARATIVE ADVANTAGE

Absolute advantage occurs when a country has a monopoly or can produce goods more efficiently than any other country. If Company A can produce 100 cars per day whereas company B produces only 90 cars per day, then Company A would have the absolute advantage over Company B.

Comparative advantage exists when a country can produce goods or services at a lower opportunity cost (they give up less) than other countries. Comparative advantage is related to more than costs as it also includes how efficiently and quickly a company can get products to market. In the United States, comparative advantage exists in having a skilled workforce, high levels of education, and an environment that promotes innovation. If a company can import items or outsource work less expensively, it helps lower costs and improves options for trade.

patpitchaya/Shutterstock.com

Comparative advantage helps explain why businesses outsource production to other countries who can manufacture products more efficiently and at lower costs. This trend has changed manufacturing in the United States and has been the source of conflict between many workers and companies. **Outsourcing** is a strategy used by companies to reduce costs by sending work to outside vendors instead of doing it internally. If properly used, outsourcing is an effective cost-saving tool. Other growing outsourcing areas include human resources and accounting when it provides cost savings to outsource rather than staff positions internally.

Absolute advantage: When a country has a monopoly or can produce goods more efficiently than any other country.

Comparative advantage: When a country can produce goods or services at a lower opportunity cost (they give up less) than other countries.

Outsourcing: Reducing costs by sending work to outside vendors.

BARRIERS TO TRADE

Even though countries need to trade globally, many barriers to trade exist. Sometimes, governments prevent trade by imposing restrictions that limit the flow of global products or services; however, cultural, social, and economic barriers can also prevent trade between nations.

Legal and political barriers include the laws and regulations that a foreign government imposes on imports. Governments sometimes set strict guidelines for others who trade with them based on their own interests or interactions with a given country. However, a country must be politically stable to be a viable trading partner. It is also important that all countries follow international laws in business transactions in order to avoid conflicts or retaliatory actions.

cbungking/Shutterstock.com

Economic barriers affect the ability of a country to trade globally. The valuation of currency, government tariffs, and investment regulations can be barriers to international trade. Another area that affects trade is the level of infrastructure that exists within a country. Infrastructure includes the availability of all communication, public works, energy, and transportation systems within a country. Countries with strong infrastructure have higher levels of success in trade.

pogonici/Shutterstock.com

Exchange rates are another area that affect global trade. Exchange rates are the rate at which currencies in one country are exchanged for currency in another country. When the United States dollar is strong, Americans can buy more overseas, but foreigners buy less of our goods due to higher costs. However, when the United States dollar is weak, Americans buy less overseas whereas foreigners buy more of our goods as a result of lower costs.

Cultural barriers refer to cultural attitudes toward, and an understanding of, a particular country. Language, customs, and religious differences can impede the acceptance of companies or products in foreign countries. For example, black and white packaging may have a negative influence on customers in Japan as those colors represent mourning, so it is important to consider culture and customs when conducting business in foreign countries. Lacking knowledge of other countries' cultural values can be detrimental to a business.

concept check

Discuss barriers to trade and what might be done to overcome them.

TRADE PROTECTIONISM

Most countries are open to trade, but some set restrictions that limit trade with other countries in order to protect their interests. In other cases, restrictions may be set to limit or protect trade. This is called protectionism, which involves government policies that restrict global trade in order to protect local businesses and jobs from foreign competition. Typical methods of protectionism are import tariffs, quotas, or embargos. Additional nontariff barriers can include: import bans, safety and health regulations, quality issues imposed on an importing country, over-valued currency, or general quotas.

When methods of protectionism are used, trade is restricted between nations and limits customer choice. When choices are limited, goods and services are either not offered or prices increase. The effects of restricting trade are generally negative in the long-run.

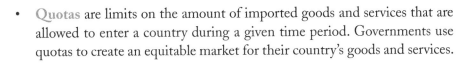

arka38/Shutterstock.com

- Tariffs are government taxes imposed on imported goods and services. These types of taxes can restrict trade as they increase the price of imported goods to consumers. Tariffs can be used to limit entry into a particular market or increase tax revenues.

- Quotas are limits on the amount of imported goods and services that are allowed to enter a country during a given time period. Governments use quotas to create an equitable market for their country's goods and services.

- Dumping involves selling goods to other countries for prices lower than they are being sold for in the domestic country. Another form of dumping involves foreign countries selling goods cheaper than it costs to produce them, which may be done to allow quick access to a market and to undercut domestic companies. Both are illegal and considered unfair trade practices.

- An embargo is the most extreme trade punishment a government can put on a foreign country. An embargo is a complete ban on imports or exports to and from a country. An embargo is usually tied to political goals or actions taken by a particular government. History has shown that embargoes have a crippling effect on a country's economic and political environment. After 60 years of an embargo with Cuba, U.S. President Barack Obama made a declaration that trade would reopen between the two countries in 2015.

rnnoa357/Shutterstock.com

Protectionism: Government policies that restrict global trade to protect local businesses and jobs from foreign competition.

Tariff: A government tax imposed on imported goods and services.

Quotas: Limits on the amount of imported goods and services that are allowed to enter a country.

Dumping: Selling goods to other countries for prices lower than they are being sold domestically.

Embargo: A complete ban on imports or exports to and from a country.

ORGANIZATIONS TO PROMOTE GLOBAL TRADE

GrAl/Shutterstock.com

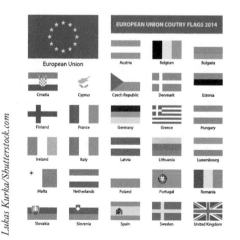

Popartic/Shutterstock.com

Lukas Kurka/Shutterstock.com

Even though barriers to trade exist, most countries recognize the importance of global trade and, therefore, have created organizations to monitor trade policies and practices. A few of the many regional or global agreements and markets that support free trade are listed below.

The North American Free Trade Agreement (NAFTA) is a comprehensive trade agreement signed in 1994 between the United States, Canada, and Mexico. NAFTA's main goal was to eliminate most tariff and nontariff barriers to free trade between these countries. Since signing this agreement, the three countries have increased their economic growth and states like Illinois, Michigan, and Ohio have seen dramatic increases in exports to Mexico and Canada. In fact, over 30 of the 50 states rank these two countries as their first or second largest exporters.[8]

The Central America-Dominican Republic Free Trade Agreement (CAFTA-DR) was signed by the United States, El Salvador, Guatemala, Honduras, and Nicaragua in 2006, by the Dominican Republic in 2007, and by Costa Rica in 2009. The agreement eliminated tariffs on many products and will continue to eliminate additional tariffs through 2020. The result is greater trade between nations, much like NAFTA for Mexico, Canada, and the United States.[9]

The European Union (EU) is a common market of 28 countries whose goals are to promote economic and social progress, increase global influence, remove barriers to trade between countries in Europe, and develop a unified currency (euro). This union works well as long as all countries remain economically and politically stable; however, if one or more countries become unstable, it can affect trade and currency rates for all nations in the union.[10]

In June of 2016, the United Kingdom voted to exit the EU (termed "Brexit"), which will inevitably cause changes in trade between the countries involved as well as globally as new agreements are negotiated. Other countries have hinted at their desire to withdraw from the EU, which creates uncertainty as partners in the agreement begin to change their minds about the trade agreement's policies and/or arrangements.

Common Market for Eastern and Southern Africa (COMESA) is a market comprised of 20 African nations. It was created in 1994 and continually strives to create a better free-trade zone. Currently, COMESA is considering allowing a common visa scheme hoping to enhance tourism to the countries.

BRICS Economies are composed of Brazil, Russia, India, China, and South Africa. Although these countries are not currently allied in any manner, they have the potential to form a powerful economic alliance in the future. Each country is developing, has huge populations, and offers low wages, which would help dominate manufacturing of many goods as well as be a major supplier of raw materials. Although there are challenges that must be overcome in each country, this will be an important group to watch in the international market in the years to come.[11]

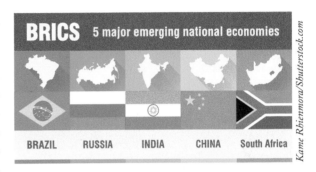

Kame Rhienmora/Shutterstock.com

concept check

What common goals do countries involved in trade agreements wish to accomplish?

INVOLVEMENT IN GLOBAL MARKETS

As mentioned earlier, one way to expand business revenue and growth is to enter foreign markets. This can be done using a variety of methods that range from minimal risk and involvement to high levels of risk and involvement. Many variables influence which strategy will work in a given country, such as product adaptation, marketing, tariff rates, and transportation costs. No strategy is applicable in all instances, so it is important for a company to align expansion efforts with their strategic plan. Common strategies for entering foreign markets are listed below and **Table 10.2** offers the pros and cons of each strategy.[12]

Taxbattuevango/Shutterstock.com

Exporting is when a company sells its products or services in a foreign market. It is relatively easy and inexpensive compared with purchasing a foreign company or directly investing in a country. However, tariffs may make this option too costly if imposed by an importing country.

Licensing is an agreement to pay for the rights to use a licensor's intangible property, such as copyrights, trademarks, patents, or other intellectual property. This allows quick access to foreign markets with little investment and may help a company enter a closed market more easily.

JuliusKielaitis/Shutterstock.com

Franchising, as discussed in Chapter 4, is paying for the use of a company's successful business model. It is a legal contract between a franchiser and the franchisee to operate a business. The franchisee pays a one-time franchise fee plus a percentage of sales (royalties) to the franchisor. In exchange, the franchisee gets instant brand name recognition, proven products or services, a standardized business model, advertising, and on-going training and support. The franchiser can rapidly develop the business and revenue under this type of expansion option. For example, Subway has become a world leader in franchising as nearly every country offers their specialty way of making sandwiches.

Coreptis VOF/Shutterstock.com

urbanbuzz/Shutterstock.com

Joint ventures are partnerships where two or more businesses form a partnership to share "markets, intellectual property, assets, knowledge, and profits (para. 7)."[13] There is no exchange of ownership but rather two firms joining forces while keeping separate entities. This is done to create a competitive advantage in the marketplace.

Contract manufacturing occurs when a manufacturer produces the same product for different companies. This can also be used to create a private label for a product or company. A manufacturer will produce similar products for multiple companies who have different labels in the marketplace. For example, there are only two freezer manufacturers, so companies like Kenmore, Whirlpool, and Frigidaire utilize contract manufacturers to produce products for all of them.

Wholly-owned subsidiaries are companies owned by a parent company. A parent company may want to expand into a foreign market by establishing a subsidiary company because it is unsure about its success in a new market. Therefore, the parent company may have another brand on the market in order to separate it from the parent company. If the new brand does not do well, it can pull it from the product mix and continue on with little damage to the parent company's reputation. The Walker's brand, a successful subsidiary of PepsiCo., is located in the United Kingdom and looks a great deal like Lays Potato Chips in the United States.

A **strategic alliance** is an arrangement between two or more companies who mutually agree upon a set of goals; however, all parties remain independent businesses. A good example would be the alliance between Starbucks and Barnes and Noble as it helped both gain a competitive advantage and increased sales. In addition, Starbucks has created strategic alliances with airlines, fast food restaurants, retail stores, and supermarkets to expand its reach.[14] Shared resources among the partners may include products, production capability, funding, capital equipment, knowledge, and expertise. **Table 10.2** recaps the pros and cons of various strategies businesses can use to enter foreign markets.

Strategic alliance: An arrangement between two or more companies who mutually agree upon a set of goals.

TABLE 10.2

Foreign Market Entrance Strategies Pros and Cons

STRATEGY	PROS	CONS
Exporting	• Quickness of market entry • Low production costs	• Costly transportation • Local information lacking • Trade barrier threats (tariffs)
Licensing	• Quickness of market entry • Immediate brand recognition	• Competition may become the licensee • Knowledge loss to potential competitor
Franchising	• Costs to start • Name recognition and support, which translates to higher success rates	• Quality control issues • Foreign market risks fall on the franchisee
Joint venture	• Great learning opportunity • Shared resources	• Dual control of business • Risk of loss of technological advantages to partner
Contract manufacturing	• Cost savings • Advanced skills • Quality	• Lack of control • Quality concerns • Outsourcing risks
Wholly-owned subsidiaries	• Total operational control • Minimal test marketing costs	• Foreign market costs and risks • Under control of parent company
Strategic alliance	• Expertise of combined workforce talent • Joint sharing of the risks and costs	• Risk of loss of technological advantages to partner • Compatibility with partner

Source: (2014). In bed with big brother: Apple and IBM form strategic alliance. Retrieved on April 26, 2015, from: http://www.theneweconomy.com/home/strategic-alliance-ibm-apple.

WRAPPING UP...

As the world becomes an open marketplace, individuals and businesses continue to navigate methods for conducting business and growing profits globally. It is important to understand what affects free trade and the benefits and drawbacks of trading globally. Most businesses you work for presently, as well as in the future, have a global presence—maybe someday, you will work in another country for a U.S. company.

In Chapter 11, we will examine the use of technology in the business world and work to explain how it has changed, as well as how it will change, the way business is conducted in the United States and globally. This is an ever-changing area and one that underpins almost every transaction that takes place in the global market.

BUSINESS TERMINOLOGY

Globalization	Dumping
Balance of trade	Embargo
Trade deficit	NAFTA
Trade surplus	CAFTA-DR
Balance of payments	COMESA
GDP per capita	BRICS
Absolute advantage	Exporting
Comparative advantage	Licensing
Outsourcing	Franchising
Infrastructure	Joint venture
Exchange rate	Contract manufacturing
Protectionism	Wholly-owned subsidiaries
Tariff	Strategic alliance
Quota	

DISCUSSION QUESTIONS

1. Discuss the pros and cons of reducing imports by 20 percent to eliminate a trade deficit.

2. Under what circumstances might a company consider expanding internationally? And, what factors should a company consider in doing so?

3. Discuss the challenges developing countries have in competing globally.

4. What are the advantages and disadvantages of having a trade agreement like NAFTA?

5. Do you consider outsourcing a necessary tool of business today? Explain.

LEARNING ACTIVITIES

1. Examine the labels on clothes, backpacks, handbags, shoes, etc., to see where they are made. In small groups, discuss how global trade affects your life and the lives of others around the globe. What would happen if all of the items you examined were made in the United States?

2. Select a country and examine the changes in its exchange rate over the past decade. How have the fluctuations in currency affected (or could it affect) the country's ability to trade with others around the world?

3. Conduct an Internet search to find an example of a failed product launch by a U.S. company in a foreign country. Be prepared to share the information in a one-minute presentation.

4. Research a company such as McDonalds, Coca-Cola, or KFC and identify whether or not it modifies its products regionally or if they offer the same types of products in every location globally. What are the advantages and disadvantages of their approach?

Note: *Because web sites often change, use a search engine to find alternative web sites to access required information when necessary.*

CASE STUDY: EXPANSION, EXPANSION: WHICH WAY TO GO?

As the owners of a fast-growing restaurant business, Mike and Debbie Schumaker have had the opportunity to begin franchising their restaurant, Homestyle Hot-dish Express. Their franchise offers regional hot-dish recipes, and in the past five years, they have franchised several restaurants that service regions throughout the United States.

A business man from Germany, who enjoys their food, approached them about the opportunity to expand into the European market. The gentleman wants to be the sole representative for the franchise and market it throughout Europe. He wants to act as the selling agent and retain a fee for each franchise agreement signed. Mike and Debbie, although successful within the United States, wonder if this would be a good way to expand globally or if they should continue to focus on U.S. expansion. They have some decisions to make before agreeing to expand globally.

CASE STUDY ANALYSIS

Based on the information provided, answer the following questions:

(1) Do you think international franchising is a viable option for Homestyle Hot-dish Express? Why or why not?

(2) If the decision is made to expand globally, how do you think Mike and Debbie should expand their business (joint venture, licensing, direct investment, etc.)?

(3) What advice would you give to Mike and Debbie in regard to this potential opportunity?

CHAPTER 11

TECHNOLOGY IN THE WORKPLACE

"The internet is becoming the town square for the global village of tomorrow."

~Bill Gates, Founder of Microsoft

OUTCOMES:

➢ Analyze the effect of technology in the workplace.
➢ Review hardware, software, and networking options that are affecting business practices today.
➢ Describe why data recovery, security, and back-up systems are necessary for a business.
➢ Explain how security and ethical issues affect information systems.
➢ Discuss current trends in technology and social media.

TECHNOLOGY AND BUSINESS

Sergey Nivens/Shutterstock.com

Technological improvements throughout history have improved our lives as well as the speed at which we operate in the business world. Inventions, such as electricity, medicines, the automobile, the telephone, and, of course, the computer have improved and affected the lives of everyone. Innovative products and methods help drive businesses to be more productive, efficient, and profitable.

Technological innovations started to steadily increase in the nineteenth century as the submission of patents to the U.S. Patent Office for new products and ideas helped many market segments emerge and evolve. These new ideas and products influenced the work environment, how people worked, and how people lived. For example, typewriters are still used but have mostly been replaced by tablets, laptops, or mobile phones. Most business transactions are automated using software and other applications.

You can easily see that technology has created a fast-paced, mobile society where business can be conducted from your home, on vacation, or other virtual means. Technology has continually changed and will continue to change for the benefit of business, people, and society. Innovation drives growth, so continued improvements in existing or new technologies is vital to the long-term success of the U.S. and global economies.

An important aspect of technology is using information wisely and knowing what to do with the technology that exists. In this chapter, we will examine how information is used in businesses, types of information systems, security, and ethical concerns related to trends in information technology and its use.

BUSINESS AND DATA

Data: Raw facts or information used to analyze, plan, or calculate something of relevance to the user.

Information: Processing data and turning it into knowledge.

Each day, decisions must be made in an organization. It is said that good decisions are made when a company has good information. When seeking information, it is important to first collect data. Data are raw facts or information used to analyze, plan, or calculate something of relevance to the user. These are all of the bits and pieces used to develop information, which is processing data and turning it into knowledge. For data to be useable as information, it must be accurate, timely, specific, organized for a purpose, relevant, and decrease uncertainty.[1]

With the advancement of information technology, it is easy to acquire and manipulate data, but processing it into useable information for use in strategic planning can be tricky for organizations. **Big data** is a comprehensive term for data sets so large or intricate that customary data processing applications are insufficient. **Data warehouses** are interactive databases designed for inquiry and analysis. They typically contain historical or past data derived from a company's internal operations; however, it can include data from other sources.

"Let's shrink Big Data into Small Data ... and hope it magically becomes Great Data."

Cartoonresource/Shutterstock.com

The main challenge is trying to extract valuable information from these enormous data warehouses. The amount of data, types of data, how data will be analyzed, and how certain an organization is that data are accurate are all factors that affect its usability. **Figure 11.1** shows the areas that make big data challenging for organizations.

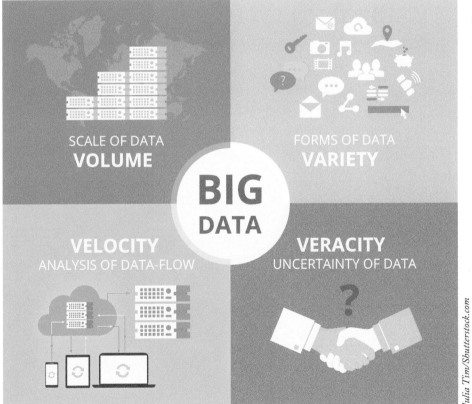

FIGURE 11.1

Four V's of Big Data

Big data: Large data sets.

Data warehouses: Interactive databases designed for inquiry and analysis.

Data mining: An analytical method used to extract usable data from data warehouses

Julia Tim/Shutterstock.com

Data mining is an analytical method used to extract usable data from data warehouses, which helps create valuable information used in developing strategic plans. Just like an individual mines for gold by sifting through dirt and rocks,

bleakstar/Shutterstock.com

individuals involved in data mining sift through data to find nuggets of useful information. Extracting information includes searching, analyzing, capturing, sharing, storing, and transferring data into useable information. In essence, the mining process helps search for consistent patterns or systemic relationships between variables to use in the decision-making process.

concept check

Compare data and information.

INFORMATION SYSTEMS

Maksim Kabakou/Shutterstock.com

Once information has been gathered, it is important to have a company-wide system in place to use it appropriately. An **information system** is a formal system used to collect, store, and process data in order to develop information, knowledge, and digital products within an organization.[2] Information is used by all business functions, such as production, marketing, and accounting. Today, companies rely on computer-based information systems to help manage processes, network with clients and vendors, and maintain a competitive advantage in the market. Information is shared between departments and technologies, such as email, intranets, and web-based applications, are used to improve communication.

Information system: A formal system used to collect, store and process data within an organization.

CIO: An individual who oversees and manages information systems.

Managing information systems takes skill and the ability to adapt quickly to change. Large companies use a **Chief Information Officer (CIO)** to oversee and manage information systems for the organization. It is the CIO's responsibility to maximize the functionality and usability of information both internally and externally. Small companies may not have an individual with the title of CIO; however, it is important for all businesses to use information systems to make effective decisions. This can be done using a multitude of information systems.

concept check

Why is having an information system important to an organization?

TYPES OF INFORMATION SYSTEMS

Basically, there are two types of information systems: operational support systems (OSS) and management information systems (MIS). OSS, also known as a business support system (BSS), are used to create and share information about business activities within the organization and externally. Organizations manage transactions (such as sales) or processes (such as a production line) in the organization using support systems called *transaction processing systems* (TPS) or *process control systems* (PCS).[3]

MIS are management support systems used to help all levels of management generate reports and make decisions. Reports should be easily obtained from the system and provide feedback to managers regarding company performance, which allows senior management to monitor the entire organization. *Decision support systems* (DSS) examine business information and prepare it in a format that allows users to make business decisions. *Executive support systems* (ESS) generate reports from all departments that executive level managers use for decision making.[4]

OSS: Information systems used to create and share information about business activities within the organization and externally.

MIS: Information systems used to guide all levels of management in generating reports and making decisions.

concept check

What is the difference between an OSS and MIS?

COMPUTER NETWORKING

Effectively linking all organizational systems together takes time, knowledge of company goals, and resources. Computer hardware includes the tangible parts or components of a computer (input, memory, output devices), such as the monitor, printer, keyboard, computer data storage, or hard disk drive (HDD). Computer software includes the programs and programming languages that direct the operations of a computer system. One of the most widely used and recognized software in the business world is Microsoft Office.

Hardware: The tangible parts or components of a computer.

Software: The programs and programming languages that direct the operations of a computer system.

Photographee.eu/Shutterstock.com

© Shutterstock.com

LAN/WAN

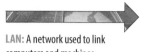

LAN: A network used to link computers and machines between short distances.

Once hardware and software have been determined, most companies look for ways to link operations within their building or between locations. This can be done by using networks. A **local area network (LAN)** is a connection method used to link computers and machines between short distances. They are usually owned and controlled by an individual or business and are commonly used in office buildings, schools, or homes. **Figure 11.2** shows an example of how several components are connected using a LAN.

FIGURE 11.2

LAN Configuration

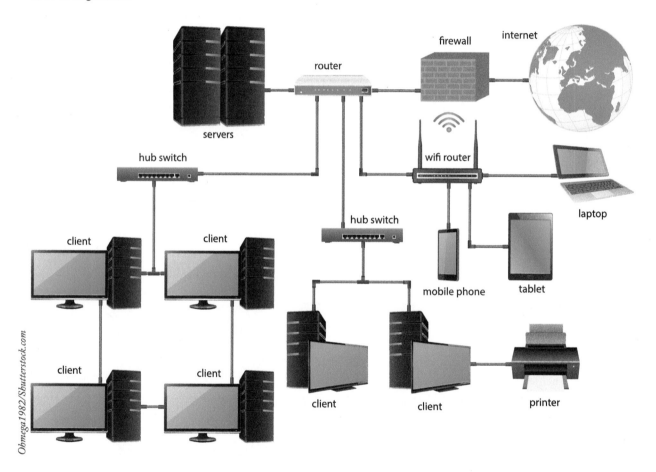

INTRODUCTION TO THE WORLD OF BUSINESS

A **wide area network (WAN)** covers a large physical distance, with the Internet being the largest WAN. Most WAN configurations use satellite services to share information with users in different geographical regions. Satellite TV or cell phone companies use WANs to connect internal equipment with outside equipment to provide higher levels of service and communication.

Wi-Fi (*wireless fidelity*) is a wireless network that allows electronic devices to communicate with each other through radio waves by using a wireless router and an Internet modem. Wi-Fi has become so common in businesses and schools that we often fail to realize how important this tool is for organizations to effectively operate.

THE INTERNET, INTRANET, AND EXTRANET

The term commonly used for networking computers globally is the Internet. However, there are differences in how individuals can access information, which leads to other types of networks such as intranets and extranets. The **Internet** (also known as the World Wide Web) is a network available to anyone with an Internet-connected device. Originally designed for use in the military, it is an enormous group of networks sharing information publicly through interlinked web pages. All web sites have a **Uniform Resource Locator (URL)**, which is the web address to reference its location on the network.

An **intranet** is a network that is only available to a small group of users, typically within companies to provide access to company files and servers. For this reason, it is commonly referred to as a private Internet. Not all intranets have access to the Internet, but if they do, firewalls or other precautions are often set up to prevent access by others to the company's information.

An **extranet** is a network that is set up and available via a web portal for users who have a valid user name and password. This makes information accessible 24/7/365 and allows remote access for a variety of needs. An organization uses this type of network to provide access to information by both in-house and outside users. For example, your school likely has access for current

TechnoVectors/Shutterstock.com

WAN: A network that covers a large physical distance.

Wi-Fi: A wireless network that allows devices to communicate through radio waves.

Internet: A network available to anyone with an Internet-connected device.

URL: The web address of a particular web site.

Intranet: A network available to a small group of users.

Extranet: A network available via a web portal for users who have a valid user name and password.

everything possible/Shutterstock.com

and prospective students, faculty, and/or parents who have user names and passwords. Each group is able to access different information, and all users can access it outside of school if they have privileges.

concept check

Explain the differences between the Internet, an intranet, and an extranet.

SECURITY AND ETHICAL CONCERNS

Although business can be conducted in almost any setting, the virtual side of business does have its challenges. As more people have access to the Internet, the potential for criminal and unethical behavior becomes more likely. Today's businesses collect personal data about customers, employees, and suppliers, so it is important to constantly work to prevent malicious attempts by perpetrators who try to access secure data. **Table 11.1** shows several recent crimes involving credit card theft or other security breaches as well as the costs to companies.[5]

TABLE 11.1

Notable Security
Breaches and Costs

COMPANY	INCIDENT/CRIME
Anthem February 2015	Theft of personal information of up to 78.8 million current and former customers. *Cost: $100 million*
Home Depot September 2014	Theft of credit/debit card information of 56 million customers. *Cost: $33 million*
Target Stores December 2013	Credit/debit card information and/or contact information of up to 110 million people was compromised. *Cost: $162 million*
Sony online entertainment services April 2011	Personal information of 78 million PlayStation network users were exposed in addition to 24.6 million users from SOE and Qriocity. *Cost: $171 million*
Department of Veterans Affairs May 2006	An unencrypted national database with names, Social Security numbers, dates of birth, and disability ratings for 26.5 million veterans, active-duty military personnel, and spouses was stolen. *Cost: $100–$500 million*

Source: Palmero, E. (2015). Ten worst data breaches of all time. Retrieved on May 23, 2016, from: http://www.tomsguide.com/us/biggest-data-breaches,news-19083.html.

marekuliasz/Shutterstock.com

Cybercrime is a crime that involves a computer or computer network and is one of the fastest growing criminal areas. Cybercrime can include national or international crime organizations engaging in Internet fraud, accessing data, altering data, or modifying computer programs. Included in cybercrime is identity theft, money laundering, attacks against computer hardware and software, fraud, penetration of online financial services, phishing, or the abuse of individuals. Many groups conduct research to study cybercrime. E-CRIME is a European-led project designed to study the effects of cybercrime as well as identify and develop processes to detect, deter, and manage it.

Malware is malicious software utilized to corrupt, disrupt, or gather sensitive information from private or public computer systems. Most computer systems have a firewall set up to protect against malware; however, many large sites have dealt with some type of attack. Recent estimates have stated that over $100 billion/year is spent dealing with malware-related attacks.[6] Malware can include the following:

Macrovector/Shutterstock.com

- **Viruses** are man-made computer programs that attach themselves to other programs without the user's knowledge or consent. They are activated when files are shared, copied, or opened. Fortunately, anti-virus software exists to protect and remove viruses, but new viruses are constantly being created, which makes it challenging to remain current.

Cartoonresource/Shutterstock.com

"That's usually not a good sign."

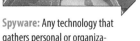

Spyware: Any technology that gathers personal or organizational information without the user's knowledge or consent.

WORM: A computer program that finds holes in networks and replicates itself over another computer network.

Trojan horse: A malicious program that claims to be one thing but is really another.

Computer security: The protection of computing systems and the data they store.

- Spyware is any technology that gathers personal or organizational information without the user's knowledge or consent. Information is gathered through the user's Internet connection and activities, typically for advertising purposes.

- WORM stands for "write once, read many" and is a computer program that finds holes in computer networks and then replicates itself over another computer network, usually to perform malicious actions.[7]

- A Trojan horse is a malicious program that claims to be one thing but is really another. For instance, a program might say that it is a game; however, when it is launched, it might delete files or gather information instead.

Computer security is the protection of computing systems and the data that they store for a company or user. Most networks have firewalls to prevent hacking; however, firewalls can sometimes be breached. Consumers can purchase products like McAfee Antivirus or Norton Antivirus programs to help eliminate computer threats. In large organizations, it is important to have recovery and back-up plans in the event a catastrophic event occurs. There are systems such as Symantec used for such purposes; however, terrorist attacks or natural disasters do not allow for such recovery, so having backups of sensitive information is important for organizations and individuals.

concept check

What types of malware exist?

TRENDS IN INFORMATION TECHNOLOGY

Several other trends in technology are taking place and will continue to evolve in the future. The need to have information stored outside of an organization has led to the creation of cloud computing. Cloud computing is used when a company stores information or uses services from the web. This helps protect information in a location outside of a physical building and provides access to large databases or certain software.[8]

Jozsef Bagota/Shutterstock.com

On-demand computing (ODC) is an enterprise-level model of technology that allows users to pay for what they use. Often referred to as *utility computing*, it is accessed on an as-needed basis. This helps companies keep up to date with rapidly changing software without investing in huge upgrades or software packages.

Internet of Everything (IoE) refers to the Internet connectivity and intelligence of everyday devices in order to give each device special functions. You currently see this in garage door openers and security devices that can be accessed and monitored via a mobile phone. You also see it in health care products, exercise trends, refrigerators, and even mattresses. There have been estimates by Cisco that the IoE will save the private sector over $4.6 trillion in productivity improvements, cost reductions, and revenues over the next few years.[9]

Praneat/Shutterstock.com

A distributed workforce occurs when geographically disbursed employees work for an organization domestically or internationally. We referred to these individuals earlier as *virtual employees* who work from *remote offices*, whereby individuals don't physically come to an office but rather work from a remote location. Key technologies permit employees to access company resources and interact with the business from various locations. Virtual meetings allow more people to join a conversation and provide input.

Dragon Images/Shutterstock.com

Cloud computing: Storing information or using services from the web.

On-demand computing: Technology that allows users to pay for what they use.

Internet of Everything: The Internet connectivity and intelligence of everyday devices in order to give each device special functions.

Distributed workforce: Geographically disbursed employees who work for an organization domestically or internationally.

Mmaxer/Shutterstock.com

Today, every business has the ability to conduct almost every aspect of business via the Internet. This ability has become vital to businesses' success, and in the past 30 years, has changed the way businesses operate globally. For better or worse, individuals can remain connected to business transactions and information on vacation, at home, or virtually anywhere outside of the office. This ability has become invaluable for businesses all over the world, so it is important to remain current and respond to customer needs.

E-business, which means electronic business, is conducting business via the Internet, Intranet or Extranet. E-business includes **e-commerce**, which includes trading merchandise with customers, suppliers, or other external members of an organization via the Internet. E-commerce relates more to commercial transactions, while e-business relates more to overall business transactions. E-business encompasses external functions but also includes internal functions related to operating the business including production, inventory, accounting, and human resources.[10]

E-business: Conducting business via the Internet, Intranet or Extranet.

E-commerce: Trading merchandise with customers, suppliers, or other external members of an organization via the Internet.

E-business helps improve effective business practices and operational efficiencies. This allows for increased communication and creates a 24/7/365 operational environment where customers and businesses can interact.[11] Many tools are used to conduct business over the Internet and the list of tools is constantly changing, just like technology. In the 1990s, very few individuals used cell phones due to the expense and relative unfamiliarity of them, but today, most adults (and many children) have cell phones. Today, the Internet is used for business transactions such as: online trading of goods and services; electronic retailing (known as *e-Tailing*); business research; business management activities; website marketing; business communications; and online staff training (known as *e-Learning*). It will be interesting to see which new applications, software, and storage options will enter the market in the future and change the way e-business is conducted.

E-business is more than just having a web site. Daily activities, such as online banking, adjusting supplies and inventory, taking sales orders, or hiring staff can be done completely online. Using e-business tools properly can improve efficiencies in business operations, so it is important for businesses to remain current.

concept check

Explain the difference between e-business and e-commerce.

SOCIAL MEDIA

fitim bushati/Sbutterstock.com

The social media craze has arrived, and businesses realize the power in its use, both good and bad. Virtually anything can be shared on the Internet, which makes social media a powerful tool but also potentially dangerous for businesses and individuals alike. Social media is any form of electronic or online communication where users share personal information, videos, personal messages, or other ideas. You are likely familiar with many of these applications, such as Twitter, Pinterest, Facebook, YouTube, or LinkedIn.[12]

Social media: Any form of electronic or online communication where users share personal information, videos, personal messages, or other ideas.

FACEBOOK

Facebook was established in 2004 and is the most popular form of social media thus far in history. With over 1.65 billion active users in the first quarter of 2016, the site allows users to create profiles and share information including updates, videos, photos, and messages with others. Facebook has become one of the most popular methods of staying in touch with individuals you know, and some that you don't want to remember!

In business, using social media tools like a Facebook fan page are popular, low-cost ways to promote businesses, generate positive buzz for new products, or connect with customers in a positive ways. Facebook has become a major marketing tool for businesses today, and special offers are frequently available through a company's Facebook page, which the company hopes you share with others using other social media, such as Twitter.

image courtesy of the author

With social media like Facebook, individuals can easily post pictures, events, and personal life happenings, such as the author's selfie in Italy!

TWITTER

Twitter is another social media tool that allows registered users to send short messages (called "tweets") to "followers". Tweeting is limited to 140 characters, so tweets must be clear and concise. Over 500 million tweets are created every day, and companies now use Twitter as a low-cost, direct marketing tool to post regular tweets about product offerings or special deals to customers.[13] It is an easy way to respond to customer queries, too. Like Facebook, Twitter can be a very effective tool in promoting a company and influencing customer behavior, but caution must be used so that negative tweets or reactions to company products don't get re-tweeted.

LINKEDIN

image courtesy of the author

Be sure all pictures posted on social media are professional and reflect what you want an employer to see.

LinkedIn is a social media tool used by business professionals. It is a method to network with others in a particular company, industry, or area of interest. Users create profiles and form professional relationships by "connecting" with other users. Users typically list their professional skills, education, and work history in their profile in hopes that others will view them and endorse their competencies and skills. Companies use LinkedIn as a low-cost recruiting tool by posting open positions or searching for keywords in individual profiles.

OTHER SOCIAL MEDIA TOOLS

There are several additional social media tools that are currently popular for business and personal use. Pinterest allows users to share collections of pictures, images, text, or web page links by creating "boards" to organize them. This is a great promotion tool for companies to use as other users can "repin" content, which increases exposure for the company.[14] Additional social media applications, such as Instagram, Vine, and Snapchat are used in the marketplace and businesses must determine how to use them appropriately to meet their strategic and marketing goals.

SOCIAL MEDIA TRENDS

With the fast-paced development of technology, social media trends continue to change. Businesses must be aware of trends and social media applications being used by individuals in order to capitalize on them for business purposes. This is

an on-going process, which will include many changes over the next few years. What is popular today will not likely be popular in the future, so it is important to develop new tools and promote innovation in businesses. With a little imagination and business acumen, maybe you will be the one to create the next "Facebook" or "Twitter" idea!

WRAPPING UP...

Technology is an area that is out of date as quickly as individuals can write or publish about it. However, it is important to understand the need for technology within business organizations and how it is used to help make better decisions, reduce costs, and increase productivity. There are many exciting developments in technology, which will shape how we work and live in the future.

In Chapters 12 and 13, we shift our focus from how an organization operates to how you, as an individual, can prepare yourself for a career and gain financial freedom. Understanding business extends beyond how a company functions and applies to you functioning in the world of business as an employee and consumer. We hope you find the information useful as you start, or broaden, your journey in the world of business.

BUSINESS TERMINOLOGY

Data	Intranet
Information	Extranet
Big data	Cybercrime
Data warehouse	Malware
Data mining	Viruses
Information system	Spyware
Chief Information Officer (CIO)	WORM
Operational support system (OSS)	Trojan horse
Management Information System (MIS)	Computer security
	Cloud computing
Hardware	On-demand computing (ODC)
Software	Internet of Everything (IoE)
Local area network (LAN)	Distributed workforce
Wide area network (WAN)	E-business
Wi-Fi	E-commerce
Internet	Social media
Uniform Resource Locator (URL)	

DISCUSSION QUESTIONS

1. Is it advantageous for businesses to offer free Wi-Fi access to patrons? Why or why not?

2. How are information systems vulnerable to disasters? And, what type of back-up systems should be in place to prevent such disasters?

3. What are companies doing to prevent hackers from attacking individual and company accounts or computer systems? Should they do more?

4. What advantages and disadvantages exist when using cloud computing?

5. Explain why is it important for managers to have access to different MIS software.

6. What e-business tools are you familiar with and/or do you use regularly?

LEARNING ACTIVITIES

1. In a small group, discuss examples of how technology has helped you personally and/or professionally. Have you experienced negative effects of using technology personally or professionally?

2. Identity theft is a concern for many individuals, particularly with the increase in incidents over the past few years. Research how to avoid identity theft and create a list of five things individuals can do to help protect themselves from becoming victims.

3. Research an example of a company who has dealt with a security breach or hacking of some type. Explain how the breach occurred, how the company handled communication with customers and the public, and how it changed its procedures to protect information moving forward.

4. Technology has changed the way education can be (and is) offered by many institutions through the use of web-blended classes, online classes, online academies, and massive open online courses (MOOCs) where students can learn and earn college credits for free. Discuss the advantages and disadvantages of having higher education accessible online for free. Would you be interested in getting a degree by taking MOOCs?

5. Debate the pros and cons of piracy in relation to music, movies, books, etc. that are available on the Internet. Do you believe that information should be free to all who have access to it or should the creators be entitled to compensation for their work? How does this affect you as a consumer?

Note: *Because web sites often change, use a search engine to find alternative web sites to access required information when necessary.*

CASE STUDY: TO HACK OR NOT TO HACK?

Alyson Cunningham was fired from a law firm in Pittsburgh, PA. In retaliation, a mutual friend, Matthew West, was encouraged to log onto the law firm's server using an internal company password provided by Alyson Cunningham over Facebook. Using a VPN proxy service located in Germany, West installed software on the server that was used to capture passwords of anyone on the company's network.

On November 29, 2011, West sent one of the partners at the law firm an email from an Anonymous account stating that their servers had been compromised and their backup files had been copied and deleted. (Anonymous is an activist group that hacks into accounts for political reasons.) The e-mail further stated that "we are not interested in ruining your business, but routinely checking that business is fair and just. Our motive is to solely capture and record 100 percent of Pittsburgh business records and operations and protect it or use it against you as we could if Anonymous had a reason and needed to (para. 4)."

In the end, the three guilty parties were caught discussing the "hack" on Alyson's Skype account. The Federal Bureau of Investigation conducted the investigation that led to the prosecution of Jonathan Cunningham, 29, and Alyson Cunningham, 25, both of Pittsburgh, PA. The couple plead guilty in federal court to charges of recklessly damaging a computer and password trafficking. The law provides for a total sentence of two years in prison, a fine of $200,000, or both.[15] After being held on bond, the couple was sentenced to 3 years of probation, computer monitoring, 300 hours of community service, and had to pay $2445.96 in restitution. In addition, the couple must inform future employers of the conviction.[16]

CASE STUDY ANALYSIS

Based on the information provided, answer the following questions:

(1) Who within the company is responsible for keeping confidential information secure?

(2) How can the business clientele know if it's safe to provide their information to this (or any) business?

(3) Was the sentence for the Cunningham's appropriate? Why or why not?

CHAPTER 12

PERSONAL FINANCE

"A good financial plan is a road map that shows us exactly how the choices we make today will affect our future."
~Alexa Von Tobel, New York Times Bestselling author of *Financially Fearless*

OUTCOMES:

➤ Understand how wealth accumulates based on interest rates and time.
➤ Differentiate between fixed and adjustable mortgage rates.
➤ Explain investment options, such as savings, stocks, bonds, and mutual funds.
➤ Compare and contrast various retirement savings options.
➤ Define whole life and term insurance options.

arka38/Shutterstock.com

In the past, employees worked for 40–45 years and often retired using Social Security payments and a pension to live on. Today, employees of all ages face the reality that Social Security may not provide the same level of benefits as it did in the past few decades. Certainly, you have heard about Social Security running out in the near future, leaving millions of workers without any form of retirement savings. This statement does not provide an accurate picture of what will really happen. Many politicians say that the system needs to be fixed, but few are providing viable plans for fixing it (at least not loudly enough for the public to hear). Although, it is true that the Social Security Trust Fund may run out if not altered, it is not true that individuals will receive nothing.

There are two components of how Social Security payments are determined, one being taxes collected and the other being the Trust Fund, which is the excess Social Security taxes collected (but not paid out). Employees pay into the system every paycheck and then money is taken out of the system to pay benefits to those who have retired. If the taxes that come from paychecks are not enough, then money is taken from the Trust Fund to cover the difference. Previously, there were more taxes collected than were paid out, thus leaving an excess in the Trust Fund. In the future, the amount in taxes will not be enough to pay retirees, so the Trust Fund will run out if the system is not altered to accommodate the change in tax revenues.

Jim Barber/Shutterstock.com

The only way that employees can keep benefits at their current rate is to raise Social Security taxes or have retirees accept lower benefits each month. Neither option is popular, which explains why politicians continue to avoid addressing this issue on a large scale. Some estimates show a drop of around 23 percent in benefits by 2030 if the Trust Fund runs out. This means that employees will have less money in their pockets during their retirement years than previously believed. Individuals will have to plan and save for their retirements in order to make up for the loss in benefits from Social Security payments. Planning for your retirement and how you will make up this difference is important to your personal well-being, financial freedom, and security.[1]

In this chapter, we will examine the importance of having a financial plan, what wealth is, types of debt, investment options, retirement savings, and life insurance options. Although one chapter is not enough to make you an expert, it will help you understand several financial terms and the need to have a financial plan in place as you move forward in your career and life.

FINANCIAL PLANNING

How much money you make determines your standard of living, but how you spend and save your money determines your financial condition. You can "live within your means", which means you spend and save only what you make. Or, you can "live beyond your means", which means you spend more than you make (go into debt) to live a particular lifestyle. Your goal is to live within your means so you gain financial freedom and, hopefully, develop wealth.

Wealth is something that must be planned and managed throughout your life, and there are advantages to starting when you are young. Wealth consists of valuable resources or material possessions. First, money is earned or acquired. Once earned, money must be saved to accumulate wealth. There are many ways to save money, but you also must invest money wisely in order to earn a rate of return that allows you to accumulate wealth. If you hide $25,000 under a mattress today, it won't buy as much 20 years from now as it would today due to inflation. In this case, you would have lost wealth as your purchasing power has decreased. Your goal in creating wealth is to increase your purchasing power and financial stability over time.

Wealth: Building up valuable resources or material possessions.

Financial plan: A road-map to help an individual reach his or her financial goals.

Net worth: The difference between your assets and liabilities.

A great way to build wealth is to create a financial plan, which is a road-map to help an individual reach his or her financial goals. A solid financial plan should include four elements: how to control expenses, how to spend money sensibly, how to save money, and how to invest wisely in order to increase wealth. The goal in developing a financial plan is to increase your net worth, or the difference between your assets and liabilities. You should review your financial plan annually to determine if your goals need to be modified.

Many individuals say that they will save when they make more money; however, saving is about discipline. Even if you save a small amount, it adds up over time and you develop the discipline to save, which is a major factor in successfully implementing your financial plan.

Along with discipline, it is important to understand the power of the interest rate at which you invest. Some investments pay higher rates of interest than others, which makes wealth accumulate at higher levels. The higher the interest rate, the better the growth over time; however, it is important to revisit the risk-reward trade-off discussed in Chapter 1 as higher rates of return come with greater risk. To illustrate, let's use a starting investment of $100 and add $100 each month for 30 years. The following chart shows the difference in the money you will accumulate simply by earning different rates of interest. At 2 percent interest, an individual would have $49,307.48 accumulated, whereas at 12 percent, an individual would have accumulated $308,197.32. The same amount of money has been invested over the 30 years; the only difference is in the interest rate earned. (see **Figure 12.1**).

FIGURE 12.1

Interest Rate Effects on Investments

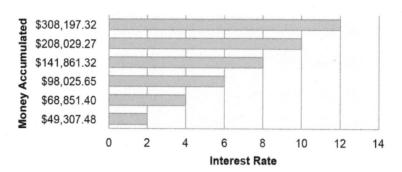

Interest Rate Effects on Investments

concept check

Explain how interest rates are connected to the creation of wealth.

CREDIT SCORES AND REPORTS

zimmytws/Shutterstock.com

Many people do not realize that their credit history can have a tremendous effect on interest rates for loans and potential job offers. Your credit rating determines the amount of risk you pose to a lending company, which is an indication of whether or not you will repay a loan. If you are considered a credit risk, your interest rates will be higher on bank loans and credit cards, your car insurance rates will be higher than others, and if a credit check is conducted by an employer, you might not be considered for a particular job if it relies on your credit rating being high. You might be asking: *How do I know my credit rating?* Understanding what a FICO score is, how it is used, and what is on a credit report will help you on the road to building and maintaining a solid credit rating.

FICO SCORE

Your credit worthiness is determined by your FICO score. Fair Isaac Corporation developed a credit scoring model known as a FICO score, which is the credit score lenders use to assess the amount of risk involved in extending loans to individuals. The main factors used to calculate an individual's FICO score include: one's bill paying history, the length of time credit accounts have been open, the total amount of credit available, and any recent credit activity. Negative factors that affect your FICO score include: late payments, bankruptcies, foreclosures, judgments, and account closures. FICO scores are not affected by race, religion, sex, national origin, or marital status.

FICO score: The credit score lenders use to assess risk in extending loans to individuals.

Once all factors are examined, FICO scores are reported to loaning institutions by three main credit reporting companies: Experian, Equifax, and TransUnion. Each company has a credit classification system that translates information into a credit score and rating, which are displayed in **Table 12.1**.

CREDIT RATING	SCORE
Excellent	750+
Good	700–749
Fair	650–699
Poor	600–649
Bad	Below 600

Table 12.1

Credit Ratings

FICO scores appear on a credit report, which is a report that details an individual's financial history. Areas shown on a credit report include an individual's bill payment history, current debt, place of residence, and information about whether or not an individual has been sued, arrested, or declared bankruptcy. It is important to check your credit report annually so you can monitor it for errors. This can be done for free once every 12 months with each company (Experian, Equifax, and TransUnion) by visiting the web site AnnualCreditReport.com. Many savvy individuals rotate when they check their credit report (for instance, January, April, and September), so they can review it for errors several times a year.

Credit Report: A report detailing your financial history.

Even if you pay your bills on time, it is important to check your credit report annually to see if the information is correct and that all credit inquiries are done by you personally, not someone else. It will not hurt your credit score if you personally review your credit report; however, if lenders continually review it in an attempt for you to open new lines of credit, then it will affect your score.[6]

Negative entries stay on your credit report for up to seven years, so you want to do your best to maintain good credit. If your credit score is not where you want it to be, you can improve it by using the following tips:

1. Pay your bills on time;

2. Do not use all credit available to you;

3. Keep older credit cards to show history with credit;

4. Diversify types of debt (credit card, auto loans, mortgages, student loans, etc.);

5. Leave established credit limits instead of increasing them.[7]

concept check

Why is understanding your credit rating important to you personally and professionally?

TYPES OF DEBT

Most lenders agree that there are good and bad reasons to have debt. Purchasing a home, going to college, or investing in a start-up business are good reasons to have debt if it is repaid within a reasonable amount of time, but buying an expensive car, a designer hand bag or exotic vacation are bad reasons to have debt. Banks use a debt ratio of 36 percent when determining how much an individual can afford to borrow. Thirty-six percent of your gross income is calculated and your monthly debt cannot exceed this amount in order to be deemed a good credit risk. Once you are over this threshold, you become less likely to pay your bills and are considered to be over-extended financially.

Credit cards: Short-term loans issued to consumers to purchase goods and services.

Oliver Hoffmann/Shutterstock.com

Credit cards are short-term loans issued to consumers to purchase goods and services and are offered by banks, credit card companies, and retail stores. Users are given a credit limit based on their income and credit history and pay a fee (in the form of interest) for using credit. Ideally, individuals should pay off the balance at the end of each month to avoid interest payments; however, the average household credit card debt carried over each month in the United States is over $7200.[2] If a cardholder pays $288/month, it will take almost 13 years at 18.9 percent interest to pay off the debt—and that is if no other purchases are made. This means that the cardholder would pay over $4500 in interest alone, so be sure that what you are purchasing on a credit card is worth the use of credit.

College loan debt is the amount of debt incurred by a student while attending a post-secondary institution. In 2016, 71 percent of individuals with a bachelor's degree held some type of college loan debt, with an average debt of $37,172, which included college tuition, text books, fees, and living expenses.[3] Although education is expensive, it is still a good investment. In 2013, individuals with bachelor's degrees made a median salary of $62,300/year, whereas those with a high school diploma made $34,000/year. Those with some college or a 2-year degree made $39,000, so having any type of education beyond high school is worthwhile. Other benefits to having a college degree include lower unemployment levels and career advancement opportunities that might not otherwise exist without the education.[4]

zimmytws/Shutterstock.com

◀ College loan debt: The amount of debt incurred by a student while attending a post-secondary institution.

It is important to have a college degree or formal training; however, if you have to take out considerable debt to complete post-secondary training or education, you might consider other options beyond loans in order to avoid huge debt. Working while attending school, attending a community college, applying for scholarships, or working for an employer who offers tuition reimbursement as part of their benefits will help reduce the amount of debt you take on as you complete your education.

Car loan: A loan from a bank, credit union, or finance company to purchase an automobile.

A car loan is a loan from a bank, credit union, or finance company to purchase an automobile. Loans usually range from 1 to 7 years depending on the year of the automobile, how much you want your monthly payment to be, and who is financing the loan. It is important to consider the value of your car when the loan is paid off as well as the cost of owning the car over the lifetime of the loan. Remember, the value of a car drops when you drive it off of the dealer's lot, so be careful not to over-pay for a car that won't be worth the investment.

◀ Mortgage: Loan used to buy real estate.

PITI: Total monthly mortgage payments including principal, interest, taxes, and insurance..

A mortgage is a loan used to buy real estate, such as a house, townhome, or condominium. Loans can be made through banks, credit unions, or other financial institutions. The mortgage loan agreement varies based on the loan amount, length of the loan, and interest rate. A term commonly used for the total monthly mortgage payment amount is PITI (pronounce "pity"), which stands for Principal, Interest, Taxes, and Insurance (PITI). *Principal* is the amount of money borrowed; *interest* refers to the interest rate paid on the loan; *taxes* depend on where you live and the value of the home; and *insurance* includes both private property insurance as well as private mortgage insurance to cover the lender if the borrower cannot repay the loan.[5]

emilie zhang/Shutterstock.com

Common types of mortgage loans include fixed-rate mortgages and adjustable-rate mortgages. A **fixed-rate mortgage** is a loan where the interest rate stays the same throughout the life of the loan. This is typically the best route for most home buyers. The benefit to this is that the payment doesn't change even if market interest rates do; however, this could be a drawback if interest rates drop lower than the interest rate you secured when you borrowed the money. If that happens, you can refinance the loan amount at the lower rate if you still owe several years on the loan.

An **adjustable-rate mortgage (ARM)**, also referred to as a "variable-rate mortgage" or a "floating-rate mortgage", is a loan where the interest rate changes with market conditions. The initial interest rate is typically fixed for a set time period (1–5 years) and adjusts based on market interest rates. If interest rates go up, the monthly interest portion of the loan goes up as well. Buyers may not be able to afford the new payment and could default on a loan if interest rates increase a great deal. This type of loan may be useful if an individual can pay off a loan in less than five years or will move to another location and pay-off the loan within that timeframe.

Visual3Dfocus/Shutterstock.com

Paying off a mortgage early allows you to reduce the interest owed on the loan. It is wise to pay a little more on the principal each month, which reduces the overall interest paid on the loan. For example, a $100,000 mortgage paid over 30 years at a 4 percent interest rate would require a monthly payment of $477. By paying $606/month (an additional $129), the borrower could pay off the home in only 20 years and save over $26,000 in interest payments. Another easy way to pay off a home more quickly is to pay one extra mortgage payment per year, which would reduce the loan by approximately 7 years and save thousands of dollars in interest.

concept check

What types of debt are considered good debt? Bad debt?

INVESTMENT OPTIONS

In order to build wealth, it is important for an investor to understand what options exist in the financial marketplace. Most investors use a combination of investment options in order to grow wealth throughout their lifetime. A **portfolio** includes all assets or financial holdings of an investor. Typically, an individual's portfolio includes many types of investments, which is known as diversification. Diversifying your portfolio means having many investment options so risk is spread between them. By doing so, an investor doesn't lose everything if one option does poorly in the market. Examples of investment options include: art, collectibles, stocks, bonds, real estate, mutual funds, and precious metals. **Figure 12.2** displays various portfolio options available to investors. The following information explains several investment options an individual may select in order to minimize risk within the portfolio and build wealth over time.

Diversification: Investing in many assets or investments to reduce risk.

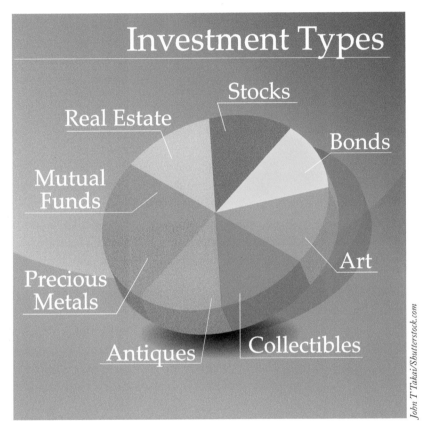

Figure 12.2

Portfolio Options for Investors

John T Takai/Shutterstock.com

Savings is the part of your income not spent or used for immediate expenses. Various saving methods include savings or checking accounts, money market accounts, a certificate of deposit (CD), or emergency cash. A certificate of deposit (CD) is an investment made in a bank for a specified length of time at a specified interest rate. Many people hold CD's as they earn a guaranteed return on their investment, although interest rates in recent years have not been very high.

Stocks are an investment that indicates ownership in a corporation as a shareholder. Holding stock offers the shareholder a claim on a corporation's assets and earnings. Two types of stock include common stock and preferred stock, with the difference being who gets paid first when a company liquidates and in how dividends (payments on each share of stock owned) are paid. Preferred stock owners

Savings: The part of your income not spent or used for immediate expenses.

Certificate of deposit (CD): An investment made in a bank for a specified length of time at a specified interest rate

Stocks: A security that shows ownership in a company.

Shareholder: An individual who owns shares of stock in a company.

Dividends: Earnings on each share of stock owned.

Preferred stock: Stock owners who get paid dividends first and who have priority over common shareholders

have a higher claim on assets and earnings than common stock holders. If the company goes bankrupt, preferred stock holders receive their money before common stock holders. In addition, dividends are paid first to preferred stock owners.

Common stock owners have the right to vote at shareholders' meetings and receive dividends, but they are paid after preferred stock holders and dividends are often less.[8] Although the stock market, over time, is a solid investment, an investor must be willing to lose everything in the stock market. Most financial planners advise clients to invest in the market, particularly when investing at younger ages, as individuals have time to recover from any downturns in the economy when the market drops.

Common stock: Shareholders who vote and earn dividends after preferred stockholders.

Mutual fund: An investment that combines several stocks into one fund.

Bonds: An IOU from an organization.

A mutual fund is managed by an investment company and combines many individual stocks into one investment option. The investment company raises money from individual shareholders and then invests in a variety of assets based on the objectives of the fund. For example, a particular fund's objective may be to invest 90 percent into technology and 10 percent into real estate, so the companies' shares held in the fund would reflect this objective. The benefit of investing in a mutual fund is that it is professionally managed and spreads risk throughout the managed fund instead of holding stocks with only one company.[9]

A bond is an I.O.U. that can be issued by cities, companies or the government for a specific amount of time or money. Grandparents or relatives often give U.S.

savings bonds when their grandchildren are born. The bonds reach their full value after several years. The purchase price of bonds is less than what it is printed on the bond. For example, if you purchase a $200 bond from the U.S. government, it might cost $100 but take 20 years to mature because it grows at a low interest rate. The reason bonds are attractive as an investment is that they are safe, secure, and help an investor diversify (spread out risk). Bonds are offered by organizations because they provide immediate cash flow and can defer payments to investors until a later date.

RETIREMENT PLANNING

As discussed earlier in the chapter, planning and saving for retirement should start early in life and continue through retirement. There are many types of retirement plans an employee can utilize to meet his or her retirement goals. A few of the most popular methods for saving involve the use of a 401K, a 403b, a traditional IRA, or a Roth IRA. Individuals often forget that a house, pension, or savings account are forms of retirement savings as well, so do not forget those assets when determining the best path toward retirement.

- A **401K** is a retirement savings plan supported by an employer in a for-profit business. It lets employees use a portion of their pre-tax or after-tax earnings to invest within various options. Taxes are paid when money is withdrawn from the account, but penalties are assessed if money is taken out early. Many companies match employee contributions up to a certain percentage, which is like getting free money in your retirement savings.

- A **403b**, also known as a tax-sheltered annuity (TSA), is a retirement plan for employees of public schools, churches, hospitals, or the government. It is similar to a 401K as money is invested before taxes are taken out, thereby reducing taxable income for contributors.

- **Traditional IRA's** allow individuals to put money into an account without paying taxes on the amount first. This helps reduce income when it is invested; however, the drawback is that taxes must be paid on the money made, called gains, when the money is withdrawn for retirement or other reasons. In addition, penalties may apply if money is taken out before reaching the age of 59½.

- A **Roth IRA** is similar to a traditional IRA except that money put into a Roth IRA has already been taxed. The benefit in paying taxes up front is that the investment grows tax-free over the investor's lifetime and can be withdrawn tax-free during retirement years if the investor meets certain requirements.[10] Individuals can withdraw investments penalty-free to purchase a home or pay for college.

401K: A retirement savings plan supported by an employer in a for-profit business.

403b: A retirement plan for employees of public schools, churches, hospitals, or the government.

Traditional IRA: A pre-tax investment option.

Roth IRA: An after-tax investment option.

There are many options when creating your individual financial plan, so you should always consult with a financial planner to determine what is best for you personally.

karenfoleyphotography/Shutterstock.com

A goal many individuals strive for is to save one million dollars by the time they retire. In order to save $1,000,000, an individual must save $100 each month at a 7 percent rate of return for 58.5 years. If you increase your savings to $200 each month, you can get to the million dollar mark ten years earlier or in 48 years. Clearly, the more you save, the less time it takes to accumulate your first million. In fact, if you save $2500/month, you will have $1 million in just 17.25 years, which means you could be a millionaire by the time a child graduates from high school if you start investing when he or she is born.[11]

Earlier, we discussed the importance of starting your financial savings at a young age. **Table 12.3** shows the expected value you can anticipate earning at age 67 if you invest $9,000/year (or $750/month) at different ages at a 7 percent interest rate.[12] You can see that waiting until you are older significantly changes the amount you accumulate toward retirement.

TABLE 12.3

Starting Young Matters

STARTING AGE	ANNUAL INVESTMENT	ANNUAL RETURN	VALUE AT AGE 67
25	$9,000	7%	$2,075,690.16
30	$9,000	7%	$1,443,036.62
35	$9,000	7%	$991,963.39
40	$9,000	7%	$670,354.41
45	$9,000	7%	$441,051.65
50	$9,000	7%	$277,561.96
55	$9,000	10%	$160,996.06

Source: IRS (2014). Types of retirement plans. Retrieved on May 13, 2015, from: http://www.irs.gov/Retirement-Plans/Plan-Sponsor/Types-of-Retirement-Plans-1.

Insurance: A risk-reduction policy. .

Another aspect of financial planning is preparing for when something unexpected or catastrophic happens in your life. **Insurance** is one way to counter these unexpected events as it helps with risk reduction. Individuals pay a premium to insurance companies in order to protect their families or their assets. There are many types of insurance including life, automobile, health, or disability insurance. Each of these allows individuals to offset the risk of an

"Do you have a moment to talk about life insurance?"

Cartoonresource/Shutterstock.com

accident and avoid major financial loss. We will discuss health benefits briefly in Chapter 13; so here, we will focus on life insurance options. The most common types of life insurance a person can purchase are whole-life or term-life insurance:

- **Whole-life insurance** is a contract that provides protection for an entire lifetime. Individuals select whole-life insurance to ensure guaranteed premiums and death benefits. In addition, policy holders can accumulate cash value and borrow against it if cash is needed throughout their lifetimes. It is more expensive than term-life insurance and is commonly used by individuals who want the options listed above.

- **Term-life insurance** is typically the cheapest and most affordable coverage because it provides protection for a specific timeframe, such as 10, 15, or 20 years.[13] This is a good option for individuals who want affordable coverage, protection for a specified period of time, help covering mortgage or college expenses should a person become deceased, or to supplement an insurance policy offered at a job. It is important to note that at the end of the term, the policy holds no value.[14]

Whole-life insurance: A contract that provides protection for an entire lifetime.

Term-life insurance: A contract that provides protection for a specified time.

concept check

Why would an individual select a term-life insurance policy over a whole-life policy?

WRAPPING UP...

There are many options for saving and investing, which should be apparent after reviewing the information in Chapter 12. The goal in planning for your financial future is to have financial freedom at every stage of your life. By carefully planning, saving, and investing, you will be able to enjoy the security that comes from financial stability and the freedom to enjoy your life.

In our final chapter, we will examine career opportunities, cover letters and resumes, interviewing skills, and how to find long-term success at work and in life. There are many areas of your career that you cannot control, but there are many areas that you can influence if you have the skills and knowledge to do so.

Brian A Jackson/Shutterstock.com

BUSINESS TERMINOLOGY

Wealth	Certificate of deposit (CD)
Financial plan	Stocks
Net worth	Shareholder
FICO score	Dividends
Credit report	Preferred stock
Credit card	Common stock
College loan debt	Mutual fund
Car loan	Bond
Mortgage	401K
PITI	403b
Fixed-rate mortgage	Traditional IRA
Adjustable-rate mortgage	Roth IRA
Portfolio	Insurance
Diversification	Whole-life insurance
Savings	Term-life insurance

DISCUSSION QUESTIONS

1. Explain the rationale for establishing a financial plan.

2. Why is investing in individual stocks riskier than investing in mutual funds?

3. What type of insurance do you feel is the most important to have? Why?

4. How can a person increase his ability to save? How can an individual on a fixed income manage to save?

5. Do you feel that credit cards are a good thing to possess? Why or why not?

6. As a college student, what steps will you take to increase your wealth moving forward?

LEARNING ACTIVITIES

1. Create a budget for the next month. Include all expenses including rent, food, utilities (cell phones, TV, electric, etc.), entertainment, savings, car payments, and other costs. How much do you earn compared to how much you spend? How much more do you have to earn to live the lifestyle you desire? Where can you cut back in order to save more?

2. Research ways to start using credit wisely, to improve your current credit score, and to understand why having good credit is important. What steps should you take in order to improve or maintain high credit scores?

3. As a college student, research suggestions for using and managing money wisely while you are in college. What types of credit cards, loans, or savings plans should you consider and why? What other areas should you consider now that will make a difference in your financial position after you graduate?

4. Is buying or renting a home better? Find 2–3 articles that support why one is preferable over the other and create a short report that clearly identifies your position.

Note: *Because web sites often change, use a search engine to find alternative web sites to access required information when necessary.*

CASE STUDY: HOW MUCH INSURANCE TO GET?

Mike (50) and Tasha (42) are a middle-aged couple who have decided to get married. Tasha also has two children, ages 15 and 18. Each partner owns a house and is employed. In a recent article, Tasha read that everyone should purchase a life insurance policy. Mike has never owned an insurance policy and feels that it is a waste of money. Tasha has a $10,000 term life policy offered by her employer.

They visited a financial planner who stated that, ideally, they should have 1½ times their annual income worth of insurance. They were both surprised at this number. As they sat down and figured this out, it was determined that Mike should have a $150,000 term policy and Tasha a $250,000 whole-life policy.

CASE STUDY ANALYSIS

Based on the information provided, answer the following questions:

(1) If you were the financial planner, how would you convince Mike of the value in buying life insurance?

(2) Do you agree with the decision to have both term and whole-life policies for Mike and Tasha? Explain your answer.

(3) Beyond providing for each other in the case of death, what other benefits might a life insurance policy provide for Mike and Tasha?

CHAPTER 13

PLANNING FOR CAREER SUCCESS

"The only way to do great work is to love what you do."
~Steve Jobs, Co-founder of Apple Inc.

OUTCOMES:

➢ Identify career options available in the marketplace and how to locate available positions.

➢ Understand the value in networking as a tool in career planning and professional development.

➢ Describe effective application materials including a cover letter and resume.

➢ Demonstrate professional behaviors related to etiquette, dressing for success, and interviewing.

➢ Analyze various benefit packages offered to employees.

Career Choices

Maridav/Shutterstock.com

Now that you have had the opportunity to learn and understand what businesss is about, it is time to examine where you want to be as you complete your degree and begin your career. Thinking about what you love to do will direct you to areas that may guide your career. Remember, every job relates to business, so regardless of what you decide to do, the information you have learned throughout the text will support your decision. In our final chapter, we will discuss how to function in the business world and how to position yourself to obtain the types of opportunities you desire as you search, apply, and interview for available positions in the workforce.

FASTEST GROWING CAREERS IN THE UNITED STATES

Making decisions about what you want to do for a career should be grounded in information and knowledge. While there are still farmers in the United States, the number has dramatically decreased over the past 125 years. It is important to understand trends and changes in employment patterns as what you choose to do today may not be in existence several years from now. Various industries tend to grow faster in job creation than others in response to societal needs and demands. **Table 13.1** shows industries with an expected growth rate of at least 25 percent between 2014–2024.[1]

TABLE 13.1

Industries and Job Positions

INDUSTRY	JOB TITLE	PERCENT GROWTH
HEALTH CARE	Ocuupational Therapy Assistant	43%
	Physical Therapist Assistant	41%
	Physical Therapy Aides	39%
	Home Health Aide	38%
BUSINESS	Statisticians	34%
	Personal Financial Advisors	30%
TECHNOLOGY	Wind Turbine Service Technicians	108%
	Information Security Analyst	36.5%
SOCIAL SERVICES	Interpreter and Translator	29%
	Genetic Counselors	29%

Source: Bureau of Labor (2016). US Department of Labor: Occupational Outlook Handbook, 2016-17 edition. Fastest growing occupations. Retrieved on May 23, 2016, from: http://bls.gov.ooh/astest-growing.htm.

Although this list is not all-inclusive, it gives a good idea about industries that will see the most growth and highest demand for workers. A closer look shows trends in the world including: caring for an aging population; catering to world needs for increased products and services; population growth; increased infrastructure and construction; increased concerns related to technology; and an increase in the need for social services as we deal with cultural barriers.

SALARY COMPARISONS BASED ON EDUCATIONAL LEVEL

Many individuals wonder if the trade-off for obtaining a post-secondary education is worth it. The simple answer is yes, it is worth it; however, there are considerable costs (as mentioned in Chapter 12) that are associated with obtaining an education. However, if an individual does receive a college degree, the earning potential over one's lifetime increases dramatically. Although an education doesn't guarantee increased earnings, the opportunities and earning potential are greater when you possess a degree than when you do not. Your motivation, desire, and work ethic play a major role in your success, with or without a degree.

Table 13.2 displays the difference in annual earnings and unemployment rates based on various levels of education. It is important to note that there is a correlation between educational level and unemployment. Not only do you make more money with a degree, but you are less likely to be unemployed.[2]

LEVEL OF EDUCATION	MEDIAN SALARY	UNEMPLOYMENT RATE
NO HIGH SCHOOL DIPLOMA	$25,376	9.0%
HIGH SCHOOL DIPLOMA	$34,736	6.0%
SOME COLLEGE, NO DEGREE	$38,532	6.0%
ASSOCIATE'S DEGREE	$41,184	4.5%
BACHELOR'S DEGREE	$57,252	3.5%
MASTER'S DEGREE	$68,952	2.5%
PROFESSIONAL DEGREE	$85,228	1.9%
DOCTORAL DEGREE	$82,732	2.1%

TABLE 13.2

Comparison Between Education, Salary, and Unemployment

Source: Bureau of Labor Statistics (2015). Employment Projections, United States Department of Labor, Retrieved on May 14, 2015, from: http://www.bls.gov/emp/ep_chart_001.htm.

NOW WHAT?

Once individuals finish a degree, they often wonder what to do next. The process of making career choices and decisions can be overwhelming and requires a great deal of time and effort. Career development is an area that you will continue to focus on throughout your working life. **Figure 13.1** displays the career development cycle, which begins with assessing yourself, exploring options, developing your skills, marketing yourself, performing, and finding success.

FIGURE 13.1

Career Development
Process

arka38/Shutterstock.com

SELF-ASSESSMENTS & EXPLORING OPTIONS

There are many individuals who are unsure about what type of job they want to do "when they grow up". Truthfully, most people evolve into the career that they retire from, so early in your career, work to find something that fits your strengths and areas of interest. Completing a self-assessment, many of which are available online, provides some guidance as to what type of position you may be interested in. Knowing what areas interest you will help you plan a pathway to success and enjoy the work you do each day.

There are a plethora of assessments that can help a person understand who they are and what interests they have. Assessments can be grouped into the following categories (although this is not an exhaustive list):

1. *Personality and Type Indicators*, such as the Myers-Briggs Type Indicator (MBTI), which indicates how individuals see the world and make decisions;

2. *Interest Inventories*, such as the RIASEC personality model, which sorts people into Realistic (Doers), Investigative (Thinkers), Artistic (Creators), Social (Helpers), Enterprising (Persuaders), and Conventional (Organizers);

3. *Skills Surveys* designed to help define abilities and qualifications;

4. *Values Inventories* which help determine what individuals value or feel is important when making career choices; and

5. *Other Tools and Resources* such as The Career Decision-making Difficulties Questionnaire (CDDQ) can help you rationalize why you might be experiencing problems making a career decision and propose a plan to help you.[3]

Sometimes businesses have candidates take assessment tests prior to being hired to see if applicants are a good fit for the organization. Using assessments may help you focus on areas where you find interest and that best fit your personality.

LOCATING AVAILABLE POSITIONS

One of the key elements to success is finding available positions. Most people rely on the newspaper or online job postings when less than 20 percent of all available positions are filled this way. The majority of available positions are filled internally (from within the organization) or through referrals from others. To be successful when job hunting, you must know and understand the tools required to find and obtain available positions.[4] Every resource should be used when searching available positions. Calling recruiters, volunteering, attending professional association conferences and meetings, and networking are all excellent methods for reaching out to individuals who may be hiring or know of positions available in a given field.

tommasolizzul/Shutterstock.com

The first and most important tool for job searching is networking. **Networking** is relationship building for employment or business purposes. Over 70 percent of job hires come through networking, so it matters who you know as well as what you know.[5] Networking can be done informally or formally, but job-seekers should be careful not to interact with others only for employment purposes as others will see that as disingenuous. Letting people know what you can do and your desire to move up in an organization or field is acceptable and encouraged when done properly.

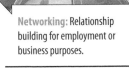

Networking: Relationship building for employment or business purposes.

Online sources include all Internet-based tools that allow job seekers to quickly identify job opportunities, research companies' information, and submit resumes. When searching the Internet, common career websites such as LinkedIn, Vault, Indeed, Monster, Glassdoor, or

iQoncept/Shutterstock.com

SimplyHired are often used to locate information, post resumes, or research companies' information. In addition to large sites, it is wise to research postings on individual company web sites as many companies post there before posting to larger sites or using other forms of advertising. Companies do search online activities and information, so be sure your Internet trail represents you professionally. **Table 13.3** provides various types of job search and networking opportunities and the type of services they offer.

TABLE 13.3

Sources to Research
Available Positions

TYPE	SERVICES
Company web sites	Allow you to search job postings within a specific company.
Government web sites	Allow you to search positions in governmental agencies.
Placement centers	Staffing companies work with companies and/or applicants to place qualified candidates.
Internships	Working for an organization prior to gaining full-time employment, can lead to a full-time position or connections for later employment.
Job shadowing	Working with a company employee to gain valuable insight about a company, allows for networking to take place as well.
Career centers	Typically part of a college or university, centers offer employment-related services such as resume development, job listings, or internship options to students and alumni.

concept check

Discuss various options for finding available jobs in the marketplace.

APPLICATION MATERIALS

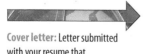

Cover letter: Letter submitted with your resume that indicates your interest in a particular position.

Once you have determined the type of job you are seeking and locate available positions, application materials must be prepared and sent. A **cover letter** is a letter submitted with your resume that indicates your interest in a particular position. It is an important selling tool because it is typically the first item human resource employees see from you.

A cover letter should contain an opening paragraph stating which job you are applying for, a paragraph that briefly describes your skills, a third paragraph that shares why you believe you are a good fit for the organization, and a conclusion that asks for the opportunity to speak with the company about the available position. If done properly, the cover letter will inspire the company to ask you for an interview. The cover letter should be one page in length and include all of your contact information (name, address, email, and phone number). Spelling and grammar are important in all written materials, so be sure to have someone review all letters and resumes prior to sending them to potential employers.

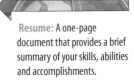

A resume provides a brief summary of your skills, abilities and accomplishments. It is a quick overview of who you are, what positions you have held in your career, and the level of education you have obtained. A resume must be clear and concise as the average time spent reviewing a resume by human resources (to determine if you are a fit for the organization) is *six seconds*. HR quickly looks for your name, your current position and how long you have been there, your former position(s) and how long you were there, and your educational level.[6] There are several types of resumes applicants can use when applying for positions. Three of the most commonly used resume formats are discussed below.

Resume: A one-page document that provides a brief summary of your skills, abilities and accomplishments.

TYPES OF RESUMES

A chronological resume is the most common type of resume because it focuses on the most recent work experience first and then works backward. Employers like this type of resume because it shows a snapshot of an applicant's history. This type of resume is best if your work experience aligns with the job you are applying for and you have had continued employment throughout your career.

A functional resume focuses on your skills and experience first and then lists work history. This type of resume is most often used by individuals who are changing careers, are new to the job market (college grads!), or have gaps in their employment history. Using a functional resume highlights the applicant's competencies, specific skills, and capabilities.

A targeted resume is customized for a specific position to which an applicant is applying. Everything on the resume mirrors what the employer is looking for in potential candidates. Creating a targeted resume is time-consuming, but, if done correctly, can be highly effective in obtaining a position. However, it is important to be truthful and accurate on your resume.[7]

Chronological resume: A resume that focuses on the most recent work experience.

Functional resume: A resume that focuses on your skills and experience first.

Targeted resume: A resume that is customized for a specific position.

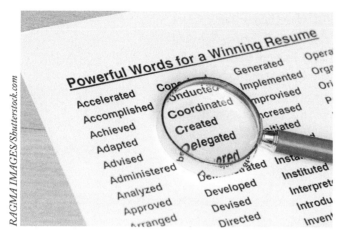
RAGMA IMAGES/Shutterstock.com

It is important to keep resumes to one-page in length, professional, and free of slang or jargon. References and salary requirements are not necessary on a resume unless specifically asked for by an employer. Finally, do not include a picture of yourself as it can be used to discriminate against you, intentionally or unintentionally.

Many companies request electronic resumes, which are formatted differently than paper versions. Electronic resumes are entered into a database, which allows human resources employees the ability to search for keywords or phrases from submitted resumes. Most companies state how to apply for open positions, but if a job posting does not specify which type of resume a company desires, consider personally submitting your cover letter and resume in order to put a face to your application materials. Be careful not to interrupt a meeting and do not expect time with the hiring manager, but personal delivery can be a positive touch when applying for a job with many applicants.[8]

concept check

Compare and contrast different types of resumes.

INTERVIEWING SKILLS

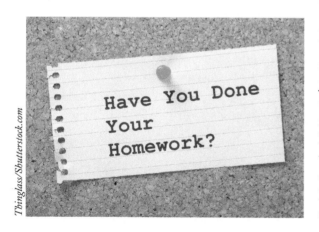
Thinglass/Shutterstock.com

It is exciting to have a company call and request an interview after reviewing your application materials, but it can also make you nervous thinking about the interviewing process. Preparing for the interview is just as important as networking and preparing quality application materials and preparation will help you be more confident. It is wise to practice interviewing and learn about the company with whom you will be interviewing. Simple research allows you to ask and answer questions intelligently, which shows you took time to learn about the company. This could give you an edge above other candidates who do not prepare.

As you prepare for and go into the interview, here are some suggestions to help you be more relaxed and ready:

- *Dress for success*: Wear proper business attire to the interview, which is determined by the type of position and environment in which you will work. The rule of thumb is to dress one or two levels above the position you are applying for, meaning if you will wear casual pants each day to the office, then wear a suit to the interview. If a suit is required, men should wear a suit and polished dress shoes, and women should wear a suit with appropriate dress shoes. Although dress codes vary by organization and industry, it is important to dress professionally as first impressions influence hiring decisions.

- *Use proper etiquette*: Show up 10 minutes before your appointment and turn off your cell phone. Give a firm handshake and address the person(s) with the appropriate title (Mr., Ms., Dr.). Be courteous and enthusiastic at all times—avoid negative comments or reactions to questions.

Paul Vasarhelyi/Shutterstock.com

- *Communicate well*: Utilize proper English and avoid using slang or inappropriate language in the interview, even if the person interviewing does this. Demonstrate that you are a professional at all times and use proper communication skills.

- *Ask questions*: Employers expect applicants to ask questions. When you ask thought-provoking questions, you collect valuable information and show that you have thoughtfully prepared for the interview. This is a good time to ask about growth opportunities within the organization, to clarify responsibilities, and ask why individuals interviewing like working for the organization. This is not the time to discuss salary, vacation time, or benefits as that discussion will come later in the process.

TYPES OF INTERVIEWS

The reason you go to a job interview is for the company to get to know you and vice versa. The employer wants to review your qualifications, and you can evaluate if you want to work for the company. There are many different types of interviews, so understanding the type of interview you will experience helps you prepare for it. Some common interviewing formats are listed below:

- *Telephone Screening Interview*: An employer may call you to screen candidates first. Be ready whenever they call and have application materials readily available. Know what your resume says and ask to call back in a few minutes if you need a moment to collect your materials, focus, or go somewhere quiet.

- *In-Person Screening Interview*: Used to verify your qualifications and select candidates to interview. It provides an initial impression of your attitude, interest, and professional style. Sell yourself as you would in a face-to-face interview as it is a step to move you closer to getting hired.

- *Selection Interview*: Used to evaluate a candidate's qualifications with in-depth questions. There may be more than one interview at this stage. Create a relationship and establish rapport with everyone you meet. Sell yourself as a positive addition to the team.

- *Behavioral Interview* (also known as a STAR interview -Situation, Task, Action, and Results): The interviewer will ask questions that require you to describe how you handled past work-related situations such as dealing with conflict, learning a new skill, or working with others. Be prepared by having examples of each type of situation so you don't have to think about it during the interview.

- *Work Sample Interview*: This type of interview provides an opportunity to showcase samples of your work and demonstrate your skills. This type of interview works well for writers, architects, salespeople, or artists.

- *Peer Group Interview*: A meeting with your prospective co-workers, who evaluate how well you fit into the organization.

- *Luncheon Interview*: Conducted in a restaurant or coffee shop to assess how well you handle yourself in social situations. Order healthy and easy things to eat so you can answer questions and pay attention to the conversation. This type of interview is common for individuals who deal with clients often and represent a firm as the company wants to be sure your professionalism and etiquette are appropriate.

- *Stress Interview*: This type of interview is designed to test how an applicant will handle stress on the job by asking questions or creating circumstances where applicants must respond to a stressful situation. Always take your time and keep your composure as it is a reflection of how you will respond in a real situation.

- *Video Conference Interview*: This interview, done using video or online meeting applications, is common for organizations that employ workers in different geographic locations such as airlines or online universities. It allows companies to have face-to-face interaction while saving time, money, and resources. Practice before a video camera or mirror if facing a camera during an interview makes you nervous.[9]

Andrey_Popov/Shutterstock.com

concept check

Understand the types of interviews you may have with an organization.

It is important to remember that an interview is a two-way conversation to determine if the job and company are the right fit for you. It is possible to have many interviews before landing the right job, so learn from each interview and develop your skills along the way. Only accept a position if you have researched the company and feel that it is a good fit for you and the company. Otherwise, you will be unhappy and will soon be looking for another position. Researching and practicing for a job interview will get you one step closer to being hired, so work at it and soon you will find the job that best suits you!

Immediately following the interview, send a thank-you letter to all of the individuals on the interviewing committee to thank them for their time and the opportunity to interview. At the very least, you should send a thank-you letter to the hiring manager. The thank-you can be sent electronically if the decision to hire will be made quickly; however, if there is time, a personal, hand-written note is highly recommended. Thank the interviewers for their time, state why you are a good fit for the organization, and close by stating that you look forward to hearing from them soon. The letter should be a few paragraphs long and only used to thank individuals for the opportunity to interview. This added touch will remind interviewers who you are and set you apart from the other candidates.

Employee Benefits Package

Summary of Benefits

zimmytws/Shutterstock.com

Total compensation package: Direct and indirect compensation paid to an employee.

Direct compensation: Salaries, hourly wages, or bonuses paid by an employer.

Indirect compensation: All non-paid benefits an employer provides to employees.

One of the greatest feelings in the world is being offered a position in an organization. When an offer is made, it is important to collect details about your **total compensation package**, which includes both the direct and indirect compensation you will receive as an employee of the organization. **Direct compensation** includes all compensation paid to an employee related to an hourly wage, base salary, or incentive pay. **Indirect compensation** involves compensation in the form of employer-paid benefits such as tuition reimbursement or paid time off. While each employer is unique in their offerings, most total compensation packages typically include the following:

- Salary or hourly pay rate;
- Medical benefits—including employee and employer-paid amounts;
- Flexible spending account information;
- Paid leave—including vacation, sick, paid-time-off (PTO), holiday, personal, bereavement, military pay, jury duty, etc.;
- Disability insurance;
- Life insurance;
- Employee assistance programs;
- Retirement benefits—including 401(k), 403(b), pension plans, etc.;
- Tuition reimbursement programs; and
- Relocation expenses.[10]

Be careful not to look only at salary or wages when deciding to accept a position. Benefits account for 20–30 percent of your total compensation package, so review what an employer offers in combination with a salary or wages. With the rising costs of health care and education, it may be wise to take a lesser salary in order to have better indirect compensation.[11]

Once you are employed and working, there will be challenges and rewards that you face on a daily basis. Knowing how to deal with different individuals and continuing to learn new skills will help you find greater levels of success. Another area that is important is maintaining a healthy work-life balance, which we discussed earlier in the textbook. Being content with your choices will allow you to focus on the good things in life. Remember that a balance between work and family will create a "healthier, happier" you.

The ability to work with others, regardless of age, gender, ability, nationality, or race is paramount to your success in a global economy. A research scientist from the Center for Creative Leadership debunks the myth that there are striking differences between generations, stating that all people have: a need for respect, value family, want to trust leadership, dislike change, appreciate feedback, and are willing to learn new things. Knowing that different generations have something to offer will help you to identify and work within those dynamics. One of the main focal points of working with others is communication and understanding. Just like in any relationship, it takes patience, determination, and the desire to get the job done.[12]

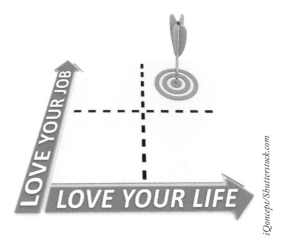

As we close this introduction to the world of business, we want to leave you with a few keys to success in the workplace. You have what it takes to succeed, but just simply need to polish your skills and keep your focus on what is important. Here are a few keys to success that will help guide your career:

- **Be competent**: Continue to improve your skills and learn new ones. The world changes quickly, so it is important to remain current.

- **Be conscientious**: Doing things well the first time allows you to complete more as well as be given more opportunities. No one gets to the top by doing nothing, so be sure that you pay attention to details and complete work on time.

- **Have common sense**: Seeing the big picture, understanding workplace and social interactions, and figuring out the unspoken rules at work and in society allow you to have common sense. This type of social intelligence is important for leaders at all levels and makes you valued and respected as a human being.[13]

WRAPPING UP...

All of the areas listed in this chapter are important for you in order to obtain a position within an organization, but the most important factor in your job search is seeking a job that makes you happy. The definition of success at work is the ability to do the job well, feeling a sense of accomplishment, having the boss and co-workers respect you, and enjoying going to work each day. While no job is perfect, taking the time to select a position in an organization that will make you happy will go a long way in helping you find success at every stage throughout your career.

BUSINESS TERMINOLOGY

Networking
Cover letter
Resume
Chronological resume
Functional resume

Targeted resume
Total compensation package
Direct compensation
Indirect compensation

DISCUSSION QUESTIONS

1. Think of at least five people you know and write their names on a piece of paper. Develop a networking model to illustrate how many people you know based on these five people and explain how they can help in your job search.

2. How can you identify your strengths and areas of improvement when searching for a job or career? How might you develop any areas needing improvement?

3. How would you explain to a prospective student that obtaining a degree can help him or her financially?

4. What type of resume would you create to best highlight your skills, educational achievements, and abilities? Explain how your choice highlights your skills better than other resume options.

5. How do you personally determine the balance between work and family life?

LEARNING ACTIVITIES

1. Select a company you would be interested in working for in the future (or one that you currently work for and wish to advance within). Research current jobs available within the company using online job web sites or the company's web site. Create a list of benefits available to employees of the company. Once your research is completed, discuss whether you believe the company and the position are still a good fit for you.

2. Using knowledge from the chapter as well as information from web sites, prepare a one-page resume that highlights your education, skills, and work history. Be sure to include only required information. Submit your resume to two other people in order to obtain feedback. Revise your resume using the feedback from others.

3. Work with your institution's Career Center (or another source) and participate in a mock interview. Dress appropriately, be professional, and ask questions. Once the interview is complete, ask the interviewer for feedback about how to improve for future interviews. Use this as practice for real interviews, where feedback is seldom offered.

4. Locate a job opening in your field of interest and write a clear, concise cover letter using the techniques listed in the chapter and on web sites. Be sure to include how your qualifications match those the employer is seeking and research why the company is a good fit for your skills, education, and experience. Submit your letter to your instructor or to classmates for feedback and then have the courage to send it to the employer and apply for the job!

Note: *Because web sites often change, use a search engine to find alternative web sites to access required information when necessary.*

CASE STUDY: MASTER THE SOCIAL NETWORKING WORLD

Job seekers could learn something from Jessie Easton about looking for work through social networks. While a graduate student in computer science at the University of Wisconsin, Jessie began using a certain collaboration platform, which she liked a great deal. She decided to contact the company to see if they currently had any part-time job openings in the Madison, WI area. She sent the company a cover letter and resume, which the company found fit their needs, so they offered her a part-time position. When Jessie moved to the West Coast after graduation, the company hired her full-time in the San Francisco Bay area.

Later, Jessie applied for and earned a new job at a different company because of a newsfeed that she had set up on one of her favorite websites. "Everyone pretty much uses social media out there," says Jessie. "It is all networking based, whether using Facebook, or Twitter, or any networking events. Social media is just another way to network."

CASE STUDY ANALYSIS

Based on the information provided, answer the following questions:

(1) What did Jessie do to get her initial job that was innovative in thought?

(2) What did Jessie do after she obtained her original job that gave her flexibility and options for future opportunities?

(3) How does using social media benefit job seekers? What drawbacks exist when using social media?

APPENDIX A

FUTURE AND PRESENT VALUE

OUTCOMES:

➤ Understand how to calculate the future value of a lump sum.
➤ Understand how to calculate the present value of a lump sum.
➤ Understand how to calculate the future value of an annuity.
➤ Understand how to calculate the present value of an annuity.

FUTURE AND PRESENT VALUE CALCULATIONS

CALCULATING THE FUTURE VALUE OF A LUMP SUM

Calculating a future value means that you want to know how much an investment today will be worth in the future. In this case, a one-time payment is deposited and left to grow at a fixed interest rate. Each number in the chart is calculated using the following formula:

$$\text{Future Value (FV)} = \text{Present Value (PV)} \times (1 + i)^n$$

i = interest rate per compounding period
n = number of compounding periods

Example 1

What is the future value of $10,000 invested for 4 years at an 8 percent interest rate, compounded quarterly?

Present Value = $10,000
Compounding Periods = 4 years $\times$ 4 times/year (quarterly) = 16
Interest Rate = 8 percent $\div$ 4 times compounding each year = 2 percent interest each quarter

From table above, find the number at the intersection of the 2 percent interest rate column and the 16 period row (1.373). Multiply this number by the amount originally invested ($10,000)

= 1.373 $\times$ $10,000 = **$13,370,** will be the total after 4 years if you invest $10,000 at 8 percent interest rate, compounded quarterly

TABLE A.1

Future Value of a Lump Sum Factors

Future value interest factor of $1 per period at i% for n periods, FVIF(i,n).																			
Period	1%	2%	3%	4%	5%	6%	7%	8%	9%	10%	11%	12%	13%	14%	15%	16%	17%	18%	19%	20%
1	1.010	1.020	1.030	1.040	1.050	1.060	1.070	1.080	1.090	1.100	1.110	1.120	1.130	1.140	1.150	1.160	1.170	1.180	1.190	1.200
2	1.020	1.040	1.061	1.082	1.103	1.124	1.145	1.166	1.188	1.210	1.232	1.254	1.277	1.300	1.323	1.346	1.369	1.392	1.416	1.440
3	1.030	1.061	1.093	1.125	1.158	1.191	1.225	1.260	1.295	1.331	1.368	1.405	1.443	1.482	1.521	1.561	1.602	1.643	1.685	1.728
4	1.041	1.082	1.126	1.170	1.216	1.262	1.311	1.360	1.412	1.464	1.518	1.574	1.630	1.689	1.749	1.811	1.874	1.939	2.005	2.074
5	1.051	1.104	1.159	1.217	1.276	1.338	1.403	1.469	1.539	1.611	1.685	1.762	1.842	1.925	2.011	2.100	2.192	2.288	2.386	2.488
6	1.062	1.126	1.194	1.265	1.340	1.419	1.501	1.587	1.677	1.772	1.870	1.974	2.082	2.195	2.313	2.436	2.565	2.700	2.840	2.986
7	1.072	1.149	1.230	1.316	1.407	1.504	1.606	1.714	1.828	1.949	2.076	2.211	2.353	2.502	2.660	2.826	3.001	3.185	3.379	3.583
8	1.083	1.172	1.267	1.369	1.477	1.594	1.718	1.851	1.993	2.144	2.305	2.476	2.658	2.853	3.059	3.278	3.511	3.759	4.021	4.300
9	1.094	1.195	1.305	1.423	1.551	1.689	1.838	1.999	2.172	2.358	2.558	2.773	3.004	3.252	3.518	3.803	4.108	4.435	4.785	5.160
10	1.105	1.219	1.344	1.480	1.629	1.791	1.967	2.159	2.367	2.594	2.839	3.106	3.395	3.707	4.046	4.411	4.807	5.234	5.695	6.192
11	1.116	1.243	1.384	1.539	1.710	1.898	2.105	2.332	2.580	2.853	3.152	3.479	3.836	4.226	4.652	5.117	5.624	6.176	6.777	7.430
12	1.127	1.268	1.426	1.601	1.796	2.012	2.252	2.518	2.813	3.138	3.498	3.896	4.335	4.818	5.350	5.936	6.580	7.288	8.064	8.916
13	1.138	1.294	1.469	1.665	1.886	2.133	2.410	2.720	3.066	3.452	3.883	4.363	4.898	5.492	6.153	6.886	7.699	8.599	9.596	10.699
14	1.149	1.319	1.513	1.732	1.980	2.261	2.579	2.937	3.342	3.797	4.310	4.887	5.535	6.261	7.076	7.988	9.007	10.147	11.420	12.839
15	1.161	1.346	1.558	1.801	2.079	2.397	2.759	3.172	3.642	4.177	4.785	5.474	6.254	7.138	8.137	9.266	10.539	11.974	13.590	15.407
16	1.173	1.373	1.605	1.873	2.183	2.540	2.952	3.426	3.970	4.595	5.311	6.130	7.067	8.137	9.358	10.748	12.330	14.129	16.172	18.488
17	1.184	1.400	1.653	1.948	2.292	2.693	3.159	3.700	4.328	5.054	5.895	6.866	7.986	9.276	10.761	12.468	14.426	16.672	19.244	22.186
18	1.196	1.428	1.702	2.026	2.407	2.854	3.380	3.996	4.717	5.560	6.544	7.690	9.024	10.575	12.375	14.463	16.879	19.673	22.901	26.623
19	1.208	1.457	1.754	2.107	2.527	3.026	3.617	4.316	5.142	6.116	7.263	8.613	10.197	12.056	14.232	16.777	19.748	23.214	27.252	31.948
20	1.220	1.486	1.806	2.191	2.653	3.207	3.870	4.661	5.604	6.727	8.062	9.646	11.523	13.743	16.367	19.461	23.106	27.393	32.429	38.338
25	1.282	1.641	2.094	2.666	3.386	4.292	5.427	6.848	8.623	10.835	13.585	17.000	21.231	26.462	32.919	40.874	50.658	62.669	77.388	95.396
30	1.348	1.811	2.427	3.243	4.322	5.743	7.612	10.063	13.268	17.449	22.892	29.960	39.116	50.950	66.212	85.850	111.065	143.371	184.675	237.376
35	1.417	2.000	2.814	3.946	5.516	7.686	10.677	14.785	20.414	28.102	38.575	52.800	72.069	98.100	133.176	180.314	243.503	327.997	440.701	590.668
40	1.489	2.208	3.262	4.801	7.040	10.286	14.974	21.725	31.409	45.259	65.001	93.051	132.782	188.884	267.864	378.721	533.869	750.378	1,051.668	1,469.772
50	1.645	2.692	4.384	7.107	11.467	18.420	29.457	46.902	74.358	117.391	184.565	289.002	450.736	700.233	1,083.657	1,870.704	2,566.215	3,927.357	5,988.914	9,100.438

CALCULATING THE PRESENT VALUE OF A LUMP SUM

Calculating the present value means that you want to know how much you need to invest today in order have it to grow to a specified amount in the future. Again, a one-time payment is deposited and left to grow at a fixed interest rate but you are waiting for the number to reach a certain amount instead of just earning interest. Each number in the chart is calculated using the following formula:

$$PV = \frac{FV}{(1 + i)^n}$$

PV = present value
FV = future value
n = number of compounding periods
i = interest rate

Example 1

What is the present value (PV) of a certificate of deposit (CD) that will pay $100.00 in 3 years if the interest rate is 5 percent compounded annually?

FV = 100.00
i = 5%
n = 3

From table above, go to the intersection of the 5 percent and period three columns, which is 0.864. Multiply 0.864 by the FV ($100):

= 0.864 × $100.00 = **$86.40,** the amount that needs to be invested today to grow to $100.00 in 3 years at 5 percent interest

TABLE A.2

Present Value of a Lump Sum Factors

Present value interest factor of $1 per period at i% for n periods, PVIF(i,n).

Period	1%	2%	3%	4%	5%	6%	7%	8%	9%	10%	11%	12%	13%	14%	15%	16%	17%	18%	19%	20%
1	0.990	0.980	0.971	0.962	0.952	0.943	0.935	0.926	0.917	0.909	0.901	0.893	0.885	0.877	0.870	0.862	0.855	0.847	0.840	0.833
2	0.980	0.961	0.943	0.925	0.907	0.890	0.873	0.857	0.842	0.826	0.812	0.797	0.783	0.769	0.756	0.743	0.731	0.718	0.706	0.694
3	0.971	0.942	0.915	0.889	0.864	0.840	0.816	0.794	0.772	0.751	0.731	0.712	0.693	0.675	0.658	0.641	0.624	0.609	0.593	0.579
4	0.961	0.924	0.888	0.855	0.823	0.792	0.763	0.735	0.708	0.683	0.659	0.636	0.613	0.592	0.572	0.552	0.534	0.516	0.499	0.482
5	0.951	0.906	0.863	0.822	0.784	0.747	0.713	0.681	0.650	0.621	0.593	0.567	0.543	0.519	0.497	0.476	0.456	0.437	0.419	0.402
6	0.942	0.888	0.837	0.790	0.746	0.705	0.666	0.630	0.596	0.564	0.535	0.507	0.480	0.456	0.432	0.410	0.390	0.370	0.352	0.335
7	0.933	0.871	0.813	0.760	0.711	0.665	0.623	0.583	0.547	0.513	0.482	0.452	0.425	0.400	0.376	0.354	0.333	0.314	0.296	0.279
8	0.923	0.853	0.789	0.731	0.677	0.627	0.582	0.540	0.502	0.467	0.434	0.404	0.376	0.351	0.327	0.305	0.285	0.266	0.249	0.233
9	0.914	0.837	0.766	0.703	0.645	0.592	0.544	0.500	0.460	0.424	0.391	0.361	0.333	0.308	0.284	0.263	0.243	0.225	0.209	0.194
10	0.905	0.820	0.744	0.676	0.614	0.558	0.508	0.463	0.422	0.386	0.352	0.322	0.295	0.270	0.247	0.227	0.208	0.191	0.176	0.162
11	0.896	0.804	0.722	0.650	0.585	0.527	0.475	0.429	0.388	0.350	0.317	0.287	0.261	0.237	0.215	0.195	0.178	0.162	0.148	0.135
12	0.887	0.788	0.701	0.625	0.557	0.497	0.444	0.397	0.356	0.319	0.286	0.257	0.231	0.208	0.187	0.168	0.152	0.137	0.124	0.112
13	0.879	0.773	0.681	0.601	0.530	0.469	0.415	0.368	0.326	0.290	0.258	0.229	0.204	0.182	0.163	0.145	0.130	0.116	0.104	0.093
14	0.870	0.758	0.661	0.577	0.505	0.442	0.388	0.340	0.299	0.263	0.232	0.205	0.181	0.160	0.141	0.125	0.111	0.099	0.088	0.078
15	0.861	0.743	0.642	0.555	0.481	0.417	0.362	0.315	0.275	0.239	0.209	0.183	0.160	0.140	0.123	0.108	0.095	0.084	0.074	0.065
16	0.853	0.728	0.623	0.534	0.458	0.394	0.339	0.292	0.252	0.218	0.188	0.163	0.141	0.123	0.107	0.093	0.081	0.071	0.062	0.054
17	0.844	0.714	0.605	0.513	0.436	0.371	0.317	0.270	0.231	0.198	0.170	0.146	0.125	0.108	0.093	0.080	0.069	0.060	0.052	0.045
18	0.836	0.700	0.587	0.494	0.416	0.350	0.296	0.250	0.212	0.180	0.153	0.130	0.111	0.095	0.081	0.069	0.059	0.051	0.044	0.038
19	0.828	0.686	0.570	0.475	0.396	0.331	0.277	0.232	0.194	0.164	0.138	0.116	0.098	0.083	0.070	0.060	0.051	0.043	0.037	0.031
20	0.820	0.673	0.554	0.456	0.377	0.312	0.258	0.215	0.178	0.149	0.124	0.104	0.087	0.073	0.061	0.051	0.043	0.037	0.031	0.026
25	0.780	0.610	0.478	0.375	0.295	0.233	0.184	0.146	0.116	0.092	0.074	0.059	0.047	0.038	0.030	0.024	0.020	0.016	0.013	0.010
30	0.742	0.552	0.412	0.308	0.231	0.174	0.131	0.099	0.075	0.057	0.044	0.033	0.026	0.020	0.015	0.012	0.009	0.007	0.005	0.004
35	0.706	0.500	0.355	0.253	0.181	0.130	0.094	0.068	0.049	0.036	0.026	0.019	0.014	0.010	0.008	0.006	0.004	0.003	0.002	0.002
40	0.672	0.453	0.307	0.208	0.142	0.097	0.067	0.046	0.032	0.022	0.015	0.011	0.008	0.005	0.004	0.003	0.002	0.001	0.001	0.001
50	0.608	0.372	0.228	0.141	0.087	0.054	0.034	0.021	0.013	0.009	0.005	0.003	0.002	0.001	0.001	0.001	0.000	0.000	0.000	0.000

CALCULATING THE FUTURE VALUE OF AN ANNUITY

Calculating the future value of an annuity means that you want to know how much your periodic investments (monthly, quarterly, yearly) will be worth in the future based on the number of years and interest rates. This is often how a financial advisor shows clients how much their money will grow toward retirement if invested at various rates. Each number in the chart is calculated using the following formula:

$$P = PMT \left[\frac{(1 + r)^n - 1}{r} \right]$$

P = future value of the annuity stream to be paid in the future
PMT = amount of each annuity payment
r = interest rate
n = number of periods over which payments are made

Example 1

The CFO of ABC Co. plans to invest $100,000 annually for five years in a long-term investment option. He expects to earn 7 percent interest, compounded annually. What will be the value of these payments at the end of the five-year period?

Look at the intersection of 7 percent and 5 periods.

= $100,000 × 5.751 = **$575,100**, the amount the investment will be worth after 5 years (*$75,100 is interest as $500,000 would be the total investment*)

TABLE A.3

Future Value of an Annuity Factors

Future value interest factor of an ordinary annuity of $1 per period at i% for n periods, FVIFA(i,n).

Period	1%	2%	3%	4%	5%	6%	7%	8%	9%	10%	11%	12%	13%	14%	15%	16%	17%	18%	19%	20%
1	1.000	1.000	1.000	1.000	1.000	1.000	1.000	1.000	1.000	1.000	1.000	1.000	1.000	1.000	1.000	1.000	1.000	1.000	1.000	1.000
2	2.010	2.020	2.030	2.040	2.050	2.060	2.070	2.080	2.090	2.100	2.110	2.120	2.130	2.140	2.150	2.160	2.170	2.180	2.190	2.200
3	3.030	3.060	3.091	3.122	3.153	3.184	3.215	3.246	3.278	3.310	3.342	3.374	3.407	3.440	3.473	3.506	3.539	3.572	3.606	3.640
4	4.060	4.122	4.184	4.246	4.310	4.375	4.440	4.506	4.573	4.641	4.710	4.779	4.850	4.921	4.993	5.066	5.141	5.215	5.291	5.368
5	5.101	5.204	5.309	5.416	5.526	5.637	5.751	5.867	5.985	6.105	6.228	6.353	6.480	6.610	6.742	6.877	7.014	7.154	7.297	7.442
6	6.152	6.308	6.468	6.633	6.802	6.975	7.153	7.336	7.523	7.716	7.913	8.115	8.323	8.536	8.754	8.977	9.207	9.442	9.683	9.930
7	7.214	7.434	7.662	7.898	8.142	8.394	8.654	8.923	9.200	9.487	9.783	10.089	10.405	10.730	11.067	11.414	11.772	12.142	12.523	12.916
8	8.286	8.583	8.892	9.214	9.549	9.897	10.260	10.637	11.028	11.436	11.859	12.300	12.757	13.233	13.727	14.240	14.773	15.327	15.902	16.499
9	9.369	9.755	10.159	10.583	11.027	11.491	11.978	12.488	13.021	13.579	14.164	14.776	15.416	16.085	16.786	17.519	18.285	19.086	19.923	20.799
10	10.462	10.950	11.464	12.006	12.578	13.181	13.816	14.487	15.193	15.937	16.722	17.549	18.420	19.337	20.304	21.321	22.393	23.521	24.709	25.959
11	11.567	12.169	12.808	13.486	14.207	14.972	15.784	16.645	17.560	18.531	19.561	20.655	21.814	23.045	24.349	25.733	27.200	28.755	30.404	32.150
12	12.683	13.412	14.192	15.026	15.917	16.870	17.888	18.977	20.141	21.384	22.713	24.133	25.650	27.271	29.002	30.850	32.824	34.931	37.180	39.581
13	13.809	14.680	15.618	16.627	17.713	18.882	20.141	21.495	22.953	24.523	26.212	28.029	29.985	32.089	34.352	36.786	39.404	42.219	45.244	48.497
14	14.947	15.974	17.086	18.292	19.599	21.015	22.550	24.215	26.019	27.975	30.095	32.393	34.883	37.581	40.505	43.672	47.103	50.818	54.841	59.196
15	16.097	17.293	18.599	20.024	21.579	23.276	25.129	27.152	29.361	31.772	34.405	37.280	40.417	43.842	47.580	51.660	56.110	60.965	66.261	72.035
16	17.258	18.639	20.157	21.825	23.657	25.673	27.888	30.324	33.003	35.950	39.190	42.753	46.672	50.980	55.717	60.925	66.649	72.939	79.850	87.442
17	18.430	20.012	21.762	23.698	25.840	28.213	30.840	33.750	36.974	40.545	44.501	48.884	53.739	59.118	65.075	71.673	78.979	87.068	96.022	105.93
18	19.615	21.412	23.414	25.645	28.132	30.906	33.999	37.450	41.301	45.599	50.396	55.750	61.725	68.394	75.836	84.141	93.406	103.74	115.27	128.12
19	20.811	22.841	25.117	27.671	30.539	33.760	37.379	41.446	46.018	51.159	56.939	63.440	70.749	78.969	88.212	98.603	110.28	123.41	138.17	154.74
20	22.019	24.297	26.870	29.778	33.066	36.786	40.995	45.762	51.160	57.275	64.203	72.052	80.947	91.025	102.44	115.38	130.03	146.63	165.42	186.69
25	28.243	32.030	36.459	41.646	47.727	54.865	63.249	73.106	84.701	98.347	114.41	133.33	155.62	181.87	212.79	249.21	292.10	342.60	402.04	471.98
30	34.785	40.568	47.575	56.085	66.439	79.058	94.461	113.28	136.31	164.49	199.02	241.33	293.20	356.79	434.75	530.31	647.44	790.95	966.71	1,181.9
35	41.660	49.994	60.462	73.652	90.320	111.43	138.24	172.32	215.71	271.02	341.59	431.66	546.68	693.57	881.17	1,120.7	1,426.5	1,816.7	2,314.2	2,948.3
40	48.886	60.402	75.401	95.026	120.80	154.76	199.64	259.06	337.88	442.59	581.83	767.09	1,013.7	1,342.0	1,779.1	2,360.8	3,134.5	4,163.2	5,529.8	7,343.9
50	64.463	84.579	112.80	152.67	209.35	290.34	406.53	573.77	815.08	1,163.9	1,668.8	2,400.0	3,459.5	4,994.5	7,217.7	10,436	15,090	21,813	31,515	45,497

CALCULATING THE PRESENT VALUE OF AN ANNUITY

Calculating the present value of an annuity means that you want to know the payment that needs to be made today in order to fulfill an obligation or meet a goal in the future. This is how lottery winners get paid a lump sum instead of taking an annual annuity for 30 years, for example. Each number in the chart is calculated using the following formula:

$$P = PMT \left[\frac{1 - \frac{1}{(1 + r)^n}}{r} \right]$$

P = future value of the annuity stream to be paid in the future
PMT = amount of each annuity payment
r = interest rate
n = number of periods over which payments are made

Example 1

Crisp Cut Industries has committed to a legal settlement that requires it to pay $50,000/year at the end of each of the next 10 years. What would it cost Crisp Cut if it were to instead settle the claim immediately with a lump-sum payment, assuming an interest rate of 5 percent?

Look at the intersection of 5 percent and 10 periods.

= 50,000 × 7.722 = **$386,100**, Crisp Cut Industries would have to pay this amount today to settle the claim in a lump-sum payout to the client.

Present Value of an Annuity Factors

Present value interest factor of an (ordinary) annuity of $1 per period at i% for n periods, PVIFA(i,n).

Period	1%	2%	3%	4%	5%	6%	7%	8%	9%	10%	11%	12%	13%	14%	15%	16%	17%	18%	19%	20%
1	0.990	0.980	0.971	0.962	0.952	0.943	0.935	0.926	0.917	0.909	0.901	0.893	0.885	0.877	0.870	0.862	0.855	0.847	0.840	0.833
2	1.970	1.942	1.913	1.886	1.859	1.833	1.808	1.783	1.759	1.736	1.713	1.690	1.668	1.647	1.626	1.605	1.585	1.566	1.547	1.528
3	2.941	2.884	2.829	2.775	2.723	2.673	2.624	2.577	2.531	2.487	2.444	2.402	2.361	2.322	2.283	2.246	2.210	2.174	2.140	2.106
4	3.902	3.808	3.717	3.630	3.546	3.465	3.387	3.312	3.240	3.170	3.102	3.037	2.974	2.914	2.855	2.798	2.743	2.690	2.639	2.589
5	4.853	4.713	4.580	4.452	4.329	4.212	4.100	3.993	3.890	3.791	3.696	3.605	3.517	3.433	3.352	3.274	3.199	3.127	3.058	2.991
6	5.795	5.601	5.417	5.242	5.076	4.917	4.767	4.623	4.486	4.355	4.231	4.111	3.998	3.889	3.784	3.685	3.589	3.498	3.410	3.326
7	6.728	6.472	6.230	6.002	5.786	5.582	5.389	5.206	5.033	4.868	4.712	4.564	4.423	4.288	4.160	4.039	3.922	3.812	3.706	3.605
8	7.652	7.325	7.020	6.733	6.463	6.210	5.971	5.747	5.535	5.335	5.146	4.968	4.799	4.639	4.487	4.344	4.207	4.078	3.954	3.837
9	8.566	8.162	7.786	7.435	7.108	6.802	6.515	6.247	5.995	5.759	5.537	5.328	5.132	4.946	4.772	4.607	4.451	4.303	4.163	4.031
10	9.471	8.983	8.530	8.111	7.722	7.360	7.024	6.710	6.418	6.145	5.889	5.650	5.426	5.216	5.019	4.833	4.659	4.494	4.339	4.192
11	10.368	9.787	9.253	8.760	8.306	7.887	7.499	7.139	6.805	6.495	6.207	5.938	5.687	5.453	5.234	5.029	4.836	4.656	4.486	4.327
12	11.255	10.575	9.954	9.385	8.863	8.384	7.943	7.536	7.161	6.814	6.492	6.194	5.918	5.660	5.421	5.197	4.988	4.793	4.611	4.439
13	12.134	11.348	10.635	9.986	9.394	8.853	8.358	7.904	7.487	7.103	6.750	6.424	6.122	5.842	5.583	5.342	5.118	4.910	4.715	4.533
14	13.004	12.106	11.296	10.563	9.899	9.295	8.745	8.244	7.786	7.367	6.982	6.628	6.302	6.002	5.724	5.468	5.229	5.008	4.802	4.611
15	13.865	12.849	11.938	11.118	10.380	9.712	9.108	8.559	8.061	7.606	7.191	6.811	6.462	6.142	5.847	5.575	5.324	5.092	4.876	4.675
16	14.718	13.578	12.561	11.652	10.838	10.106	9.447	8.851	8.313	7.824	7.379	6.974	6.604	6.265	5.954	5.668	5.405	5.162	4.938	4.730
17	15.562	14.292	13.166	12.166	11.274	10.477	9.763	9.122	8.544	8.022	7.549	7.120	6.729	6.373	6.047	5.749	5.475	5.222	4.990	4.775
18	16.398	14.992	13.754	12.659	11.690	10.828	10.059	9.372	8.756	8.201	7.702	7.250	6.840	6.467	6.128	5.818	5.534	5.273	5.033	4.812
19	17.226	15.678	14.324	13.134	12.085	11.158	10.336	9.604	8.950	8.365	7.839	7.366	6.938	6.550	6.198	5.877	5.584	5.316	5.070	4.843
20	18.046	16.351	14.877	13.590	12.462	11.470	10.594	9.818	9.129	8.514	7.963	7.469	7.025	6.623	6.259	5.929	5.628	5.353	5.101	4.870
25	22.023	19.523	17.413	15.622	14.094	12.783	11.654	10.675	9.823	9.077	8.422	7.843	7.330	6.873	6.464	6.097	5.766	5.467	5.195	4.948
30	25.808	22.396	19.600	17.292	15.372	13.765	12.409	11.258	10.274	9.427	8.694	8.055	7.496	7.003	6.566	6.177	5.829	5.517	5.235	4.979
35	29.409	24.999	21.487	18.665	16.374	14.498	12.948	11.655	10.567	9.644	8.855	8.176	7.586	7.070	6.617	6.215	5.858	5.539	5.251	4.992
40	32.835	27.355	23.115	19.793	17.159	15.046	13.332	11.925	10.757	9.779	8.951	8.244	7.634	7.105	6.642	6.233	5.871	5.548	5.258	4.997
50	39.196	31.424	25.730	21.482	18.256	15.762	13.801	12.233	10.962	9.915	9.042	8.304	7.675	7.133	6.661	6.246	5.880	5.554	5.262	4.999

FUTURE AND PRESENT VALUE PROBLEMS

Use the tables on the previous pages to solve the following problems related to future and present value:

1. What is the future value of $25,000 invested for 10 years at 6 percent interest, compounded bi-annually?

2. What is the future value of $10,000 invested for 30 years at 10 percent interest, compounded annually?

3. What is the present value (PV) of a bond that will be worth $1000.00 in 10 years if the interest rate is 3 percent compounded annually?

4. What is the present value (PV) of a certificate of deposit (CD) that will pay $25,000.00 in 20 years if the interest rate is 6 percent compounded annually?

5. John wants to start his own business in ten years and plans to invest $10,000 annually in order to achieve his dream. He expects to earn 6 percent interest, compounded annually. How much money will John have to start his business at the end of the 10-year period?

6. The CFO of XYZ Co. plans to invest $50,000 annually for 20 years in a long-term investment option. She expects to earn 4 percent interest annually. What will be the value of these payments at the end of the 20-year period?

7. Jill just won the lottery and wants to collect all of her earnings in a lump-sum today instead of receiving annual payments of $100,000 for the next 30 years. How much would the Lottery Commission owe Jill if it were to pay her a lump-sum today, assuming a 3 percent interest rate, compounded annually?

8. You were the unfortunate victim in a car accident and agreed to a settlement with the insurance company that will pay you $10,000/year for the next 10 years. However, you have the option to take a lump-sum payment instead. How much would your lump-sum payment be if you agreed to a 5 percent interest rate, compounded annually? And, explain if you would take the money as a lump-sum or yearly annuity.

SELF-CHECK

1.   = 1.806 × $25,000 = $45,150

2.   = 17.449 × $10,000 = $174,490

3.   = 0.744 × $1,000 = $744

4.   = 0.312 × $25,000 = $7800

5.   = 13.181 × $10,000 = $131,810

6.   = 29.778 × $50,000 = $1,488,900

7.   = 19.600 × $100,000 = $1,960,000

8.   = 7.722 × $10,000 = $77,220

APPENDIX B

CREATING A BUSINESS PLAN

OUTCOMES:

> Understand the sections of a business plan.
> Develop a business plan using Small Business Administration guidelines.
> Create a solid beginning for an emerging business through the creation of a business plan.

SAMPLE BUSINESS PLAN FORMAT

DT10/Shutterstock.com

One of the first steps in creating a new business is to develop a business plan. The business plan describes a business and its products or services, market, people, and financing needs. Although individuals can open businesses without the amount of detail included here, completing a formal business plan will help you understand the business world better as well as develop solid plans (not just ideas) about the viability of your plan.

Consider taking a course through the Small Business Administration, which will provide mentors and guidelines for developing each aspect of your business plan. Most classes can be taken online or through local community education programs for a minimal fee, which is well worth the money and time to help you create a solid business plan.

Use the following information, based on the Small Business Administration guidelines, as a guide to create your business plan.[1] Include the following sections:

I. SUMMARY

The summary should concisely describe the key elements of the business plan. For a firm seeking capital, the summary should convince the lender or venture capitalists that it is worthwhile to review the plan in detail. The summary should briefly cover the following items:

- Name of the business;
- Business location and plan description;
- Discussion of the product, market, and competition;
- Expertise of the management team;
- Summary of financial projections;
- Amount of financing requested (if applicable);
- Form of and purpose for financing (if applicable);
- Purpose for undertaking the project (if financing is sought); and
- Business goals.

II. THE COMPANY

This section provides background information on the company. It commonly includes a general description of the business, including the product or service, and may describe the historical development of the business, legal structure, significant changes in ownership, organizational structure, products or lines, acquisitions, subsidiaries, and degree of ownership as well as the principals and the roles they played in the formation of the company.

III. THE PRODUCT OR SERVICE

This is a detailed description of product or service lines, including the relative importance of each product or service to the company. Include sales projections if possible. If available, include product evaluations, comparison to competitors' products or product lines, competitive advantages over other producers, and the elasticity or inelasticity of demand for this product (i.e., does demand respond to factors other than price?). Possible sources of information for this section include competitors' web sites, business directories, and census data similar to what is published in the U.S. Industrial Outlook.

IV. THE PROJECT

If financing is sought for a specific project, describe the project, the purpose for which it is undertaken, its cost, the amount, and form of the financing needed.

V. MANAGEMENT

Discuss the firm's management. Provide an organizational chart. Discuss key management and supervisory personnel who add special or unique value to the organization. Describe their responsibilities and provide resumés describing their skills and experience as they relate to activities of the business. Discuss planned staff additions. Describe other employees, including the number of employees at year end, total payroll expenses for each of the previous five years (break down by wages, benefits, etc.), method of comparison, and the departmental or divisional breakdown of the work force.

VI. OWNERSHIP

Provide names, addresses, and business affiliations of principal holders of the firm's common stock and other types of equity securities. Discuss the degree to which principal holders are involved in management. Describe principal non-management owners. Provide the names of the board of directors, their areas of expertise, and the role of the board. Specify the amount of stock currently authorized and issued.

VII. MARKETING STRATEGY/MARKET ANALYSIS

Describe the industry and the industry outlook. Identify the principal markets (commercial/industrial, consumer, governmental, international). Include current industry size as well as its anticipated size in the next ten years. Explain the sources of your projections. Describe major characteristics of the industry and the effects of major social, economic, technological or regulatory trends in the industry.

Describe major customers, including names, locations, products or services sold to each, percentage of annual sales volume for each customer over the previous five years, and the duration and condition of contracts in place.

Describe the market and its major segments. Describe principal market participants and their performance. Identify the firm's target market. For each market, include the requirements of each and the current ways of filling these requirements. Also include information on the buying habits of the customers and the impact on the customer of using the product or service.

Describe the companies with which the business competes and how the business compares with the competition. This is a more detailed narrative than that contained in the description of the product or service above.

Describe prospective customers and their reaction to the firm and any of the firm's products or services they have seen or tested.

Describe the firm's marketing strategy, including overall strategy, pricing policy, method of selling, distributing and servicing the product, geographic penetration, field/product support, advertising, public relations and promotion, and priorities among these activities.

Describe how the firm will identify prospective customers and how and in what order the firm will contact the relevant decision-makers. Also, describe the sales effort the firm will have (e.g., sales channels and terms, number of salespersons, number of sales contacts, anticipated time, and initial order size) and estimated sales and market share.

Sources of information include census data (on both industry and consumer demographics), business directories, specific industry reports (either from government or private sources), and competitors' web sites.

VIII. TECHNOLOGY

Describe the technical status of your product (i.e., idea stage, development stage, prototype state, etc.) and the relevant activities, milestones, and other steps necessary to bring the product into production. Discuss the firm's patent or copyright position. Include how much is patented and how much can be patented (i.e., how comprehensive and effective the patents or copyrights will be). Include a list of patents, copyrights, licenses, or statements of proprietary interest in the product or product line.

Describe new technologies that may become practical in the next five years which may affect the product. Also describe new products the firm plans to develop to meet changing market needs. Describe regulatory or approval requirements and status and discuss any other technical and legal considerations that may be relevant to the technological development of the product. Include a discussion or research and development efforts and future plans for research and development. Technologies are also requirements that your competitors are using that customers expect you to have such as new software, signs, gimmicks, etc.

IX. PRODUCTION/OPERATING PLAN

Explain how the firm will execute production or deliver its service. Describe capacity and status in terms of physical facilities: are they owned or leased; size and location; sales volume and unit capacity; expansion capabilities; capital equipment, etc. Include a facilities plan and description of planned capital improvements as well as a timetable for those improvements.

Describe suppliers including name and location of principal suppliers; length of lead time required; usual terms of purchase; amounts, duration and conditions of contracts; and subcontractors. Also describe the current and planned labor supply, including number of employees; unionization; stability (seasonal or cyclical); and fringe benefits (insurance, profit sharing, pension, etc.).

Provide a profile of key patents and describe technologies and skills required to develop and manufacture the products. Provide a cost breakdown for material, labor and manufacturing overhead for each product, plus cost versus volume curves for each product. Provide block and workflow diagrams of the manufacturing process where appropriate and provide a schedule of work for the next 1–2 years. Describe the production or operating advantages of the firm. Discuss whether they are expected to continue.

X. FINANCIAL/ADMINISTRATIVE PLAN

Provide the names and addresses of key advisors, including an auditor, legal counsel, and banker.

Describe financial controls including the cost system and budgets used. Describe cash requirements and how over the next five years these funds will be used. Specify financial needs to be raised from debt and from equity. Discuss plans to "go public." Relate this to future value and liquidity of investments.

Provide financial statements and projections for the next five years. These should include profit and loss or income statements by month (at least until breakeven and then by quarter); balance sheets (end of each year); cash budgets and cash flow projections; capital budgets for equipment and other capital acquisitions; and include key assumptions made in pro forma statements and how these assumptions reflect industry performance.

If financing is sought, most lenders and venture capitalists will require a funding request indicating the described financing, capitalization, use of funds, and future financing; a financial statement for the past three years; current financial statements; monthly cash flow financial projections including the proposed financing for two years, and projected balance sheets, income statement and statement of changes in financial position for two years including the proposed financing.

APPENDIX C

SUPPLEMENTAL
CASE STUDIES

CASES:

➤ NASA: Deadly Decision-Making?
➤ McDonald's: Expanding the Arches
➤ Leadership: Joining Cultures
➤ Elmira Lilic: Aspiring Artist and Entrepreneur

NASA: DEADLY DECISION-MAKING?

© Shutterstock.com

© Shutterstock.com

The launch of NASA's space shuttle, Challenger, was originally planned for January 20, 1986. It was delayed several times due to technical problems and severe weather. After six unsuccessful attempts, the seventh attempt took place on the cold morning of January, 28, 1986. Seventy-three seconds into the flight, the shuttle exploded leaving behind a cloud of gas as it burned nearly two million liters of fuel in a matter of seconds. Seven astronauts lost their lives as family, friends, and television viewers watched. This mission was distinctive as among the crew was the first civilian astronaut, school teacher Christa McAuliffe, and the second African-American astronaut to fly in space, Ron McNair (Raval, 2014).

A presidential commission was created to investigate the disaster and published a report determining that the O-Ring was responsible for the explosion. The O-Ring joint failure occurred in the right Solid Rocket Booster (SRB) allowing for a trail of hot gasses to escape and cause the explosion. Problems with the shuttle's O-Rings were well known by the team of engineers assigned to work on the SRB. The abnormal O-Ring erosion had been observed in prior flights, yet rather than investigating this matter, NASA Management ignored the problem and chose to increase the tolerance level. In fact, the night before the launch, NASA had a conference call with Morton Thiokol, manufacturer of the SRB, where serious apprehension was raised over the possibility of O-Ring failure due to the cold temperatures predicted during the launch. The engineers recommended postponing the launch, which NASA did not support. Morton Thiokol's management succumbed to pressure from NASA and gave approval for the launch. Following the explosion, it took 81 days to collect the Challenger's debris from the ocean (Raval, 2014).

Following this great tragedy, the shuttle program was grounded for almost three years until several procedural and management changes were implemented to ensure safety in the operation of the program.

1. What management and leadership concepts and/or terminology from the text relate to the unfortunate outcome of the Challenger?

2. How did NASA's management structure and/or culture contribute to the Challenger tragedy?

3. What role did communication play in this tragedy?

REFERENCES

Raval, S. (2014). Challenger: A Management Failure. *Space Safety Magazine*. Retrieved on May 21, 2016, from http://www.spacesafetymagazine.com/space-disasters/challenger-disaster/challenger-management-failure/.

MCDONALD'S: EXPANDING THE ARCHES

© Shutterstock.com

McDonald's is the world's leading global food service retailer with over 36,000 locations serving approximately 69 million customers in over 100 countries each day. Around the globe, McDonald's offers various cultures local flavors as well as its standard offerings. More than 80% of McDonald's restaurants worldwide are owned and operated by independent, local business men and women. McDonald's stresses quality in its products in order to align with their mission statement: *"Our overall vision is for McDonald's to become a modern, progressive burger company delivering a contemporary customer experience"* (McDonald's, 2016, para. 3).

However, in an age where nutrition and health matter, McDonald's has struggled to keep pace with fast-food chains such as Subway, Chipotle, and Burger King, which offer healthier food options to customers. In an effort to increase sales, McDonald's released a limited All-Day Breakfast advertising campaign in 2015 with discontentment from franchise owners who stated that it would slow down service, crowd their kitchens, and create more work. Customers complained that some of their favorites were not on the menu, so McDonald's later added the McGriddle in several markets around the country (Taylor, 2016).

A 2016 McDonald's report stated that although they experienced a sales increase of 5.7 percent in the last three months of 2015, it was not revealed how the all-day breakfast offering benefitted the chain or if its affects will last. CNBC reported that sales growth came from a variety of changes including the All-Day breakfast, the Pick-Two promotion, as well as from an increase in sales in Asia.

QUESTIONS:

1. Discuss how offering an All-Day Breakfast menu aligns with McDonald's mission statement to promote "...a progressive burger company...and a contemporary customer experience".

2. Identify areas you feel McDonald's could expand upon or eliminate.

3. Do you feel that offering an All-Day Breakfast menu will enhance long-term sales for McDonald's? Explain.

REFERENCES

McDonald's (2016). Company profile. Retrieved on May 12, 2016, from: http://www.aboutmcdonalds.com/mcd/investors/company-overview/company-overview-segment-information.html.

Taylor, K. (2016). McDonald's is fixing its biggest problem with all-day breakfast at more than 1,000 locations. Retrieved on May 12, 2016, from: http://www.businessinsider.com/mcdonalds-tests-mcgriddle-all-day-menu-2016-3.

© *Shutterstock.com*

Bear River Community College celebrated 50-Years of Transforming Lives during the 2015-2016 year at the Colgate Campus and Centerville Campus. From its start in 1965, more than 216,000 people have attended courses at one or both of the campuses in Centerville and Colgate. Courses range from short-term training/certificate programs to two-year, four-year, and graduate degrees in an attempt to meet the diverse needs of students.

The past President, Dr. James Smyth, served for 20 years and established a culture where employees were not encouraged to develop professionally or personally nor interact with other campuses. After his retirement, the interim president tried to bridge the gap between the campuses until President Branson was selected. Branson was hired as president over Bear River Community College (BRCC) and Ash Technical College (ATC) and to oversee the successful alignment of three campuses: BRCC-Centerville, BRCC-Colgate, and ATC. The alignment involved streamlining operations between campuses in order to increase efficiencies, unifying the three cultures, and developing one vision for all three campuses.

The process of unifying the distinct cultures of three separate campuses was a goal of Dr. Branson's; however, the consolidation of operations between the three campuses resulted in the eliminated of several positions. Dismayed ATC employees viewed this transition as a hostile takeover rather than a friendly "alignment". Poor communication by administration further escalated the situation and isolated campus employees. Furthermore, ineffective management processes and misaligned personnel failed to create a fluid system that optimized employee strengths, productivity, and the interests of all stakeholders.

Dr. Branson worked to lead his employees through these changes with integrity and transparency to start the work of rebuilding a caring and student-oriented culture. Recent changes in leadership made it difficult for the existing cultures within campuses to transition to the new system. Leadership's failure to effectively communicate their vision and unify the employees at BRCC and ATC, resulted in a blurring of the benefits of the alignment and the continued miscommunication of the long term goals for all three of the campuses.

QUESTIONS:

1. How would you suggest Dr. Branson develop a culture that allows employees to feel safe and secure in their positions if the possibility of cuts exist?

2. What type of leadership style would you recommend Dr. Branson utilize? Explain.

3. What suggestions would you offer Dr. Branson to improve relationships between leadership, management, and employees?

ELMIRA LILIC: ASPIRING ARTIST AND ENTREPRENEUR

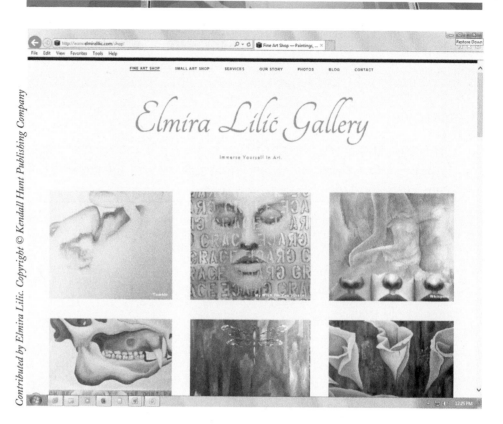

Elmira Lilic is an artist who wants to revolutionize the Los Angeles art scene by using art to create a myriad of business opportunities. Currently, she works to bring artists together on one website in order to promote and sell their work as well as sell her own artwork and greeting cards. In addition, she has a children's book and custom designed scarves that she would like to better promote and sell.

Her ideas are on the cutting edge and she has characteristics of an entrepreneur that will allow her to succeed, such as motivation, interpersonal skills, solid business acumen, and practical experience. However, she has several common tendencies of new entrepreneurs such as creating too high of expectations for herself and the business, not setting goals, and lacking a business plan. The commitment to overcome and conquer challenges in getting started has been overwhelming for Elmira. Her previous sales were $2000; however, her projected sales for the upcoming year are $50,000.

Networking is a practice that Elmira works at regularly. She networks continually through friends, business acquaintances, professional organizations, in addition to researching various topics. These opportunities continue to afford her business opportunities and may allow her to expand into new or additional markets. Pros and cons about Elmira's efforts and abilities in starting a new business are presented below:

PROS:	CONS:
Past industry success	Limited business experience
Industry professional connections	Limited working capital
Creative ideas	No partnerships established
Unlimited opportunities for expansion	Incomplete business plan

Elmira's goals for the future are to increase exposure and sales, promote her artwork and children's book, find a manufacturer for her scarves, and market her products on ShopNBC and in local, high-end furniture stores. Her website is: http://www.elmiralilic.com/shop/.

DISCUSSION QUESTIONS:

1. How would you explain the importance of developing a sustainable business plan to Elmira?

2. What new ideas or markets do you feel Elmira might consider as she continues to grow her business?

3. After reviewing Elmira's current website, what suggestions would you offer about the content or markets that she might not have considered? Explain.

REFERENCES

CHAPTER 1

1 NCCS Business Master File 11/2015, http://nccs.urban.org/statistics/quickfacts.cfm

2 Lawrence, A. (2012). Five customer retention tips for entrepreneurs. http://www.forbes.com/sites/alexlawrence/2012/11/01/five-customer-retention-tips-for-entrepreneurs/. Accessed 28 Feb 2015.

3 US Census Bureau. (2012). 2012 National projection: Summary tables. www.census.gov/population/projections/data/national/2012/summarytables.html. Accessed 9 Dec 2014.

4 D'Onfro, D. (2014). Google employees reveal their favorite perks about working for the company. http://www.businessinsider.com/google-employees-favorite-perks-2014-7?op=1. Accessed 28 Feb 2015.

5 US Department of Labor. (n.d.). Summary of the major laws of the Department of Labor. http://www.dol.gov/opa/aboutdol/lawsprog.htm. Accessed 28 Feb 2015.

6 Greechie, S. (n.d.). Role of government in business. http://smallbusiness.chron.com/role-government-business-803.html. Accessed 28 Feb 2015.

CHAPTER 2

1 Trader Joe's Settlement Site. Class Action 2014 Lawsuit. https://tjallnaturalclassaction.com. Accessed 9 Sept 2014.

2 Ziaja, S. (2011). We can't stop the twisters, but we can stop price gouging. http://lawblog.legalmatch.com/2011/05/05/we-cant-stop-the-twisters-but-we-can-stop-price-gouging/. Accessed 12 Dec 2014.

3 Jennings, M. (2008). *Business, its legal, ethical, and global environment* (7th ed.). South-Western College/West.

4 Ethics Resource Center. (2013). National Business Ethics Survey. http://www.ethics.org/resource/national-business-ethics-survey%C2%AE-us-workplace. Accessed 4 Feb 2014.

5 Sharp-Paine, L. (1994). Managing for organizational integrity. [2] *Harvard Business Review*, 105–117.

6   Perry, D. (n.d.). Keys to creating an effective ethics program. http://home.earthlink.net/
    ~davidlperry/healthex.htm. Accessed 9 Dec 2014.

7   Grace, N. (2015). Comprehensive list of federal employment laws. http://smallbusiness.chron.com/
    comprehensive-list-federal-employment-laws-1330.html. Accessed 1 March 2015.

8   US Sentencing Commission. (n.d.). http://www.ussc.gov. Accessed 12 Jan 2015.

9   Matthews, C. (2012). Most whistleblowers report internally, study finds. http://blogs.wsj.com/
    corruption-currents/2012/05/30/most-whistleblowers-report-internally-study-finds/. Accessed
    14 Dec 2014.

10 Hardcastle, J. (2006). Two views of social responsibility. http://ezinearticles.com/?Two-Views-of-
    Social-Responsibility&id=319944. Accessed 14 Dec 2014.

11 Kanaan, F. (2014). Pros & cons of corporate social responsibility. http://we-initiative.com/
    pros-cons-of-corporate-social-responsibility/. Accessed 9 Dec 2014.

12 Jennings, M. (2008). *Business, its legal, ethical, and global environment* (7th ed.). South-Western
    College/West.

13 Kanaan, F. (2014). Pros & cons of corporate social responsibility. http://we-initiative.com/
    pros-cons-of-corporate-social-responsibility/. Accessed 9 Dec 2014.

14 Fallon, N. (2014). What is corporate social responsibility? http://www.businessnewsdaily.
    com/4679-corporate-social-responsibility.html. Accessed 9 Dec 2014.

15 Forbes (2013). America's 10 most generous companies. http://www.forbes.com/pictures/
    efkk45ekmdh/no-10-google-2/. Accessed 9 Dec 2014.

16 Williams, O. (n.d.). Social responsibility challenges in business. http://yourbusiness.azcentral.com/
    social-responsibility-challenges-business-11340.html. Accessed 12 Dec 2014.

17 Fallon, N. (2014). What is corporate social responsibility? http://www.businessnewsdaily.
    com/4679-corporate-social-responsibility.html. Accessed 9 Dec 2014.

18 MacIntyre, D. (2014). 10 major clothing brands caught in shocking sweatshop scandals. http://
    www.therichest.com/rich-list/most-shocking/10-major-clothing-brands-caught-in-shocking-
    sweatshop-scandals/. Accessed 9 Dec 2014.

19 Williams, O. (n.d.). Social responsibility challenges in business. http://yourbusiness.azcentral.com/
    social-responsibility-challenges-business-11340.html. Accessed 12 Dec 2014.

20 Koch, W. (2012). FTC toughens green marketing guidelines. http://www.usatoday.com/story/news/
    nation/2012/10/01/ftc-revises-green-guidelines-for-marketing-products/1605953/. Accessed
    12 Dec 2014.

CHAPTER 3

1   American Economic Association. (n.d.). What is economics? https://www.aeaweb.org/students/
    WhatIsEconomics.php. Accessed 21 Dec 2014.

2   Macroeconomics. (n.d.). http://www.investinganswers.com/financial-dictionary/economics/
    macroeconomics-937. Accessed 21 Dec 2014.

3   Moffatt, M. (n.d.). Definition of gross domestic product (GDP). http://economics.about.com/cs/
    economicsglossary/g/gross_domestic.htm. Accessed 21 Dec 2014.

4   Investopedia. (n.d.). http://www.investopedia.com/terms/c/consumerpriceindex.asp. Accessed 21 Dec 2014.

5   Bureau of Labor Statistics. (n.d.). http://www.bls.gov/dolfaq/bls_ques23.htm. Accessed 27 Jan 2015.

6   Amadeo, K. (2013). What is the business cycle? Stages and definition. http://useconomy.about.com/od/glossary/g/business_cycle.htm. Accessed 18 Dec 2014.

7   Dictionary.com. (n.d.). http://dictionary.reference.com/browse/mixed%20economies?s=t. Accessed 19 Dec 2014.

8   Zheng, K. (n.d.). http://yourbusiness.azcentral.com/examples-oligopoly-markets-6720.html. Accessed 18 Dec 2014.

9   Federal Reserve. (n.d.). http://www.federalreserve.gov/faqs/banking-financial-system.htm. Accessed 19 Dec 2014.

10 Federal Reserve. (n.d.). http://www.federalreserve.gov/faqs/banking-financial-system.htm. Accessed 19 Dec 2014.

11 Federal Reserve Bank of San Fransisco. (2015). What is the Fed: Supervision and regulation. http://www.frbsf.org/education/teacher-resources/what-is-the-fed/supervision-regulation. Accessed 20 Dec 2014.

12 Kosakowski, P. (n.d.). The fall of the market in the fall of 2008. http://www.investopedia.com/articles/economics/09/subprime-market-2008.asp. Accessed 11 Feb 2015.

13 2008 Financial Crisis and Global Recession. (n.d.). http://2008financialcrisis.umwblogs.org/introduction/. Accessed 18 Dec 2014.

CHAPTER 4

1   Pofeldt, E. (n.d.). Gallup: The 10 qualities of highly successful entrepreneurs. http://www.forbes.com/sites/elainepofeldt/. Accessed 10 Jan 2015.

2   Blank, S. (2010). You're not a real entrepreneur. http://innovationfactory.ca/the-four-types-of-entrepreneurship/. Accessed 9 Jan 2015.

3   Mark Cuban. (n.d.). BrainyQuote.com. http://www.brainyquote.com/quotes/quotes/m/markcuban417210.html. Accessed 9 March 2015.

4   Ashoka (n.d.) What is a social entrepreneur? https://www.ashoka.org/social_entrepreneur. Accessed 9 Jan 2015.

5   SBA. (2014). Frequently asked questions. Advocacy: The voice of small business in government. https://www.sba.gov/advocacy. Accessed 10 March 2015.

6   Brown, J. (n.d.). How important are small businesses to local economies? http://smallbusiness.chron.com/important-small-businesses-local-economies-5251.html. Accessed 11 Jan 2015.

7   Risk Management. (n.d.). http://toolkit.smallbiz.nsw.gov.au/part/18/89/387. Accessed 16 Jan 2015.

8   Finklestein, R. (2006). What successful businesses have in common. http://www.entrepreneur.com/article/83764. Accessed 15 Jan 2015.

9   Statistic Brain. (2015). Startup business failure rate by industry. http://www.statisticbrain.com/startup-failure-by-industry/. Accessed 11 March 2015.

10 US Small Business Administration. (n.d.). What are the major reasons for small business failure? https://www.sba.gov/content/what-are-major-reasons-small-business-failure. Accessed 12 Jan 2015.

11 US Small Business Administration. (n.d.). https://www.sba.gov/about-sba/what_we_do=2. Accessed 12 Jan 2015.

12 Cohn, M. (2015). SEC Commissioner rejects IFRS. Retrieved on March 30, 2015, from: http://www.acountingtoday.com.

13 US Small Business Administration. (n.d.). https://www.sba.gov/tools/business-plan/1. Accessed 12 Jan 2015.

14 US Small Business Administration. (n.d.). Sole proprietorship. https://www.sba.gov/content/sole-proprietorship-0. Accessed 12 Jan 2015.

15 US Small Business Administration. (n.d.). Partnerships. https://www.sba.gov/content/partnership. Accessed 12 Jan 2015.

16 US Small Business Administration. (n.d.). Corporation. https://www.sba.gov/content/corporation. Accessed 12 Jan 2015.

17 US Small Business Administration. (n.d.). Limited liability company. https://www.sba.gov/content/limited-liability-company-llc. Accessed 12 Jan 2015.

18 International Franchising Association. (n.d.). What are the advantages and disadvantages of owning a franchise? http://www.franchise.org/franchiseesecondary.aspx?id=52630. Accessed 12 Jan 2015.

19 Yarrow, J. (2011). The dumbest acquisitions in the history of tech. http://www.businessinsider.com/bad-acquisitions-2011-8?op=1. Accessed 24 March 2015.

20 DiMaggio, M. (2009). The top ten best (and worst) corporate mergers of all time...or the good, the bad, and the ugly. http://www.rasmussen.edu/degrees/business/blog/best-and-worst-corporate-mergers/. Accessed 24 March 2015.

21 US Small Business Administration. (n.d.). Microloan program. https://www.sba.gov/content/microloan-program. Accessed 13 Jan 2015.

22 Berry, T. (n.d.). How to get your business funded. http://articles.bplans.com/author/tim-berry/. Accessed 12 Jan 2015.

CHAPTER 5

1 American Accounting Association. (n.d.). http://aaahq.org. Accessed 2 Feb 2015.

2 Types of Accounting. (n.d.). http://accounting-simplified.com/financial/types-of-accounting.html. Accessed 2 Feb 2015.

3 Introduction to Accounting. (n.d.). http://accounting-simplified.com/financial/users-of-accounting-information.html. Accessed 2 Feb 2015.

4 Facts about FASB. (n.d.). http://www.fasb.org/facts/. Accessed 2 Feb 2015.

5 Morrow, S. (2009). General accepted accounting principles or GAAP: What does it mean? https://www.legalzoom.com/articles/general-accepted-accounting-principles-or-gaap-what-does-it-mean. Accessed 2 Feb 2015.

6   Hill, R. (2015). Liquidity ratio: Definition, calculation, and analysis. http://education-portal.com/academy/lesson/liquidity-ratio-definition-calculation-analysis.html. Accessed 4 Feb 2015.

7   Investing Answers. (2015). Leverage ratio. http://www.investinganswers.com/financial-dictionary/debt-bankruptcy/leverage-ratio-5287. Accessed 4 Feb 2015.

8   Grimsley, S. (2015). Profitability ratio. http://education-portal.com/academy/lesson/profitability-ratio-definition-formula-analysis-example.html. Accessed 4 Feb 2015.

9   Loth, R. (2015). Profitability indicator ratios: Return on equity. http://www.investopedia.com/university/ratios/profitability-indicator/ratio4.asp. Accessed 8 April 2015.

10 Ratio Analysis. (n.d.). Financial ratio analysis. http://ratio-analysis.org/activity-ratios.php. Accessed 4 Feb 2015.

11 CSI Market. (n.d.). Inventory turnover ratio screening. http://csimarket.com/screening/index.php?s=it&pageS=1&fis=. Accessed 8 April 2015.

12 IFRS. (n.d.). IASB. http://www.ifrs.org/About-us/IASB/Pages/Home.aspx. Accessed 5 Feb 2015.

13 Management study guide (2013). Role of a Financial Manager. http://managementstudyguide.com/role-of-financial-manager.htm. Accessed 5 Feb 2015.

14 Entrepreneur. (2013). How to determine your working capital needs. http://www.entrepreneur.com/article/225658. Accessed 5 Feb 2015.

15 Entrepreneur. (n.d.). Undercapitalization. http://www.entrepreneur.com/encyclopedia/undercapitalization. Accessed 5 Feb 2015.

CHAPTER 6

1   Cohan, H. (2011). 72 marketing definitions. http://heidicohen.com/marketing-definition/. Accessed 12 Feb 2015.

2   Linton, I. (2015). What are the four types of business marketing utilities? http://smallbusiness.chron.com/four-types-business-marketing-utilities-20698.html. Accessed 12 Feb 2015.

3   Linton, I. (2015). What are the four types of business marketing utilities? http://smallbusiness.chron.com/four-types-business-marketing-utilities-20698.html. Accessed 12 Feb 2015.

4   Merritt, C. (n.d.). What are the five eras of marketing? http://yourbusiness.azcentral.com/five-eras-marketing-3411.html. Accessed 12 Feb 2015.

5   Templeman, M. (2014). Three key differences in strategy of B2B marketing vs. B2C marketing. http://foxtailmarketing.com/3-key-differences-strategy-b2b-marketing-vs-b2c-marketing/. Accessed 12 Feb 2015.

6   Lavinsky, D. (2013). Marketing plan template: Exactly what to include. http://www.forbes.com/sites/davelavinsky/2013/09/30/marketing-plan-template-exactly-what-to-include/. Accessed 12 Feb 2015.

7   Lesonsky, R. (2014). Do you have a marketing plan? https://www.sba.gov/blogs/do-you-have-marketing-plan. Accessed 12 Feb 2015.

8   Perner, L. (2010). Consumer behavior: The psychology of marketing. http://www.consumerpsychologist.com/. Accessed 11 Jan 2015.

9   Chand, S. (2015). 7 stages or steps involved in marketing research process. http://www. yourarticlelibrary.com/marketing/7-stages-or-steps-involved-in-marketing-research-process/27953/. Accessed 9 Jan 2015.

10 Market research. (2015). http://www.entrepreneur.com/encyclopedia/market-research. Accessed 9 Jan 2015.

11 The marketing mix and the 4Ps of marketing. (n.d.). http://www.mindtools.com/pages/article/ newSTR_94.htm. Accessed 14 Jan 2015.

12 United States Patent and Trademark Office (2013). Trademark, Patent, or Copyright? http://www. uspto.gov/trademarks-getting-started/trademark-basics/trademark-patent-or-copyright. Accessed 12 Jan 2015.

13 Types of product classification. (2015). http://www.mbanetbook.co.in/2011/01/types-of-product-classification-product.html. Accessed 29 March 2015.

14 Uhlig, D., (2015). Four types of pricing objectives. http://smallbusiness.chron.com/four-types-pricing-objectives-33873.html. Accessed 29 March 2015.

15 Odd even pricing. (n.d.). http://www.businessdictionary.com/definition/odd-even-pricing.html. Accessed 29 March 2015.

16 What is odd pricing–definition, example, meaning. (n.d.). http://www.psychologicalpricing.net/ odd-pricing/. Accessed 29 March 2015.

17 Distribution channel. (2015). http://www.businessdictionary.com/definition/distribution-channel. html. Accessed 3 Feb 2015.

18 Level of distribution coverage. (n.d.). http://www.knowthis.com/distribution-decisions/level-of-distribution-coverage. Accessed 3 Feb 2015.

19 Adaso, H., (2013). 5 differences between push marketing and pull marketing. http://www.dmn3.com/ dmn3-blog/five-differences-between-push-marketing-and-pull-marketing. Accessed 11 Feb 2015.

20 O'Reilly, L. (2015). These are the 10 companies that spend the most on advertising. Retrieved on March 1, 2016, from: http://www.businessinsider.com.

21 Edwards, J. (2014). The 10 biggest advertisers in America, ranked by dollars spent annually. http:// www.businessinsider.com. Accessed 11 May 2015.

22 Brookins, M. (2015). Examples of cause marketing. http://smallbusiness.chron.com/examples-cause-marketing-21133.html. Accessed 12 March 2015.

23 Hauwa, L. (2015). Product life cycle changes. http://www.academia.edu/5441144/Product_Life_ Cycle_Stages. Accessed 3 Feb 2015.

24 Sharma, N. (2013). Market strategy on different stages PLC and its marketing implications on FMCG products. International Journal of Marketing, Financial Services & Management Research, 2(3). http://indianresearchjournals.com/pdf/IJMFSMR/2013/March/12.pdf. Accessed 3 Feb 2015.

CHAPTER 7

1 Definition of management. (n.d.). http://www.businessdictionary.com/definition/management.html. Accessed 13 March 2015.

2 Norman, L. (2015). What are the four basic functions that make up the management process? http://smallbusiness.chron.com/four-basic-functions-make-up-management-process-23852.html. Accessed 1 March 2015.

3 Levels of management. (2015). http://www.managementstudyguide.com/management_levels.htm. Accessed 31 March 2015.

4 AMA's list of must-have management skills. (2015). http://www.amanet.org/training/promotions/six-skills-for-managers-and-leaders.aspx. Accessed 22 March 2015.

5 Romero, J. (2015). Sample vision statements. http://www.skills2lead.com/sample-vision-statements.html. Accessed 3 March 2015.

6 Examples of mission statements. (2015). http://examples.yourdictionary.com/examples-of-mission-statements.html. Accessed 3 March 2015.

7 Detailing types of plans. (2014). http://www.cliffsnotes.com/more-subjects/principles-of-management/organizational-planning/detailing-types-of-plans. Accessed 31 March 2015.

8 Richards-Gustafson, F. (2015). What is the difference between programmed & unprogrammed decisions from a business perspective? http://smallbusiness.chron.com/difference-between-programmed-unprogrammed-decisions-business-perspective-25876.html. Accessed 4 March 2015.

9 The Wall Street Journal (2015). Leadership styles. http://guides.wsj.com/management/developing-a-leadership-style/how-to-develop-a-leadership-style/. Accessed 2 March 2015.

10 Johnson, R. (n.d.). 5 different types of leadership styles. http://smallbusiness.chron.com/5-different-types-leadership-styles-17584.html. Accessed 1 April 2015.

11 Hersey-Blanchard Situational Leadership Theory. (n.d.). http://www.leadership-central.com/situational-leadership-theory.html#axzz3T0PKiEYU. Accessed 30 March 2015.

12 Friesen, W. (2012). Are you a Theory X or a Theory Y leader? http://www.inplantgraphics.com/article/are-you-theory-x-theory-y-leader/1. Accessed 1 April 2015.

13 Theory Z. (n.d.). http://www.businessdictionary.com/definition/theory-Z.html. Accessed 1 April 2015.

14 Doyle, A. (2015). Top 10 communication skills. http://jobsearch.about.com/od/skills/qt/communication-skills.htm. Accessed 2 April 2015.

15 Dodrill, P. (2014). Transparency through open communication. https://www.zendesk.com/blog/transparency-open-communication. Accessed 31 March 2015.

16 Bunnow, R. (2001). Noise in the communication process. https://www.wisc-online.com/learn/career-clusters/arts-audio-video-technology-and-communications/oic2501/noise-in-the-communication-process. Accessed 2 April 2015.

17 Sandilands, T. (2015). What are types of departmentalization that would be used in a restaurant? http://smallbusiness.chron.com/two-types-departmentalization-would-used-restaurant-38424.html. Accessed 1 March 2015.

18 Moore, S. (2012). Advantages of the span of control. http://www.ehow.com/about_4760759_ advantages-spanofcontrol.html. Accessed 1 April 2015.

19 Centralization versus decentralization of authority. (n.d.). http://business-basics.org/centralization-versus-decentralization-of-authority/. Accessed 1 April 2015.

20 Committee organizational structure. (n.d.). http://www.mbaknol.com/management-principles/ committee-organizational-structure/. Accessed 22 March 2015.

21 Matrix organization. (2015). http://www.businessdictionary.com/definition/matrix-organization. html. Accessed 24 March 2015.

CHAPTER 8

1 The people solution. (1998). Calculating employee turnover rates. http://www.beta.mmb.state. mn.us/doc/wfp/turnover.pdf. Accessed 17 March 2015.

2 Morgan, R. (2014). 5 key elements to hiring a first class team. http://realbusiness.co.uk/ article/26678-5-key-elements-to-hiring-a-first-class-team. Accessed 18 March 2015.

3 Brookins, M. (n.d.). The advantages & disadvantages of job enrichment. http://smallbusiness. chron.com/advantages-disadvantages-job-enrichment-11960.html. Accessed 16 March 2015.

4 HRSmart. (2013). Employee performance management. 360 appraisals. https://www.hrsmart.com/ solutions/performance-management/360-appraisals. Accessed 19 March 2015.

5 The different forms of compensation. (2013). http://businessecon.org/2013/01/the-different-forms-of-compensation/. Accessed 20 March 2015.

6 U.S. Department of Labor. (n.d.). Employment cost statistics. http://www.dol.gov/dol/topic/ statistics/industries.htm. Accessed 20 March 2015.

7 Summary of labor laws. (n.d.). http://www.dol.gov/opa/aboutdol/lawsprog.htm. Accessed 17 March 2015.

8 EEOC. (n.d.). The Americans with disabilities act: A primer for small business. http://www.eeoc. gov/eeoc/publications/adahandbook.cfm. Accessed 18 March 2015.

9 U.S. Department of Labor. (n.d.). Family and medical leave. http://www.dol.gov/dol/topic/ benefits-leave/fmla.htm. Accessed 18 March 2015.

10 Herzberg's motivators and hygiene factors. (n.d.). http://www.mindtools.com/pages/article/ newTMM_74.htm. Accessed 20 March 2015.

11 Expectancy theory of motivation. (2013). http://www.managementstudyguide.com/expectancy-theory-motivation.htm. Accessed 20 March 2015.

12 Management by objectives. (n.d.). http://www.investopedia.com/terms/m/management-by-objectives.asp. Accessed 23 March 2015.

13 Kadian-Baumeyer, K. (2015). Locke's goal-setting theory: Using goals to advance motivation. http://study.com/academy/lesson/lockes-goal-setting-theory-using-goals-to-advance-motivation. html. Accessed 23 March 2015.

14 The history of labor unions & fight for fairness at work. (2015). http://www.unionplus.org/about/ labor-unions/history-origin. Accessed 24 March 2015.

15   Wagner Act. (n.d.). http://legal-dictionary.thefreedictionary.com/Wagner+Act. Accessed 24 March 2015.

16   U.S. Department of Labor. (2015). The Fair Labor Standards Act (FLSA). http://www.dol.gov/compliance/laws/comp-flsa.htm. Accessed 24 March 2015.

17   Taft-Hartley Act. (n.d.) http://www.investopedia.com/terms/t/tafthartleyact.asp. Accessed 24 March 2015.

18   Landrum-Griffin Act. (2015). http://employment.laws.com/landrum-griffin-act. Accessed 24 March 2015.

19   Flemer, R. (2013). The future of labor unions in the U.S. http://www.jdsupra.com/legalnews/the-future-of-labor-unions-in-the-us-21121/. Accessed 24 March 2015.

CHAPTER 9

1   The various types of production systems and their importance. (n.d.). http://www.scribd.com/doc/28207305/The-Various-Types-of-Production-Systems-and-their-Importance#scribd. Accessed 26 March 2015.

2   Flexible manufacturing system. (n.d.). http://encyclopedia2.thefreedictionary.com/Flexible+production. Accessed 11 April 2015.

3   Holstein, W. (2015). Production system. http://www.britannica.com/EBchecked/topic/478032/production-system. Accessed 11 April 2015.

4   EPA. (2015). Lean manufacturing and the environment. http://www.epa.gov/lean/environment/. Accessed 13 April 2015.

5   Lean.org. (n.d.). What is lean? http://www.lean.org/WhatsLean/. Accessed 13 April 2015.

6   P2P foundation. (n.d.). Rapid manufacturing. http://p2pfoundation.net/Rapid_Manufacturing. Accessed 18 April 2015.

7   National Council for Advanced Manufacturing. (2008). Sustainable manufacturing. http://www.nacfam.org/PolicyInitiatives/SustainableManufacturing/tabid/64/Default.aspx. Accessed 19 April 2015.

8   U.S. Green Building Council. (2015). LEED. http://www.usgbc.org/leed. Accessed 19 April 2015.

9   Rouse, M. (2015) PERT (Program Evaluation Review Technique) chart. http://searchsoftwarequality.techtarget.com/definition/PERT-chart. Accessed 19 April 2015.

10   iSix Sigma. (2015). What is six sigma? http://www.isixsigma.com/new-to-six-sigma/getting-started/what-six-sigma/. Accessed 19 April 2015.

11   ISO. (n.d.). ISO 9000—Quality management. http://www.iso.org/iso/iso_9000. Accessed 20 April 2015.

CHAPTER 10

1   The most populous continents in the world 2015. (2015). http://www.blatantworld.com/data/the-most-populous-continents-in-the-world-2015/. Accessed 21 May 2015.

2   U.S. exports of goods by state, zip code based, by NAICS-Based Product. (2015). http://www.census.gov/foreign-trade/statistics/state/zip/2014/12/zipstate.txt. Accessed 22 April 2015.

3   Top trading partners. (2015). http://www.census.gov/foreign-trade/statistics/highlights/toppartners.html#total. Accessed 22 April 2015.

4   U.S. international trade in goods and services. (2016). http://www.bea.gov/newsreleases/international/trade/tradnewsrelease.htm. Accessed 20 May 2016.

5   Latest U.S. international trade in goods and services report. (2016). http://www.census.gov/foreign-trade/data/. Accessed 20 May 2016.

6   Per capita GDP. (2015). http://www.investopedia.com/terms/p/per-capita-gdp.asp. Accessed 27 April 2015.

7   GDP per capita ranking. (2015). http://knoema.com/sijweyg/gdp-per-capita-ranking-2015-data-and-charts. Accessed 27 April 2015.

8   North American Free Trade Agreement (NAFTA). (2011). https://ustr.gov/trade-agreements/free-trade-agreements/north-american-free-trade-agreement-nafta. Accessed 22 April 2015.

9   Central America-Dominican Republic Free Trade Agreement (CAFTA-DR). (2014). http://export.gov/%5C/FTA/cafta-dr/index.asp. Accessed 22 April 2015.

10 European Union (EU). (n.d.). http://www.britannica.com/EBchecked/topic/196399/European-Union-EU. Accessed 23 April 2015.

11 Brazil, Russia, India and China. (n.d.). http://www.investopedia.com/terms/b/bric.asp. Accessed 23 April 2015.

12 Market entry strategies. (n.d.). http://www.tradestart.ca/market-entry-strategies. Accessed 25 April 2015.

13 Allen, S. (n.d.). What is a joint venture and how do they work? http://entrepreneurs.about.com/od/beyondstartup/a/jointventures.htm. Accessed 26 April 2015.

14 The New Economy. (2014). In bed with big brother: Apple and IBM form strategic alliance. http://www.theneweconomy.com/home/strategic-alliance-ibm-apple. Accessed 26 April 2015.

CHAPTER 11

1   Information. (n.d.). http://www.businessdictionary.com/definition/information.html. Accessed 28 April 2015.

2   Zwass, V. (2015). Information systems. http://www.britannica.com/EBchecked/topic/287895/information-system. Accessed 28 April 2015.

3   Techopedia. (2015). Operational support system (OSS). http://www.techopedia.com/definition/24238/operational-support-system-oss. Accessed 29 April 2015.

4   Management information systems (MIS). (n.d.). http://www.inc.com/encyclopedia/management-information-systems-mis.html. Accessed 1 May 2015.

5   Aremerding, T. (2012). The 15 worst data security breaches of the 21st century. http://www. csoonline.com/article/2130877/data-protection/data-protection-the-15-worst-data-security-breaches-of-the-21st-century.html. Accessed 1 May 2015.

6   Steiner, D. (2014). Staggering cost of malware is now over $100 billion a year. http://www. smallbusiness.yahoo.com. Accessed 26 May 2015.

7   Worm. (2015). http://www.webopedia.com/TERM/W/worm.html. Accessed 30 April 2015.

8   McAfee, A. (2011). What every CEO needs to know about the cloud. *Harvard Business Review*. https://hbr.org/2011/11/what-every-ceo-needs-to-know-about-the-cloud/ar/1. Accessed 28 April 2015.

9   Bajarin, T. (2014). The next big thing for tech: The Internet of everything. http://time.com/539/ the-next-big-thing-for-tech-the-internet-of-everything/. Accessed 26 May 2015.

10   Bartels, A. (2000). The difference between e-business and e-commerce. *Computerworld*. http:// www.computerworld.com/article/2588708/e-commerce/the-difference--between-e-business-and-e-commerce.html. Accessed 6 May 2015.

11   Northern Territory Government Department of Business. (n.d.). What is e-business? http://www. dob.nt.gov.au/business/starting-business/ebusiness/Pages/ebusiness.aspx. Accessed 20 May 2015.

12   Ward, S. (2015). Social media definition. http://sbinfocanada.about.com/od/socialmedia/g/social-media.htm. Accessed 21 May 2015.

13   McMahon, D. (2010). Twitter. http://whatis.techtarget.com/definition/Twitter. Accessed 21 May 2015.

14   Janssen, C. (n.d.). Pinterest. http://www.techopedia.com/definition/28407/pinterest. Accessed 22 May 2015.

15   U.S. Attorney's Office-Federal Bureau of Investigation. (2013). Couple pleads guilty in computer hacking case. http://www.fbi.gov/pittsburgh/press-releases/2013/couple-pleads-guilty-in-computer-hacking-case. Accessed 4 May 2015.

16   Goldman, J. (2013). Pittsburgh couple sentenced for hacking law firm. http://www.esecurityplanet. com/hackers/pittsburgh-couple-sentenced-for-hacking-law-firm.html. Accessed 26 May 2015.

CHAPTER 12

1   Vernon, S. (2013). Will Social Security run out of money? http://www.cbsnews.com/news/will-social-security-run-out-of-money/. Accessed 28 May 2015.

2   Picchi, A. (2015). America's skyrocketing credit card debt. http://www.cbsnews.com/news/ americas-skyrocketing-credit-card-debt/. Accessed 28 May 2015.

3   Student Loan Hero (2016). A look at the shocking student loan debt statistics for 2016. Retrieved on May 24, 2016, from: https://studentloanhero.com.

4   The Domestic Policy Council and the Council of Economic Advisors. (2014). Taking action: Higher education and student debt. https://www.whitehouse.gov/sites/default/files/docs/student_ debt_report_final.pdf. Accessed 28 May 2015.

5   Investopedia. (n.d.). Principal, interest, taxes, insurance– PITI. http://www.investopedia.com/ terms/p/piti.asp. Accessed 11 May 2015.

6   Five common myths about your credit reports. (2016) Star Tribune, Business section, D4. Retrieved on May 23, 2016, from: http://www.startribune.com.

7   Fair Isaac Corporation (2016). How my FICO scores are calculated. Retrieved on May 24, 2016, from: http://www.myfico.com.

8   Investopedia. (n.d.). Stock. http://www.investopedia.com/terms/s/stock.asp. Accessed 11 May 2015.

9   Mutual fund. (n.d.). http://www.investorwords.com/3173/mutual_fund.html. Accessed 12 May 2015.

10 IRS. (2015). Roth IRAs. http://www.irs.gov/Retirement-Plans/Roth-IRAs. Accessed 13 May 2015.

11 Pant, P. (2015). How to be a millionaire. http://budgeting.about.com/od/Why_Budget/a/How-To-Be-A-Millionaire.htm. Accessed 28 May 2015.

12 IRS. (2014). Types of retirement plans. http://www.irs.gov/Retirement-Plans/Plan-Sponsor/Types-of-Retirement-Plans-1. Accessed 13 May 2015.

13 Metlife. (2014). Term life insurance. https://www.metlife.com/individual/insurance/life-insurance/term-life-insurance.html. Accessed 13 May 2015.

14 Solin, D. (2014). Which is better for you: Term or permanent life insurance? http://money.usnews.com/money/blogs/the-smarter-mutual-fund-investor/2014/02/26/which-is-better-for-you-term-or-permanent-life-insurance. Accessed 28 May 2015.

CHAPTER 13

1   Graves, J. (2014). The 20 fastest-growing jobs this decade. *U.S. News*. http://money.usnews.com/money/careers/articles/2014/03/06/the-20-fastest-growing-jobs-this-decade. Accessed 14 May 2015.

2   Bureau of Labor Statistics. (2015). Employment projections, United States Department of Labor. http://www.bls.gov/emp/ep_chart_001.htm. Accessed 14 May 2015.

3   The Riley Guide. (2014). Self-assessment resources. http://www.rileyguide.com/assess.html. Accessed 14 May 2015.

4   Morgan, H. (2014). Don't believe these 8 job search myths. http://money.usnews.com/money/blogs/outside-voices-careers/2014/09/17/dont-believe-these-8-job-search-myths. Accessed 29 May 2015.

5   Morgan, H. (2014). Don't believe these 8 job search myths. http://money.usnews.com/money/blogs/outside-voices-careers/2014/09/17/dont-believe-these-8-job-search-myths. Accessed 29 May 2015.

6   Giang, V. (2012). What recruiters look at during the 6 seconds they spend on your resume. http://www.businessinsider.com/heres-what-recruiters-look-at-during-the-6-seconds-they-spend-on-your-resume-2012-4. Accessed 29 May 2015.

7   What are the different types of resume formats? (2015). http://www.americasjobexchange.com/career-advice/types-of-resume-formats. Accessed 29 May 2015.

8   ULS. (2014). Paper resume vs. electronic resume: what to send when. http://www.

universitylanguage.com/resumes/paper-or-electronic-resume/. Accessed 16 May 2015.

9   Minnesota Department of Employment and Economic Development. (n.d.). Types of interviews. http://mn.gov/deed/job-seekers/job-guide/job-interview/types.jsp. Accessed 16 May 2015.

10 SHRM. (2015). What should be included in a total compensation statement. http://www.shrm. org/templatestools/hrqa/pages/totalcompensationstatement.aspx. Accessed 16 May 2015.

11 Bureau of Labor Statistics. (2014). Employer costs for employee compensation. http://www.bls. gov/news.release/ecec.nr0.htm. Accessed 16 May 2015.

12 American Management Association (2014). The myth of generational differences in the workplace. http://www.amanet.org/training/articles/The-Myth-of-Generational-Differences-in-the-Workplace.aspx. Accessed 29 May 2015.

13 Riggio, R. (2013). The 3 keys to workplace success. Psychology Today. https://www. psychologytoday.com/blog/cutting-edge-leadership/201301/the-3-keys-workplace-success. Accessed 16 May 2015.

APPENDIX B

1   U.S. Small Business Administration 8(a) Business Plan-Form 1010C. (2010). https://www.sba.gov/ sites/default/files/SBA%201010C.pdf. Accessed 25 April 2015.

GLOSSARY

360-degree feedback: A comprehensive evaluation tool that gathers information from multiple sources.

401K: A retirement savings plan supported by an employer in a for-profit business.

403b: A retirement plan for employees of public schools, churches, hospitals, or the government.

Absolute advantage: When a country has a monopoly or can produce goods more efficiently than any other country.

Accounting: The act of collecting, organizing, and interpreting financial data.

Accounting cycle: Identifying, collecting and analyzing documents and transactions to create financial statements.

Accounting equation: Assets = Liabilities + Owner's Equity

Acid test (quick ratio): Measures ability to convert assets into cash.

Acquisition: One firm purchasing most or all of another company's assets in order to assume control of the target firm.

Action research: Research used to solve an immediate problem within an organization.

Activity ratios: Measure how effectively management uses organizational assets.

Adam Smith: The father of modern economics.

Adjustable-rate mortgage (ARM): A loan where the interest rate changes with market conditions.

Advertising: Calling public attention to a company's product or service through paid advertisements.

Affirmative action: Programs designed to hire underrepresented individuals in the workplace.

Agile manufacturing: Using flexibility and speed as a competitive advantage.

Analytic production: Breaking down raw materials into one or more products.

Angel investors: Wealthy individuals who provide capital in exchange for ownership equity.

Assets: Valuable items that are owned by a business.

Autocratic leadership: Manager makes most decisions with little input from others.

Average collection period: Shows how long a company waits to collect money from customers.

B2B: Businesses selling products or services to other businesses.

B2C: Businesses selling products or services to end-users (consumers).

Balance of payments: The flow of money in and out of a country in a given year.

Balance of trade: A nation's total exports minus the total imports over a given time period.

Balance sheet: Summarizes a company's assets, liabilities, and owner's equity.

Big data: Large data sets.

Bona fide occupational qualifications (BFOQ): Qualifications that an employee must hold in order to fulfill the duties of a given job.

Bonds: An IOU from an organization.

Bookkeeping: Keeping the financial records of a firm.

Boycott: Completely stopping the use or purchase of a company's goods or services.

Brand equity: The value that a company's name gives to a product or service.

Brand loyalty: Consumers' faithfulness to a specific brand.

Branding: Creating an exclusive name, image, or symbol for a company or product that differentiates it from its competition.

Breakeven analysis: The point at which the number of units sold covers the cost of producing the products.

Business: An organized effort of producing and selling goods and services.

Business cycle: The phases of growth and decline in an economy.

Business ethics: The practical application of moral standards within business situations.

Business incubator: Shared facilities to nurture startup firms.

Business law: Laws that dictate how to establish and operate a business.

Business plan: A detailed plan of how a company plans to achieve its goals.

C-corporation: A business entity owned by shareholders but separates assets and liabilities from them.

Capitalism: An economic system characterized by a free market and private control of production and consumption exists.

Car loan: A loan from a bank, credit union, or finance company to purchase an automobile.

Carbon footprint: Carbon compounds released into the atmosphere by an individual, company, or country.

Centralization: Decisions are made from the top-down in an organization.

Certificate of deposit (CD): An investment made in a bank for a specified length of time at a specified interest rate.

Certified Public Accountant (CPA): An individual who passes an exam and meets specific requirements in order to become an accountant.

Chronological resume: A resume that focuses on the most recent work experience.

CIO: An individual who oversees and manages information systems.

Cloud computing: Storing information or using services from the web.

Code of ethics: A written statement of how an organization expects employees to behave within the organization.

Collective bargaining: The process by which union representation negotiates employee contracts with employers.

College loan debt: The amount of debt incurred by a student while attending a post-secondary institution.

Commercial paper: Short-term debt issued by a corporation to raise money.

Committee organization: Utilizes a group or committee for authority and oversight instead of a single manager.

Common stock: Shareholders who vote and earn dividends after preferred stockholders.

Communism: An economic system in which all activity is controlled by a centralized government.

Comparative advantage: When a country can produce goods or services at a lower opportunity cost (they give up less) than other countries.

Compensation: The total of all wages and benefits paid to employees.

Competitive advantage: A distinct advantage a business has over its competition.

Competitive pricing: Matching competitors' pricing.

Compressed work week: Shifting a 40-hour work week into less than five days.

Compliance-based: Rules and regulations to ensure ethics compliance in an organization.

Computer-Aided Design (CAD): System that uses a computer to design and test products before producing them.

Computer-Aided Manufacturing (CAM): Uses technology to analyze each machine in the production process.

Computer-Integrated Manufacturing (CIM): Unifies all processes in manufacturing and with workers to effectively manage operations.

Computer security: The protection of computing systems and the data they store.

Conceptual skills: Skills that allow a manager to view the organization as a whole.

Consumer behavior: The study of buyers and the processes they use to select products or services that satisfy their needs and wants.

Consumer Bill of Rights: Six basic rights introduced by President John F. Kennedy in 1962 to protect consumers.

Consumer Price Index (CPI): Measures the average prices of a basket of consumer goods and services in order to determine inflation rates.

Consumerism: Actions taken to protect consumer rights.

Contingency plan: Alternative course of action that can be utilized if the original plan needs revision.

Continuous production: Assembly line production where there is a continuous flow of products.

Contract manufacturing: When a manufacturer produces the same product for different companies.

Copyright: Legal protection for an author's original works.

Corporate entrepreneurship: The development of new ideas and opportunities within large or established businesses.

Corporate philanthropy: Contributions of time, money, or resources given by an organization to charity.

Corporate social responsibility (CSR): A business's duty to maximize its positive impact on all stakeholders, the community, and the environment.

Cover letter: Letter submitted with your resume that indicates your interest in a particular position.

Credit cards: Short-term loans issued to consumers to purchase goods and services.

Credit report: A report detailing your financial history.

Critical path: The highest number of days to complete a project.

Crowdfunding: Raising money from individuals for a project.

Current ratio: Compares ratio of assets to liabilities in an organization.

Customer-driven production: A process where products are produced by linking directly to customer demand.

Cybercrime: Crime that involves a computer or computer network.

Data: Raw facts or information used to analyze, plan, or calculate something of relevance to the user.

Data mining: An analytical method used to extract usable data from data warehouses

Data warehouses: Interactive databases designed for inquiry and analysis.

Debt financing: Borrowing money that must be repaid.

Debt ratio: Measures how much debt a company has for each dollar in assets.

Debt-to-equity: Measures relationship between liabilities and the owners' capital.

Decentralization: Decisions are made from the bottom-up in an organization.

Delegation: Assigning responsibility and authority to employees to accomplish tasks.

Demand: The readiness and capability of buyers to purchase goods or services at different price levels.

Demographics: The study of a population that analyzes factors such as race, age, sex, etc.

Departmentalization: Dividing a company by functional units or other criteria.

Direct compensation: Salaries, hourly wages, or bonuses paid by an employer.

Direct selling: The use of independent sales representatives who use person-to-person sales directly to consumers.

Discount pricing: Short-term price drops designed to increase sales.

Discouraged workers: Individuals who have given up looking for employment.

Distributed workforce: Geographically disbursed employees who work for an organization domestically or internationally.

Distribution channel: The route a product travels between the producer and the consumer.

Distribution intensity: How widely available a company's products are distributed in the market place.

Diversification: Investing in many assets or investments to reduce risk.

Dividends: Earnings on each share of stock owned.

Doctrine of equity: Requires a court to resolve a case based on principles of fairness and justness.

Dodd-Frank Act: Law passed in 2010 to help lower risks in the financial system and protect consumers.

Double-entry bookkeeping: Transactions are recorded in two areas that offset one another.

Dumping: Selling goods to other countries for prices lower than they are being sold domestically.

E-business: Conducting business via the Internet, Intranet, or Extranet.

E-commerce: Trading merchandise with customers, suppliers, or other external members of an organization via the Internet.

Economic model: Focused on maximizing profits and returns to shareholders.

Economics: An analysis of how societies use scarce resources to produce, distribute, and monitor consumption of goods and services around the world.

EDLP: Continuous low prices.

Embargo: A complete ban on imports or exports to and from a country.

Emotional intelligence (EI): The ability to identify, understand, and manage one's emotions in positive ways.

Employee retention: A company's ability to retain employees.

Employee turnover: The number of employees who leave an organization after initial training is completed.

Entrepreneur: A person who starts a business and is willing to risk loss in order to make money.

Environmental Protection Agency (EPA): Governmental agency that regulates business effects on the environment.

Environmentalism: The effort made by an organization to protect the environment.

Equilibrium price: The point at which supply matches demand for a particular good or service.

Equity financing: Investments by others for an exchange of ownership in the business.

Ethics: The study of right and wrong within a society.

Exchange rates: The rate at which currencies in one country are exchanged for currency in another country.

Expansionary monetary policy: Stimulating the economy by increasing the money supply and lowering interest rates.

Expectancy: A person's belief that effort leads to an expected performance.

Exporting: Selling products or services in a foreign market.

External recruiting: Hiring employees from outside of the organization.

External stakeholders: Individuals outside a firm who are affected by its actions.

External users: Secondary users outside of an organization.

Extranet: A network available via a web portal for users who have a valid user name and password.

Factoring: Selling accounts receivables in order to gain funding for a business.

FASB: Establishes accounting standards for financial reporting.

Federal Reserve Bank: The central bank of the United States, which regulates banking institutions.

FICO score: The credit score lenders use to assess risk in extending loans to individuals.

Financial manager: Individual who examines, plans, assesses, and manages financial functions of the organization.

Financial plan: A road-map to help an individual reach his or her financial goals.

Financing activities: Transactions directly involved with financing the company from startup to expansion.

First-level management: Supervisory managers responsible for employees and front-line tasks.

Fiscal policy: The actions of the Federal government to achieve macroeconomic policy objectives through "tax and spend" policies.

Fixed costs: Costs that do not fluctuate based on sales volume.

Fixed-rate mortgage: A loan where the interest rate stays the same throughout the life of the loan.

Flexible benefits: The ability to select benefits that best fit an employee's needs.

Flexible manufacturing: A process that produces smaller quantities through the use of computer-based systems.

Flextime: Offering a variety of shifts for employees to select from in an organization.

For-profit organization: A company engaged in selling a product or service primarily for a profit.

Four P's: Product, price, place, and promotion.

Franchisee: An individual or business that purchases a franchise.

Franchising: Paying for the use of a firm's successful business model and brand for a prescribed period of time.

Franchisor: The supplier who allows a franchisee to use the supplier's trademark and distribute the supplier's products or services.

Fringe benefits: Indirect compensation paid to employees.

Functional resume: A resume that focuses on your skills and experience first.

GAAP: Generally accepted accounting principles used for reporting financial information.

Gantt chart: A bar graph to show what task is being worked on and how long it will take to complete each task.

GDP per capita: A country's total output (GDP) divided by the number of people in the country, used to determine standard of living.

Globalization: The integration of world-wide economics, trade, financial systems, and communications.

Good faith: Honesty in business transactions and conduct.

Great Depression: A severe worldwide economic depression during the late 1930s through the middle 1940s.

Green manufacturing: Incorporating environmentally-friendly operating processes within an organization.

Gross margin: Shows what percentage of each dollar results in profit after expenses are paid.

Green marketing: The practice of selling products and/or services based on their environmental benefits.

Gross Domestic Product (GDP): The total value of goods and services produced within a country's borders over some unit of time.

Hardware: The tangible parts or components of a computer.

Human relation skills: Skills that enable managers to effectively communicate with and motivate people.

Human resources (HR): Department that attracts, trains, develops, and retains employees who help the organization reach its goals and objectives.

Hygiene factors: Factors related to the work environment that affect satisfaction.

IASB: Board developed to promote consistent financial reporting around the globe.

Income statement: Profit and loss statement.

IFRS: International reporting standards.

Indirect compensation: All non-paid benefits an employer provides to employees.

Inflation: A sustained increase in the general price level of goods and services.

Information: Processing data and turning it into knowledge.

Information system: A formal system used to collect, store and process data within an organization.

Infrastructure: The availability of all communication, public works, energy, and transportation systems within a country.

Inputs: Raw materials or ideas used to create another product or service.

Integrated marketing communications (IMC): The process of coordinating all promotional activities within an organization.

Integrity-based: Views ethics as an opportunity to implement core values of the organization.

Internet: A network available to anyone with an Internet-connected device.

Internet of Everything: The Internet connectivity and intelligence of everyday devices in order to give each device special functions.

Intranet: A network available to a small group of users.

Instrumentality: Belief that the company will deliver promised rewards.

Insurance: A risk reduction policy.

Internal recruiting: Hiring employees from within the organization to fill open positions.

Internal stakeholders: Individuals within a firm who are affected by its actions.

Internal users: Primary users within an organization.

Intermittent production: A system with interrupted intervals in the material flow process.

Intrapreneurs: Employees within a company who are assigned a special idea or project and have the resources and capabilities of the firm at their disposal.

Inventory turnover rate: Measures how long it takes to convert inventory into sales.

Investing activities: Transactions used for investing purposes.

Invisible Hand: Smith's philosophy that describes how an individual's personal gain benefits others and the economy.

ISO 9000: Principles to demonstrate work toward customer satisfaction and continual quality improvement as an organization.

ISO 14000: Standards to support companies who work to minimize environmental harm.

JIT manufacturing: Reducing inventory and production costs by producing and ordering on demand.

Job enlargement: Adding to the number of tasks associated with a certain job.

Job enrichment: Empowering employees to make the job more challenging by adding new skills, knowledge, and decision-making ability.

Job rotation: Learning several jobs within an organization.

Job sharing: Two employees sharing one full-time position.

Joint venture: A partnership in which two or more companies agree to develop a new, combined organization.

Keynesian: School of economic thought that supports government intervention to stabilize the economy.

Labor union: A group of workers who join forces to improve working conditions and pay.

Laissez-faire/Free-rein leadership: Employees determine policies and methods used to achieve goals.

LAN: A network used to link computers and machines between short distances.

Lean manufacturing: Aims to reduce waste while providing high-quality products.

LEED: Certification that recognizes sustainability in the construction of new buildings.

Leverage ratios: Ratios used to measure how much a firm relies on debt to operate the business.

Liabilities: Debt that businesses owe to others.

Licensing: An agreement to pay for the rights to use a licensor's intangible property.

Limited liability corporation (LLC): A hybrid type of legal structure that provides limited liability like a corporation with the tax benefits and flexibility of a partnership.

Line-and-staff organization: Two types of managerial authority granted by an organizational structure, line and staff.

Line organization: The chain of command flows from top-level management to employees.

Liquidity ratios: Ratios used to measure the ability of a firm to pay short-term debt.

Lockout: Ordering a temporary stop to work to force compliance in negotiations.

Long-term financing: Funds needed for more than one year.

Macroeconomics: The study of economic indicators such as unemployment, inflation, and gross domestic product, and their influence on the economy as a whole.

Malware: Software utilized to corrupt, disrupt, or gather sensitive information from private or public computer systems.

Management: The organization and coordination of business activities, resources, and people in order to achieve strategic goals.

Marketing: The process of creating, communicating, delivering, and exchanging goods and services that have value.

Marketing concept: A philosophy focused on customer orientation, customer satisfaction, and profit.

Marketing mix: The strategic mix of the controllable elements within a product's marketing plan.

Marketing plan: A written document that shows how a business will use its resources, establish objectives, develop marketing strategy, and implement and control the plan.

Marketing research: The process of gathering, analyzing, and interpreting data about a market, product or service, and consumers.

Marketing segmentation: Subdividing a large market into identifiable segments that have similar needs, wants, or characteristics.

Marketing strategy: A plan to determine the target market and proper marketing mix.

Marxism: Theory that states it is best to allow a centralized government to control production and to share resources equally among citizens.

Mass production: The production of large quantities, typically on an assembly line.

Matrix organization: Managing employees with more than one reporting line.

Merger: Combining of two or more companies into one company.

Microeconomics: A division of economics that studies the behavior of individual consumers and suppliers as they make decisions.

Microloans: SBA loans up to $50,000 to help small businesses start up or expand.

Micromanagement: Providing too much oversight or control over employees after delegating.

Middle-level management: Mid-level managers responsible for specific areas and who report to top managers.

MIS: Information systems used to guide all levels of management in generating reports and making decisions.

Mission statement: A statement describing the reason a company exists.

Mixed economies: Economies that combine elements of capitalism and socialism.

Monetarism: School of thought that the Federal Reserve System should control the supply of money as the chief method of stabilizing the economy.

Monetary policy: The actions of the Federal Reserve System to achieve macroeconomic policy objectives such as price stability, full employment, and economic growth.

Monopolistic competition: Many heterogeneous products are sold by firms and are differentiated in the marketplace.

Monopoly: A market environment where only one provider of a certain economic good or service exists.

Mortgage: Loan used to buy real estate.

Motivational factors: Factors related to the job itself that affect motivation.

Mutual fund: An investment that combines several stocks into one fund.

Net worth: The difference between your assets and liabilities.

Networking: Relationship building for employment or business purposes.

Noise: Anything that interferes with communicating a message properly.

Non-profit marketing: Marketing related to non-profit business activities.

Non-profit organization: An organization whose primary purpose is to serve society versus making a profit.

Non-programmed decisions: Decisions made in situations where no established policies or protocols have been determined.

Odd pricing: Using odd number to price products.

Oligopoly: A small group of firms control the market.

On-demand computing: Technology that allows users to pay for what they use.

Operating activities: Day-to-day business operations of an organization.

Operational plan: A plan that is very specific and outlines the standards and schedules needed to achieve tactical objectives.

Operations management: The process of managing people and processes to transform raw materials into finished products and services.

Organizational chart: Illustrates reporting relationships within an organization.

Organizational structure: The organization of employees, jobs, and the way work will get done.

Orientation: Process to help new employees become acquainted with the company, employees, and policies.

OSS: Information systems used to create and share information about business activities within the organization and externally.

Outputs: The finished products created by processing inputs.

Outsourcing: Reducing costs by sending work to outside vendors.

Owner's equity: Amount owner has invested plus profits not distributed.

Paid time off (PTO): Flexible time given to employees to use for vacation, sick, or holiday time.

Participative/democratic leadership: Employees are involved in the decision-making process.

Partnership: A business where two or more people share ownership.

Patent: Legal protection for an invention.

Per capita GDP: A measure of a country's economic strength and standard of living as compared to other countries.

Performance appraisals: A formal evaluation of employees' skills and productivity.

Personal selling: A salesperson sells a product, service, or solution to a customer.

PERT chart: A project management tool utilized for scheduling, organizing, and coordinating project tasks.

Penetration pricing: Setting a low initial price to gain a greater percentage of the overall market.

Picketing: Standing or walking in front of a business in order to discourage customer patronage.

PITI: Total monthly mortgage payments including principal, interest, taxes, and insurance.

Portfolio: All assets or financial holdings of an investor.

Preferred stock: Stock owners who get paid dividends first and who have priority over common shareholders

Price objective: A marketing strategy that helps guide businesses in setting the selling price of products or services.

Price skimming: Setting the initial price high to maximize profits.

Primary data: Data collected first-hand by the company.

Product life cycle (PLC): The four stages of a product's life in the marketplace.

Product line: A group of similar products aimed at the same target market.

Product mix: All the product lines that a company sells.

Production: The process of utilizing resources to transform raw materials into finished products and services.

Production control: The list of activities used in any production process.

Productivity: A measure of how much is produced with available resources.

Profit: Income after costs and expenses are deducted from sales revenue.

Profitability ratios: Ratios used to measure how well managers use available resources to make a profit.

Programmed decisions: Simple, common, and typically frequent decisions where the outcome is fairly predictable.

Project system: A one-time-use system to develop a product or project.

Promotion: Creating consumer awareness of a product or brand, generating sales, and creating brand loyalty.

Promotional objectives: Specific goals to be achieved through various marketing activities.

Protectionism: Government policies that restrict global trade to protect local businesses and jobs from foreign competition.

Public relations: Actions by a business to create a strong and favorable public image.

Publicity: Unpaid promotion of a company's products or services.

Pulling strategy: Creating demand for products through customers.

Pure competition: Many competitors with little influence on price exist in the market.

Pushing strategy: Creating demand for products within the distribution channel.

Qualitative research: Inquiry research used to uncover trends in thoughts and opinions.

Quality control: Monitoring the production process to determine if company and customer standards have been met.

Quantitative research: Uses numbers to formulate facts and uncover patterns in a set of data.

Quotas: Limits on the amount of imported goods and services that are allowed to enter a country.

Rapid manufacturing: A process used to design, create, and manufacture products rapidly.

Ratio analysis: Using ratios to calculate the financial health of the organization.

Recruiting: The process of attracting qualified candidates to fill open positions in an organization.

Remote offices: Working from home to complete job responsibilities.

Restrictive monetary policy: Slowing down the economy by decreasing the money supply and raising interest rates.

Resume: A one-page document that provides a brief summary of your skills, abilities and accomplishments.

Return on equity: Shows how much a company earns on each dollar invested by shareholders of the company.

Return on sales (operating margin): Shows how well a firm generates income from sales.

Reverse discrimination: Discrimination against majority groups in hiring practices.

Risk/Reward tradeoff: The potential gain one might receive when taking a risk.

Roth IRA: An after-tax investment option.

S-corporation: A special type of corporation that has less than 100 stockholders and avoids double taxation by distributing remaining profits as dividends.

Sales promotion: Activities that attempt to provide added value or incentives to customers to encourage immediate purchase.

Sarbanes Oxley Act of 2002 (SOX): Federal legislation that established new rules and regulations for accounting practices and securities trading.

Savings: The part of your income not spent or used for immediate expenses.

Scalable entrepreneurs: Those seeking to create large businesses by starting on a smaller scale.

Secondary data: Data collected by outside sources used to make internal decisions.

Seed capital: The initial capital used to start a business.

Selection process: Gathering applicants' information and basing hiring decisions on qualifications and education.

Serial entrepreneur: An individual who continuously comes up with new ideas and/or starts new businesses.

Service mark: Legal protection for a service.

Shareholder: An individual who owns shares of stock in a company.

Short-term financing: Funds needed for less than one year.

Situational leadership: Changing leadership styles based on employees' maturity and readiness to complete tasks.

Six Sigma: A data-driven approach designed to eliminate defects.

Skunkworks: A special or secret project worked on by a group of employees in an organization.

Small business: A business with 500 or less employees.

Small Business Administration (SBA): Governmental agency designed to aid in small business development.

Small business entrepreneurs: People who start a small business with their own savings or money acquired from relatives or friends.

Social entrepreneur: An individual with innovative solutions to social problems.

Social media: Any form of electronic or online communication where users share personal information, videos, personal messages, or other ideas.

Social responsibility: A business or individual who acts for the benefit of society at large.

Socialism: An economic system in which major industries are controlled by the government, while private owners operate noncritical industry businesses.

Socioeconomic model: Business has responsibilities to society at large beyond maximizing profits.

Software: The programs and programming languages that direct the operations of a computer system.

Sole proprietorship: The simplest form of business ownership operated by one individual.

Span of control: The number of employees who report to a manager.

Sponsorships: A company pays for costs associated with a project or program in exchange for advertising or recognition.

Spyware: Any technology that gathers personal or organizational information without the user's knowledge or consent.

Stakeholder: A person, group, or organization affected by the operations of a business.

Statement of Cash Flows: Reports cash generated and used in a specific time period.

Statement of Owner's Equity: Displays owner's equity in the firm.

Stocks: A security that shows ownership in a company.

Stockholder/shareholder: An investor who owns shares of an organization.

Strategic alliance: An arrangement between two or more companies who mutually agree upon a set of goals.

Strategic plan: A plan that defines the goals of the entire organization.

Strikebreaker: An individual who works for the company when employees are on strike.

Strikes: Employees stop working to inflict financial hardship on an organization.

Supply: The amount of goods or services producers are willing and able to produce in the market at different prices.

Sustainable manufacturing: Recognizing present and future needs of the environment in manufacturing practices.

Sustainability: Methods used to promote proper use and extension of ecological resources.

Sweatshops: A workplace that has socially unacceptable working conditions.

Synthetic production: Combining two or more raw materials to create another product.

Tactical plan: A plan that specifies what must be done and how goals should be met, typically one year or less.

Target audience: A specific cluster of people within the target market.

Target market: A specific consumer group that a company focuses its marketing efforts toward.

Targeted resume: A resume that is customized for a specific position.

Tariff: A government tax imposed on imported goods and services.

Technical skills: Skills related to discipline- or departmental-specific tasks.

Term-life insurance: A contract that provides protection for a specified time.

Theory X: The belief that employees inherently dislike work and will avoid it when possible.

Theory Y: The belief that employees are motivated to work and accept responsibility.

Theory Z: Japanese management style that focuses on empowerment and the team over the individual.

Top-level management: Upper management tasked with developing vision, goals, and objectives of the firm.

Total compensation package: Direct and indirect compensation paid to an employee.

Total labor force: All individuals who are 16 years or older and actively seeking employment.

Total quality management (TQM): An organization-wide philosophy that seeks to continuously improve its capacity to deliver the highest quality goods to customers.

Trade deficit: When imports are greater than exports.

Trade surplus: When exports are greater than imports.

Trademark: Legal protection for a brand or product.

Traditional IRA: A pre-tax investment option.

Transactional leadership: Provides rewards or punishments based on performance outcomes.

Transformational leadership: Emphasizes employee motivation and morale to change behavior.

Transparency: Making financial information and documentation available for public review.

Trojan horse: A malicious program that claims to be one thing but is really another.

Troubled Asset Relief Program (TARP): Plan created in 2008 by the U.S. Congress to assist failing financial institutions and save the U.S. economy from collapse.

Unemployment rate: Total unemployed workers in the total labor force.

Undercapitalization: Not having enough capital to operate or expand a business.

Underemployed workers: Individuals working but not utilizing their skills or education.

Unlimited liability: All debts of the business are the responsibility of the owner.

URL: The web address of a particular web site.

Utility: How products and services satisfy the needs and wants of those who use them.

Valence: Value given to a reward.

Variable costs: Costs that change directly with sales volume.

Venture capital: Investors who provide funds in exchange for ownership in a company.

Viruses: Man-made computer programs that attach themselves to other programs without the user's knowledge or consent.

Vision statement: An explanation of what a business is currently and where it wants to go in the future.

WAN: A network that covers a large physical distance.

Wealth: Building up valuable resources or material possessions.

Whistleblowers: Employees who disclose illegal, unethical, or immoral business practices committed by a company.

Whole-life insurance: A contract that provides protection for an entire lifetime

Wholly-owned subsidiaries: Companies owned by a parent company.

Wi-Fi: A wireless network that allows devices to communicate through radio waves.

Work-life balance: Balancing one's professional and personal life in order to remain productive and satisfied in both worlds.

Workplace diversity: Similarities and differences among employees related to race, age, gender, religion, physical and mental disabilities, sexual orientation, and cultural background.

WORM: A computer program that finds holes in networks and replicates itself over another computer network.

INDEX

A

Accounting
  versus bookkeeping, 90
  defined, 90
  international, 104–105
  types of, 91–92
  undercapitalization, effects of, 109
Accounting cycle, 95–96
Accounting equation, 96
Accounting information, users of
  external users, 94
  internal users, 93
Acid test (quick ratio), 100
Acquisitions, 81
Action research, 126
Activity ratios, 103–104
Additive fabrication, 208
Adjustable-rate mortgage (ARM), 260
Advertising, 138
Agents, 134
Agile manufacturing, 208
American Accounting Association (AAA), 90
American Federation of Labor (AFL), 193
American Marketing Association (AMA), 114
Analytic production, 206
Angel investors, 84
Anthony, Susan B., 68(t)
Application for job, 272–274
Assembly line, 206
Assets, 96
Autocratic leadership, 159
Average collection period, 103

B

Baby Boomer generation (1946–1964), 11
Balance of payments, 222–224
Balance of trade, 222–224
  in United States, 223(f)
Balance sheet, 97
  structure for, 97(t)
Behavioral interview, 276
Bhave, Vinoba, 68(t)
Big data, 237
  four V's of, 237(f)
Bona fide occupational qualifications
  (BFOQ), 179
Bonds, 262
Bookkeeping
  versus accounting, 90
  double-entry, 96
  purpose of, 90
Boycott, 195
Brand equity, 129
Branding, 128
Brand loyalty, 129
Breakeven analysis, 132
Brexit, 229
BRICS Economies, 229
Brokers, 134
Bureau of Labor Statistics (BLS), 47, 193
Business
  contract enforcement, 15
  government's role in, 15–17
  history of, 4–8
    colonial period, 5
    eras in, 5(t)

long-term, 108

short-term, 107

Financing activities, 92

Financing life cycle, 82

Fiscal policy, 55

Fixed costs, 132

Fixed-rate mortgage, 260

Flexible manufacturing, 205

Flextime, 185

Ford, Henry, 7

Form utility, 114

For-profit organizations, 3

Forty-niners, 6

401K (retirement savings plan), 263

403b (retirement plan for employees), 263

Franchisee, 78

Franchises, 78–81

advantages and disadvantages of, 79

steps to franchising, 80

Franchising, 230

Franchisor, 78

Free-rein leadership, 160

Fringe benefits, 185

Functional resumes, 275

Fundings, available for businesses, 82–85

angel investors, 84

commercial lenders, 84

other lenders, 85

Small Business Administration (SBA), 84

venture capital, 83–84

Future and present value, calculation of, 286–293

G

Gantt chart, 211, 211(f)

Gantt, Henry, 211

GDP per capita, 223–224

poorest countries by, 224(f)

wealthiest countries by, 224(f)

Generally Accepted Accounting Principles (GAAP), 95, 105

Globalization, concept of, 221

Global trade, 220–221

absolute *versus* comparative advantage, 225

balance of

payment, 222–224

trade, 222–224

barriers to, 225–226

exports and imports, 221–222

foreign market entrance strategies, pros and cons, 231(t)

involvement in, 229–231

organizations to promote

BRICS Economies, 229

Central America-Dominican Republic Free Trade Agreement (CAFTA-DR), 228

Common Market for Eastern and Southern Africa (COMESA), 229

European Union (EU), 228–229

North American Free Trade Agreement (NAFTA), 228

Goleman, Daniel, 158

Gompers, Samuel, 193

Good faith and fair dealing, 31–33

Google, 13

Great Depression of the 1930s, 7, 48, 53, 57

Great Recession of 2008, 56–57

Green manufacturing, 209

Green marketing, 38

Gross domestic product (GDP), 45

boom stage, 48

countries with highest, 46

expansion stage, 48

Gross profit margin, 101

H

Hardware, computer, 239

Hedge funds, 108

Herzberg, Frederick, 190

two-factor model, 190, 190(f)

Hierarchy of company, 166

Holistic marketing, 117

Human capital

civilian labor force, 12(t)

population and labor pool, 11–12

K

Kennedy, John F., 27
Keynesian school of economic thought, 53

L

Labor laws, 186–189
  affirmative action programs, 188
  Age Discrimination in Employment
    Act (1967), 188
  Americans with Disabilities Act
    (ADA, 1990), 188
  Family and Medical Leave Act
    (FMLA, 1993), 188–189
  federal employment laws, 187(t)
  on reverse discrimination, 188
  Title VII of the Civil Rights Act of 1964, 188
Labor–management relations, 192–196
  evolution of, 193
  laws related to, 193–195
    Fair Labor Standards Act (1938), 193
    Landrum-Griffin Act (1959), 194
    Taft-Hartley Act (1947), 194
    Wagner Act (1935), 193
Labor union, 192
  development of, 193
  future of, 196
Laissez-faire leadership, 160
Leadership
  emotional intelligence (EI), 157
  versus management, 156
  styles of, 158
  theories of, 161–162
    Hersey and Blanchard's, 161
    theory X, 161
    theory Y, 161
    theory Z, 161
  types of, 158–162, 159(f)
Lean manufacturing, 207
Lehman Brothers, 57
Lenders
  commercial, 84
  other lenders, 85

Leverage ratios, 100–101
Liabilities, 96
Licensing agreement, 230
Lilic, Elmira, 310–311
Limited-liability corporations (LLC), 77
  advantages and disadvantages of, 78
Line-and-staff organizations, 168
  structure of, 168(f)
Line organization, 167
  structure of, 168(f)
LinkedIn, 248
Liquid assets, 100
Liquidity ratios, 99–100
Local area network (LAN), 240
Locke's Goal Setting Theory, 192
Lockout, 195
Luncheon interview, 278

M

McAfee Antivirus program, 244
Macroeconomics, 45
Malware, 243–244
Management
  basic functions, 148–151, 149(t)
  communication, 162–164
  contingency plans, 155
  decisions, programmed *versus* non-
    programmed, 155–156
  first-level, 150
  versus leadership, 156
  meaning of, 148
  middle-level, 150
  operational plans, 155
  and responsibilities, 151(t)
  skills, 151–152
    conceptual, 152
    critical, 152(t)
    human relation, 151–152
    technical, 151
  strategic plans, 154
  tactical plans, 154
  top-level, 149
  vision and mission statements, 153

O

Occupational Health and Safety Administration (OSHA), 17
Oligopoly, 51, 52(f)
On-demand computing (ODC), 245
"One-time use" system, 205
Operating activities, 92
Operational support systems (OSS), 239
Operations management, 204
Organizational structures, 165–167
    centralization, 166, 167(t)
    chart, 165
    decentralization, 166, 167(t)
    delegation, 166
    departmentalization, 165
    micromanagement, 166
    span of control, 166
    types of, 167–169
Ouchi, William, 162
Outsourcing, 13, 195, 225
    countries to outsource business, 14(t)
    reasons for, 13(t)
Owner's equity, 96
    statement of, 98
Ownership (possession) utility, 115

P

Paid time off (PTO), 185
Paid-time-off (PTO), 278
Participative leadership, 159
Partnership
    advantges and disadvantages of, 76
    general, 76
    limited, 76
Patents, 129
PayPal, 115
Peer group interview, 278
Penetration pricing, 132
Pension funds, 108
Per capita GDP, 45
Performance appraisals, 182

Permission, to conduct business, 15
Personal finance
    credit scores and reports, 256–258
        FICO score, 257
    debt, types of, 258–260
    financial changes, 254
    financial planning, 255–256
    investment options, 260–262
    retirement planning, 263–265
    Social Security payments, 254
Personal selling, 138
Picketing, 195
Pinterest, 248
Place utility, 115
Portfolio, 260
Preferred stocks, 261–262
Price, 131–133
    breakeven analysis, 132
    case study, 146
    competitive, 133
    discount, 133
    everyday low pricing (EDLP), 132–133
    objectives, 131
        type of, 131(t)
    odd pricing/psychological, 133
        frequency of, 133(f)
    penetration pricing, 132
    pricing strategies, 131–133
Price-gouging, practice of, 24
Price skimming, 132
Principal, Interest, Taxes, and Insurance (PITI), 259
Private equity funds, 108
Private placements, 108
Process control systems (PCS), 239
Producers, 134
Production
    additional manufacturing processes, 207–208
    analytic *versus* synthetic, 206
    assembly line, 206
    classic system of, 202(t)
    continuous *versus* intermittent, 206
    customer-driven production, 205
    era of, 6–7, 116